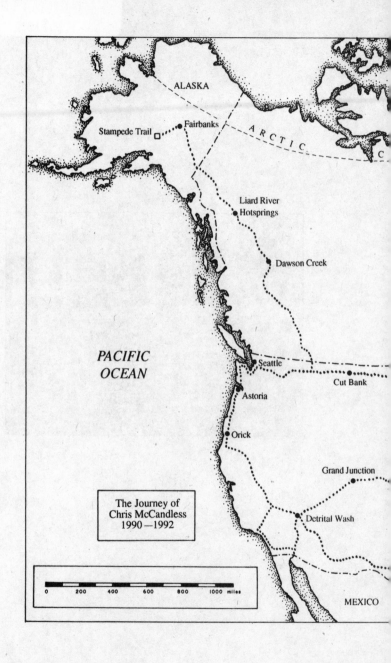

ALASKA

Stampede Trail Fairbanks

ARCTIC

Liard River
Hotsprings

Dawson Creek

*PACIFIC
OCEAN*

Seattle

Cut Bank

Astoria

Orick

Grand Junction

The Journey of
Chris McCandless
1990 — 1992

Detrital Wash

0   200   400   600   800   1000 miles

MEXICO

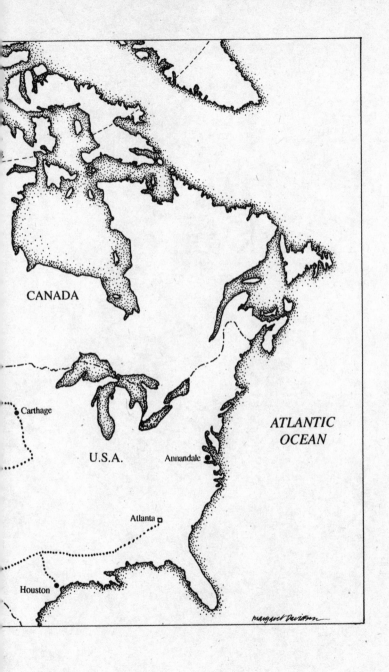

CANADA

Carthage

U.S.A.

Annandale

Atlanta

Houston

ATLANTIC
OCEAN

margaret davidson

Jon
Krakauer

INTO THE
WILD

ANCHOR BOOKS

A DIVISION OF PENGUIN RANDOM HOUSE LLC

NEW YORK

ANCHOR BOOKS EDITIONS, 1997, 2015

Library of Congress Cataloging-in-Publication Data
Krakauer, Jon.
Into the wild / Jon Krakauer.
p.   cm.
Originally published: New York : Villard, © 1996.
1. McCandless, Christopher Johnson, 1968–1992.   2. Adventure and
adventurers—United States—Biography.   3. Wayfaring life—Alaska.
4. Wayfaring life—West (U.S.)   5. Hitchhiking—Alaska.
6. Hitchhiking—West (U.S.)   7. Alaska—Biography.   8. West (U.S.)
Biography. · I Title.
[CT9971.M38K73   1997]
917.9804'5—dc20   96-43566
CIP

Anchor Books Trade Paperback ISBN: 978-0-385-48680-4
eBook ISBN: 978-0-307-47686-9

Author photograph © Linda M. Moore

www.anchorbooks.com

Printed in the United States of America
146 145 144 143 142 141

FOR LINDA

AUTHOR'S NOTE

In April 1992, a young man from a well-to-do East Coast family hitchhiked to Alaska and walked alone into the wilderness north of Mt. McKinley. Four months later his decomposed body was found by a party of moose hunters.

Shortly after the discovery of the corpse, I was asked by the editor of *Outside* magazine to report on the puzzling circumstances of the boy's death. His name turned out to be Christopher Johnson McCandless. He'd grown up, I learned, in an affluent suburb of Washington, D.C., where he'd excelled academically and had been an elite athlete.

Immediately after graduating, with honors, from Emory University in the summer of 1990, McCandless dropped out of sight. He changed his name, gave the entire balance of a twenty-four-thousand-dollar savings account to charity, abandoned his car and most of his possessions, burned all the cash in his wallet. And then he invented a new life for himself, taking up residence at the ragged margin of our society, wandering across North America in search of raw, transcendent experience. His family had no idea where he was or what had become of him until his remains turned up in Alaska.

Working on a tight deadline, I wrote a nine-thousand-word article, which ran in the January 1993 issue of the magazine, but my fascination with McCandless remained long after that issue of *Outside* was replaced on the newsstands by more current journalistic fare. I was haunted by the particulars of the boy's starvation and by vague, unsettling parallels between events in his life and those in my own. Unwilling to let McCandless go, I spent more than a year retracing the convoluted path that led to his death in the Alaska taiga, chasing down details of his peregrinations with an interest that bordered on obsession. In trying to understand McCandless, I inevitably came to reflect on other, larger subjects as well: the grip wilderness has on the American imagination, the allure high-risk activities hold for young men of a certain mind, the complicated, highly charged bond that exists between fathers and sons. The result of this meandering inquiry is the book now before you.

I won't claim to be an impartial biographer. McCandless's strange tale struck a personal note that made a dispassionate rendering of the tragedy impossible. Through most of the book, I have tried—and largely succeeded, I think—to minimize my authorial presence. But let the reader be warned: I interrupt McCandless's story with fragments of a narrative drawn from my own youth. I do so in the hope that my experiences will throw some oblique light on the enigma of Chris McCandless.

He was an extremely intense young man and possessed a streak of stubborn idealism that did not mesh readily with modern existence. Long captivated by the writing of Leo Tolstoy, McCandless particularly admired how the great novelist had forsaken a life of wealth and privilege to wander among the destitute. In college McCandless began emulating Tolstoy's asceticism and moral rigor to a degree that first astonished, and then alarmed, those who were close to him. When the boy headed off into the Alaska bush, he entertained no illusions that he was trekking into a land of milk and honey; peril, adversity, and Tolstoyan renunciation were precisely what he was seeking. And that is what he found, in abundance.

For most of the sixteen-week ordeal, nevertheless, McCandless more than held his own. Indeed, were it not for one or two seemingly insignificant blunders, he would have walked out of the woods in August 1992 as anonymously as he had walked into them in April. Instead, his innocent mistakes turned out to be pivotal and irreversible, his name became the stuff of tabloid headlines, and his bewildered family was left clutching the shards of a fierce and painful love.

A surprising number of people have been affected by the story of Chris McCandless's life and death. In the weeks and months following the publication of the article in *Outside,* it generated more mail than any other article in the magazine's history. This correspondence, as one might expect, reflected sharply divergent points of view: Some readers admired the boy immensely for his courage and noble ideals; others fulminated that he was a reckless idiot, a wacko, a narcissist who perished out of arrogance and stupidity—and was undeserving of the considerable media attention he received. My convictions should be apparent soon enough, but I will leave it to the reader to form his or her own opinion of Chris McCandless.

JON KRAKAUER
SEATTLE
APRIL 1995

INTO THE
WILD

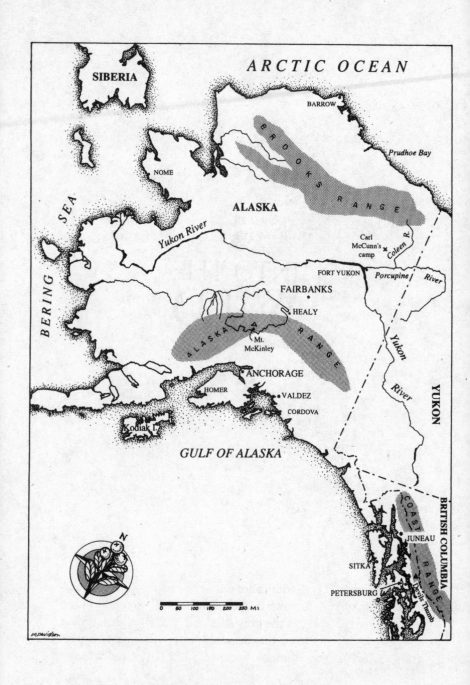

CHAPTER ONE

THE ALASKA INTERIOR

April 27th, 1992

Greetings from Fairbanks! This is the last you shall hear from me Wayne. Arrived here 2 days ago. It was very difficult to catch rides in the Yukon Territory. But I finally got here.

Please return all mail I receive to the sender. It might be a very long time before I return South. If this adventure proves fatal and you don't ever hear from me again I want you to know you're a great man. I now walk into the wild. Alex.

POSTCARD RECEIVED BY WAYNE WESTERBERG
IN CARTHAGE, SOUTH DAKOTA

Jim Gallien had driven four miles out of Fairbanks when he spotted the hitchhiker standing in the snow beside the road, thumb raised high, shivering in the gray Alaska dawn. He didn't appear to be very old: eighteen, maybe nineteen at most. A rifle protruded from the young man's backpack, but he looked friendly enough; a hitchhiker with a Remington semiautomatic isn't the sort of thing that gives motorists pause in the forty-ninth state. Gallien steered his truck onto the shoulder and told the kid to climb in.

The hitchhiker swung his pack into the bed of the Ford and introduced himself as Alex. "Alex?" Gallien responded, fishing for a last name.

"Just Alex," the young man replied, pointedly rejecting the bait. Five feet seven or eight with a wiry build, he claimed to be twenty-four years old and said he was from South Dakota. He explained that he wanted a ride as far as the edge of Denali National Park, where he intended to walk deep into the bush and "live off the land for a few months."

Gallien, a union electrician, was on his way to Anchorage, 240 miles beyond Denali on the George Parks Highway; he told Alex he'd drop him off wherever he wanted. Alex's backpack looked as though it weighed only twenty-five or thirty pounds, which struck Gallien—an accomplished hunter and woodsman—as an improbably light load for a stay of several months in the back-country, especially so early in the spring. "He wasn't carrying anywhere near as much food and gear as you'd expect a guy to be carrying for that kind of trip," Gallien recalls.

The sun came up. As they rolled down from the forested ridges above the Tanana River, Alex gazed across the expanse of windswept muskeg stretching to the south. Gallien wondered whether he'd picked up one of those crackpots from the lower forty-eight who come north to live out ill-considered Jack London fantasies. Alaska has long been a magnet for dreamers and misfits, people who think the unsullied enormity of the Last Frontier will patch all the holes in their lives. The bush is an unforgiving place, however, that cares nothing for hope or longing.

"People from Outside," reports Gallien in a slow, sonorous drawl, "they'll pick up a copy of *Alaska* magazine, thumb through it, get to thinkin' 'Hey, I'm goin' to get on up there, live off the land, go claim me a piece of the good life.' But when they get here and actually head out into the bush—well, it isn't like the magazines make it out to be. The rivers are big and fast. The mosquitoes eat you alive. Most places, there aren't a lot of animals to hunt. Livin' in the bush isn't no picnic."

It was a two-hour drive from Fairbanks to the edge of Denali Park. The more they talked, the less Alex struck Gallien as a nutcase. He was congenial, and seemed well educated. He peppered Gallien with thoughtful questions about the kind of small game that live in the country, the kinds of berries he could eat—"that kind of thing."

Still, Gallien was concerned. Alex admitted that the only food in his pack was a ten-pound bag of rice. His gear seemed exceedingly minimal for the harsh conditions of the interior, which in April still lay buried under the winter snowpack. Alex's cheap leather hiking boots were neither waterproof nor well insulated. His rifle was only .22 caliber, a bore too small to rely on if he expected to kill large animals like moose and caribou, which he would have to eat if he hoped to remain very long in the country. He had no ax, no bug dope, no snowshoes, no compass. The only navigational aid in his possession was a tattered state road map he'd scrounged at a gas station.

A hundred miles out of Fairbanks the highway begins to climb into the foothills of the Alaska Range. Alex pulled out his crude map and pointed to a dashed red line that intersected the road near the coal-mining town of Healy. It represented a route called the Stampede Trail. Seldom traveled, it isn't even marked on most road maps of Alaska. On Alex's map, nevertheless, the broken line meandered west from the Parks Highway for forty miles or so before petering out in the middle of trackless wilderness north of Mt. McKinley. This, Alex announced to Gallien, was where he intended to go.

Gallien thought the hitchhiker's scheme was foolhardy and tried repeatedly to dissuade him: "I said the hunting wasn't easy where he was going, that he could go for days without killing any game. When that didn't work, I tried to scare him with bear stories. I told him that a twenty-two probably wouldn't do anything to a grizzly except make him mad. Alex didn't seem too worried. 'I'll climb a tree' is all he said. So I explained that trees don't grow real big in that part of the state, that a bear could knock down one of them skinny little black spruce without even trying. But he wouldn't give an inch. He had an answer for everything I threw at him."

Gallien offered to drive Alex all the way to Anchorage, buy him some decent gear, and then drive him back to wherever he wanted to go.

"No, thanks anyway," Alex replied, "I'll be fine with what I've got."

Gallien asked whether he had a hunting license.

"Hell, no," Alex scoffed. "How I feed myself is none of the government's business. Fuck their stupid rules."

When Gallien asked whether his parents or a friend knew what he was up to—whether there was anyone who would sound the alarm if he got into trouble and was overdue—Alex answered calmly that no, nobody knew of his plans, that in fact he hadn't spoken to his family in nearly two years. "I'm absolutely positive," he assured Gallien, "I won't run into anything I can't deal with on my own."

"There was just no talking the guy out of it," Gallien remembers. "He was determined. Real gung ho. The word that comes to mind is *excited.* He couldn't wait to head out there and get started."

Three hours out of Fairbanks, Gallien turned off the highway and steered his beat-up 4 x 4 down a snow-packed side road. For the first few miles the Stampede Trail was well graded and led past cabins scattered among weedy stands of spruce and aspen. Beyond the last of the log shacks, however, the road rapidly deteriorated. Washed out and overgrown with alders, it turned into a rough, unmaintained track.

In summer the road here would have been sketchy but passable; now it was made unnavigable by a foot and a half of mushy spring snow. Ten miles from the highway, worried that he'd get stuck if he drove farther, Gallien stopped his rig on the crest of a low rise. The icy summits of the highest mountain range in North America gleamed on the southwestern horizon.

Alex insisted on giving Gallien his watch, his comb, and what he said was all his money: eighty-five cents in loose change. "I don't want your money," Gallien protested, "and I already have a watch."

"If you don't take it, I'm going to throw it away," Alex cheerfully retorted. "I don't want to know what time it is. I don't want to know what day it is or where I am. None of that matters."

Before Alex left the pickup, Gallien reached behind the seat, pulled out an old pair of rubber work boots, and persuaded the boy to take them. "They were too big for him," Gallien recalls. "But I said, 'Wear two pair of socks, and your feet ought to stay halfway warm and dry.'"

"How much do I owe you?"

"Don't worry about it," Gallien answered. Then he gave the kid a slip of paper with his phone number on it, which Alex carefully tucked into a nylon wallet.

"If you make it out alive, give me a call, and I'll tell you how to get the boots back to me."

Gallien's wife had packed him two grilled-cheese-and-tuna sandwiches and a bag of corn chips for lunch; he persuaded the young hitchhiker to accept the food as well. Alex pulled a camera from his backpack and asked Gallien to snap a picture of him shouldering his rifle at the trailhead. Then, smiling broadly, he disappeared down the snow-covered track. The date was Tuesday, April 28, 1992.

Gallien turned the truck around, made his way back to the Parks Highway, and continued toward Anchorage. A few miles down the road he came to the small community of Healy, where the Alaska State Troopers maintain a post. Gallien briefly considered stopping and telling the authorities about Alex, then thought better of it. "I figured he'd be OK," he explains. "I thought he'd probably get hungry pretty quick and just walk out to the highway. That's what any normal person would do."

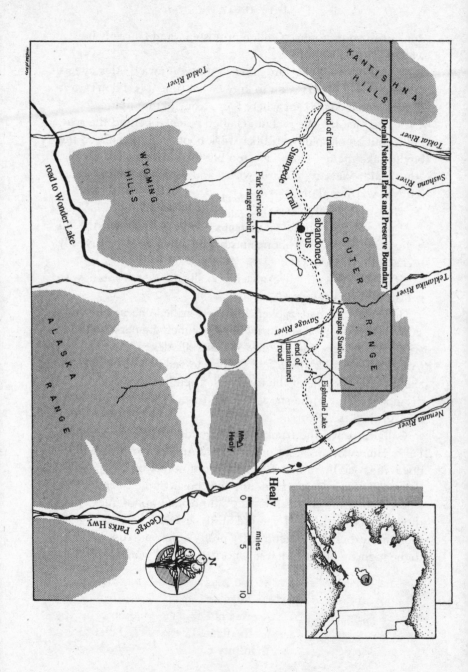

CHAPTER TWO

THE STAMPEDE TRAIL

Jack London is <u>King</u>
Alexander Supertramp
May 1992
GRAFFITO CARVED INTO A PIECE OF WOOD DISCOVERED
AT THE SITE OF CHRIS MCCANDLESS'S DEATH

Dark spruce forest frowned on either side the frozen waterway.
The trees had been stripped by a recent wind of their white cov-
ering of frost, and they seemed to lean toward each other, black
and ominous, in the fading light. A vast silence reigned over the
land. The land itself was a desolation, lifeless, without move-
ment, so lone and cold that the spirit of it was not even that of
sadness. There was a hint in it of laughter, but of a laughter
more terrible than any sadness—a laughter that was mirthless
as the smile of the Sphinx, a laughter cold as the frost and par-
taking of the grimness of infallibility. It was the masterful and
incommunicable wisdom of eternity laughing at the futility
of life and the effort of life. It was the Wild, the savage, frozen-
hearted Northland Wild.

JACK LONDON,
WHITE FANG

On the northern margin of the Alaska Range, just before the
hulking ramparts of Mt. McKinley and its satellites surrender to
the low Kantishna plain, a series of lesser ridges, known as the
Outer Range, sprawls across the flats like a rumpled blanket on
an unmade bed. Between the flinty crests of the two outermost

escarpments of the Outer Range runs an east-west trough, maybe five miles across, carpeted in a boggy amalgam of muskeg, alder thickets, and veins of scrawny spruce. Meandering through the tangled, rolling bottomland is the Stampede Trail, the route Chris McCandless followed into the wilderness.

The trail was blazed in the 1930s by a legendary Alaska miner named Earl Pilgrim; it led to antimony claims he'd staked on Stampede Creek, above the Clearwater Fork of the Toklat River. In 1961, a Fairbanks company, Yutan Construction, won a contract from the new state of Alaska (statehood having been granted just two years earlier) to upgrade the trail, building it into a road on which trucks could haul ore from the mine year-round. To house construction workers while the road was going in, Yutan purchased three junked buses, outfitted each with bunks and a simple barrel stove, and skidded them into the wilderness behind a D-9 Caterpillar.

The project was halted in 1963: some fifty miles of road were eventually built, but no bridges were ever erected over the many rivers it transected, and the route was shortly rendered impassable by thawing permafrost and seasonal floods. Yutan hauled two of the buses back to the highway. The third bus was left about halfway out the trail to serve as backcountry shelter for hunters and trappers. In the three decades since construction ended, much of the roadbed has been obliterated by washouts, brush, and beaver ponds, but the bus is still there.

A vintage International Harvester from the 1940s, the derelict vehicle is located twenty-five miles west of Healy as the raven flies, rusting incongruously in the fireweed beside the Stampede Trail, just beyond the boundary of Denali National Park. The engine is gone. Several windows are cracked or missing altogether, and broken whiskey bottles litter the floor. The green-and-white paint is badly oxidized. Weathered lettering indicates that the old machine was once part of the Fairbanks City Transit System: bus 142. These days it isn't unusual for six or seven months to pass without the bus seeing a human visitor, but in early September 1992, six people in three separate parties happened to visit the remote vehicle on the same afternoon.

In 1980, Denali National Park was expanded to include the Kantishna Hills and the northernmost cordillera of the Outer Range, but a parcel of low terrain within the new park acreage was omitted: a long arm of land known as the Wolf Townships, which encompasses the first half of the Stampede Trail. Because this seven-by-twenty-mile tract is surrounded on three sides by the protected acreage of the national park, it harbors more than its share of wolf, bear, caribou, moose, and other game, a local secret that's jealously guarded by those hunters and trappers who are aware of the anomaly. As soon as moose season opens in the fall, a handful of hunters typically pays a visit to the old bus, which sits beside the Sushana River at the westernmost end of the nonpark tract, within two miles of the park boundary.

Ken Thompson, the owner of an Anchorage auto-body shop, Gordon Samel, his employee, and their friend Ferdie Swanson, a construction worker, set out for the bus on September 6, 1992, stalking moose. It isn't an easy place to reach. About ten miles past the end of the improved road the Stampede Trail crosses the Teklanika River, a fast, icy stream whose waters are opaque with glacial till. The trail comes down to the riverbank just upstream from a narrow gorge, through which the Teklanika surges in a boil of white water. The prospect of fording this *latte*-colored torrent discourages most people from traveling any farther.

Thompson, Samel, and Swanson, however, are contumacious Alaskans with a special fondness for driving motor vehicles where motor vehicles aren't really designed to be driven. Upon arriving at the Teklanika, they scouted the banks until they located a wide, braided section with relatively shallow channels, and then they steered headlong into the flood.

"I went first," Thompson says. "The river was probably seventy-five feet across and real swift. My rig is a jacked-up eighty-two Dodge four by four with thirty-eight-inch rubber on it, and the water was right up to the hood. At one point I didn't think I'd get across. Gordon has a eight-thousand-pound winch on the front of his rig; I had him follow right behind so he could pull me out if I went out of sight."

Thompson made it to the far bank without incident, followed

by Samel and Swanson in their trucks. In the beds of two of the pickups were light-weight all-terrain vehicles: a three-wheeler and a four-wheeler. They parked the big rigs on a gravel bar, unloaded the ATVs, and continued toward the bus in the smaller, more maneuverable machines.

A few hundred yards beyond the river the trail disappeared into a series of chest-deep beaver ponds. Undeterred, the three Alaskans dynamited the offending stick dams and drained the ponds. Then they motored onward, up a rocky creek bed and through dense alder thickets. It was late afternoon by the time they finally arrived at the bus. When they got there, according to Thompson, they found "a guy and a girl from Anchorage standing fifty feet away, looking kinda spooked."

Neither of them had been in the bus, but they'd been close enough to notice "a real bad smell from inside." A makeshift signal flag—a red knitted leg warmer of the sort worn by dancers— was knotted to the end of an alder branch by the vehicle's rear exit. The door was ajar, and taped to it was a disquieting note. Handwritten in neat block letters on a page torn from a novel by Nikolay Gogol, it read:

> S.O.S. I NEED YOUR HELP. I AM INJURED, NEAR DEATH, AND TOO WEAK
> TO HIKE OUT OF HERE. I AM ALL ALONE, THIS IS NO JOKE. IN THE NAME
> OF GOD, PLEASE REMAIN TO SAVE ME. I AM OUT COLLECTING BERRIES
> CLOSE BY AND SHALL RETURN THIS EVENING. THANK YOU, CHRIS
> MCCANDLESS. AUGUST?

The Anchorage couple had been too upset by the implication of the note and the overpowering odor of decay to examine the bus's interior, so Samel steeled himself to take a look. A peek through a window revealed a Remington rifle, a plastic box of shells, eight or nine paperback books, some torn jeans, cooking utensils, and an expensive backpack. In the very rear of the vehicle, on a jerry-built bunk, was a blue sleeping bag that appeared to have something or someone inside it, although, says Samel, "it was hard to be absolutely sure.

"I stood on a stump," Samel continues, "reached through a

back window, and gave the bag a shake. There was definitely something in it, but whatever it was didn't weigh much. It wasn't until I walked around to the other side and saw a head sticking out that I knew for certain what it was." Chris McCandless had been dead for two and a half weeks.

Samel, a man of strong opinions, decided the body should be evacuated right away. There wasn't room on his or Thompson's small machine to haul the dead person out, however, nor was there space on the Anchorage couple's ATV. A short while later a sixth person appeared on the scene, a hunter from Healy named Butch Killian. Because Killian was driving an Argo—a large amphibious eight-wheeled ATV—Samel suggested that Killian evacuate the remains, but Killian declined, insisting it was a task more properly left to the Alaska State Troopers.

Killian, a coal miner who moonlights as an emergency medical technician for the Healy Volunteer Fire Department, had a two-way radio on the Argo. When he couldn't raise anybody from where he was, he started driving back toward the highway; five miles down the trail, just before dark, he managed to make contact with the radio operator at the Healy power plant. "Dispatch," he reported, "this is Butch. You better call the troopers. There's a man back in the bus by the Sushana. Looks like he's been dead for a while."

At eight-thirty the next morning, a police helicopter touched down noisily beside the bus in a blizzard of dust and swirling aspen leaves. The troopers made a cursory examination of the vehicle and its environs for signs of foul play and then departed. When they flew away, they took McCandless's remains, a camera with five rolls of exposed film, the SOS note, and a diary—written across the last two pages of a field guide to edible plants—that recorded the young man's final weeks in 113 terse, enigmatic entries.

The body was taken to Anchorage, where an autopsy was performed at the Scientific Crime Detection Laboratory. The remains were so badly decomposed that it was impossible to determine exactly when McCandless had died, but the coroner could find no sign of massive internal injuries or broken bones.

Virtually no subcutaneous fat remained on the body, and the muscles had withered significantly in the days or weeks prior to death. At the time of the autopsy, McCandless's remains weighed sixty-seven pounds. Starvation was posited as the most probable cause of death.

McCandless's signature had been penned at the bottom of the SOS note, and the photos, when developed, included many self-portraits. But because he had been carrying no identification, the authorities didn't know who he was, where he was from, or why he was there.

CHAPTER THREE

CARTHAGE

I wanted movement and not a calm course of existence. I wanted excitement and danger and the chance to sacrifice myself for my love. I felt in myself a superabundance of energy which found no outlet in our quiet life.

LEO TOLSTOY,
"FAMILY HAPPINESS"
PASSAGE HIGHLIGHTED IN ONE OF THE BOOKS FOUND
WITH CHRIS MCCANDLESS'S REMAINS

It should not be denied . . . that being footloose has always exhilarated us. It is associated in our minds with escape from history and oppression and law and irksome obligations, with absolute freedom, and the road has always led west.

WALLACE STEGNER,
THE AMERICAN WEST AS LIVING SPACE

Carthage, South Dakota, population 274, is a sleepy little cluster of clapboard houses; tidy yards, and weathered brick storefronts rising humbly from the immensity of the northern plains, set adrift in time. Stately rows of cottonwoods shade a grid of streets seldom disturbed by moving vehicles. There's one grocery in town, one bank, a single gas station, a lone bar—the Cabaret, where Wayne Westerberg is sipping a cocktail and chewing on a sweet cigar, remembering the odd young man he knew as Alex.

The Cabaret's plywood-paneled walls are hung with deer antlers, Old Milwaukee beer promos, and mawkish paintings of game birds taking flight. Tendrils of cigarette smoke rise from clumps of farmers in overalls and dusty feed caps, their tired faces as grimy as coal miners'. Speaking in short, matter-of-fact phrases, they worry aloud over the fickle weather and fields of sunflowers still too wet to cut, while above their heads Ross Perot's sneering visage flickers across a silent television screen. In eight days the nation will elect Bill Clinton president. It's been nearly two months now since the body of Chris McCandless turned up in Alaska.

"These are what Alex used to drink," says Westerberg with a frown, swirling the ice in his White Russian. "He used to sit right there at the end of the bar and tell us these amazing stories of his travels. He could talk for hours. A lot of folks here in town got pretty attached to old Alex. Kind of a strange deal what happened to him."

Westerberg, a hyperkinetic man with thick shoulders and a black goatee, owns a grain elevator in Carthage and another one a few miles out of town but spends every summer running a custom combine crew that follows the harvest from Texas north to the Canadian border. In the fall of 1990, he was wrapping up the season in north-central Montana, cutting barley for Coors and Anheuser-Busch. On the afternoon of September 10, driving out of Cut Bank after buying some parts for a malfunctioning combine, he pulled over for a hitchhiker, an amiable kid who said his name was Alex McCandless.

McCandless was smallish with the hard, stringy physique of an itinerant laborer. There was something arresting about the youngster's eyes. Dark and emotive, they suggested a trace of exotic blood in his heritage—Greek, maybe, or Chippewa—and conveyed a vulnerability that made Westerberg want to take the kid under his wing. He had the kind of sensitive good looks that women made a big fuss over, Westerberg imagined. His face had a strange elasticity: It would be slack and expressionless one minute, only to twist suddenly into a gaping, oversize grin that distorted his features and exposed a mouthful of horsy teeth. He was nearsighted and wore steel-rimmed glasses. He looked hungry.

Ten minutes after picking up McCandless, Westerberg stopped in the town of Ethridge to deliver a package to a friend. "He offered us both a beer," says Westerberg, "and asked Alex how long it'd been since he ate. Alex allowed how it'd been a couple of days. Said he'd kind of run out of money." Overhearing this, the friend's wife insisted on cooking Alex a big dinner, which he wolfed down, and then he fell asleep at the table.

McCandless had told Westerberg that his destination was Saco Hot Springs, 240 miles to the east on U.S. Highway 2, a place he'd heard about from some "rubber tramps" (i.e., vagabonds who owned a vehicle; as distinguished from "leather tramps," who lacked personal transportation and were thus forced to hitchhike or walk). Westerberg had replied that he could take McCandless only ten miles down the road, at which point he would be turning north toward Sunburst, where he kept a trailer near the fields he was cutting. By the time Westerberg steered over to the shoulder to drop McCandless off, it was ten-thirty at night and raining hard. "Jeeze," Westerberg told him, "I hate to leave you out here in the goddamn rain. You got a sleeping bag—why don't you come on up to Sunburst, spend the night in the trailer?"

McCandless stayed with Westerberg for three days, riding out with his crew each morning as the workers piloted their lumbering machines across the ocean of ripe blond grain. Before McCandless and Westerberg went their separate ways, Westerberg told the young man to look him up in Carthage if he ever needed a job.

"Was only a couple of weeks that went by before Alex showed up in town," Westerberg remembers. He gave McCandless employment at the grain elevator and rented him a cheap room in one of the two houses he owned.

"I've given jobs to lots of hitchhikers over the years," says Westerberg. "Most of them weren't much good, didn't really want to work. It was a different story with Alex. He was the hardest worker I've ever seen. Didn't matter what it was, he'd do it: hard physical labor, mucking rotten grain and dead rats out of the bottom of the hole—jobs where you'd get so damn dirty you couldn't even tell what you looked like at the end of the day. And he never quit in the middle of something. If he started a job, he'd finish it. It was almost like a moral thing for him. He was what you'd call extremely ethical. He set pretty high standards for himself.

Alex's work ethic + personality [handwritten marginal note]

"You could tell right away that Alex was intelligent," Westerberg reflects, draining his third drink. "He read a lot. Used a lot of big words. I think maybe part of what got him into trouble was that he did too much thinking. Sometimes he tried too hard to make sense of the world, to figure out why people were bad to each other so often. A couple of times I tried to tell him it was a mistake to get too deep into that kind of stuff, but Alex got stuck on things. He always had to know the absolute right answer before he could go on to the next thing."

At one point Westerberg discovered from a tax form that McCandless's real name was Chris, not Alex. "He never explained why he'd changed his name," says Westerberg. "From things he said, you could tell something wasn't right between him and his family, but I don't like to pry into other people's business, so I never asked about it."

If McCandless felt estranged from his parents and siblings, he found a surrogate family in Westerberg and his employees, most of whom lived in Westerberg's Carthage home. A few blocks from the center of town, it is a simple, two-story Victorian in the Queen Anne style, with a big cottonwood towering over the front yard. The living arrangements were loose and convivial. The four or five inhabitants took turns cooking for one another, went drinking together, and chased women together, without success.

McCandless quickly became enamored of Carthage. He liked the community's stasis, its plebeian virtues and unassuming mien. The place was a back eddy, a pool of jetsam beyond the pull of the main current, and that suited him just fine. That fall he developed a lasting bond with both the town and Wayne Wester-berg.

Westerberg, in his mid-thirties, was brought to Carthage as a young boy by adoptive parents. A Renaissance man of the plains, he is a farmer, welder, businessman, machinist, ace mechanic, commodities speculator, licensed airplane pilot, computer pro-grammer, electronics troubleshooter, video-game repairman. Shortly before he met McCandless, however, one of his talents had got him in trouble with the law.

Westerberg had been drawn into a scheme to build and sell "black boxes," which illegally unscramble satellite-television transmissions, allowing people to watch encrypted cable pro-gramming without paying for it. The FBI caught wind of this, set up a sting, and arrested Westerberg. Contrite, he copped a plea to a single felony count and on October 10, 1990, some two weeks after McCandless arrived in Carthage, began serving a four-month sentence in Sioux Falls. With Westerberg in stir, there was no work at the grain elevator for McCandless, so on October 23, sooner than he might have under different circumstances, the boy left town and resumed a nomadic existence.

The attachment McCandless felt for Carthage remained pow-erful, however. Before departing, he gave Westerberg a treasured 1942 edition of Tolstoy's *War and Peace*. On the title page he in-scribed, "Transferred to Wayne Westerberg from <u>Alexander</u>. Oc-tober, 1990. Listen to <u>Pierre</u>." (The latter is a reference to Tolstoy's protagonist and alter ego, Pierre Bezuhov—altruistic, questing, illegitimately born.) And McCandless stayed in touch with Westerberg as he roamed the West, calling or writing Carthage every month or two. He had all his mail forwarded to Westerberg's address and told almost everyone he met thereafter that South Dakota was his home.

In truth McCandless had been raised in the comfortable upper-middle-class environs of Annandale, Virginia. His father, Walt, is an eminent aerospace engineer who designed advanced radar systems for the space shuttle and other high-profile projects while in the employ of NASA and Hughes Aircraft in the 1960s and '70s. In 1978, Walt went into business for himself, launching a small but eventually prosperous consulting firm, User Systems, Incorporated. His partner in the venture was Chris's mother, Billie. There were eight children in the extended family: a younger sister, Carine, with whom Chris was extremely close, and six half-brothers and sisters from Walt's first marriage.

In May 1990, Chris graduated from Emory University in Atlanta, where he'd been a columnist for, and editor of, the student newspaper, *The Emory Wheel*, and had distinguished himself as a history and anthropology major with a 3.72 grade-point average. He was offered membership in Phi Beta Kappa but declined, insisting that titles and honors are irrelevant.

The final two years of his college education had been paid for with a forty-thousand-dollar bequest left by a friend of the family's; more than twenty-four thousand dollars remained at the time of Chris's graduation, money his parents thought he intended to use for law school. "We misread him," his father admits. What Walt, Billie, and Carine didn't know when they flew down to Atlanta to attend Chris's commencement—what nobody knew—was that he would shortly donate all the money in his college fund to OXFAM America, a charity dedicated to fighting hunger.

The graduation ceremony was on May 12, a Saturday. The family sat through a long-winded commencement address delivered by Secretary of Labor Elizabeth Dole, and then Billie snapped pictures of a grinning Chris traversing the stage to receive his diploma.

The next day was Mother's Day. Chris gave Billie candy, flowers, a sentimental card. She was surprised and extremely touched: It was the first present she had received from her son in more than two years, since he had announced to his parents that, on principle, he would no longer give or accept gifts. Indeed, Chris had only recently upbraided Walt and Billie for expressing their desire to buy him a new car as a graduation present and offering to pay for law school if there wasn't enough money left in his college fund to cover it.

He already had a perfectly good car, he insisted: a beloved 1982 Datsun B210, slightly dented but mechanically sound, with 128,000 miles on the odometer. "I can't believe they'd try and buy me a car," he later complained in a letter to Carine,

or that they think I'd actually let them pay for my law school if I was going to go. . . . I've told them a million times that I have the best car in the world, a car that has spanned the continent from Miami to Alaska, a car that has in all those thousands of miles not given me a single problem, a car that I will never trade in, a car that I am very strongly attached to—yet they ignore what I say and think I'd actually accept a new car from them! I'm going to have to be real careful not to accept any gifts from them in the future because they will think they have bought my respect.

Chris had purchased the secondhand yellow Datsun when he was a senior in high school. In the years since, he'd been in the habit of taking it on extended solo road trips when classes weren't in session, and during that graduation weekend he casually mentioned to his parents that he intended to spend the upcoming summer on the road as well. His exact words were "I think I'm going to disappear for a while."

Neither parent made anything of this announcement at the time, although Walt did gently admonish his son, saying "Hey, make sure you come see us before you go." Chris smiled and sort of nodded, a response that Walt and Billie took as an affirmation that he would visit them in Annandale before the summer was out, and then they said their good-byes.

Toward the end of June, Chris, still in Atlanta, mailed his parents a copy of his final grade report: A in Apartheid and South African Society and History of Anthropological Thought; A minus in Contemporary African Politics and the Food Crisis in Africa. A brief note was attached:

Here is a copy of my final transcript. Gradewise things went pretty well and I ended up with a high cumulative average.

Thankyou for the pictures, the shaving gear, and the postcard from Paris. It seems that you really enjoyed your trip there. It must have been a lot of fun.

I gave Lloyd [Chris's closest friend at Emory] his picture, and he was very grateful; he did not have a shot of his diploma getting handed to him.

Not much else happening, but it's starting to get real hot and humid down here. Say Hi to everyone for me.

It was the last anyone in Chris's family would ever hear from him.

During that final year in Atlanta, Chris had lived off campus in a monkish room furnished with little more than a thin mattress on the floor, milk crates, and a table. He kept it as orderly and spotless as a military barracks. And he didn't have a phone, so Walt and Billie had no way of calling him.

By the beginning of August 1990, Chris's parents had heard nothing from their son since they'd received his grades in the mail, so they decided to drive down to Atlanta for a visit. When they arrived at his apartment, it was empty and a FOR RENT sign was taped to the window. The manager said that Chris had moved out at the end of June. Walt and Billie returned home to find that all the letters they'd sent their son that summer had been returned in a bundle. "Chris had instructed the post office to hold them until August 1, apparently so we wouldn't know anything was up," says Billie. "It made us very, very worried."

By then Chris was long gone. Five weeks earlier he'd loaded all his belongings into his little car and headed west without an itinerary. The trip was to be an odyssey in the fullest sense of the word, an epic journey that would change everything. He had spent the previous four years, as he saw it, preparing to fulfill an absurd and onerous duty: to graduate from college. At long last he was unencumbered, emancipated from the stifling world of his parents and peers, a world of abstraction and security and material excess, a world in which he felt grievously cut off from the raw throb of existence.

Driving west out of Atlanta, he intended to invent an utterly new life for himself, one in which he would be free to wallow in unfiltered experience. To symbolize the complete severance from his previous life, he even adopted a new name. No longer would he answer to Chris McCandless; he was now Alexander Supertramp, master of his own destiny.

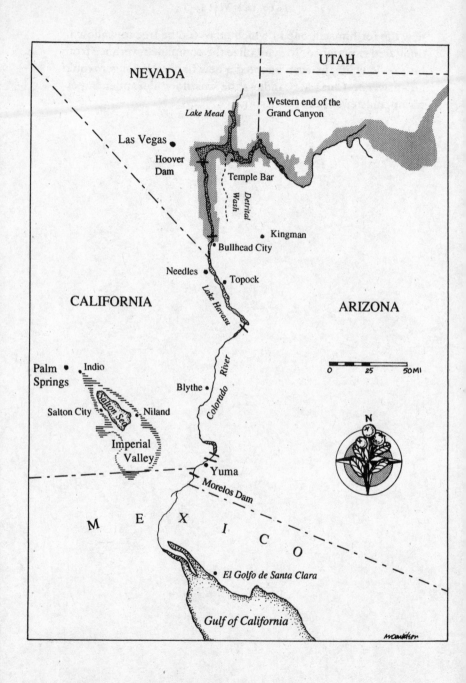

CHAPTER FOUR

DETRITAL WASH

The desert is the environment of revelation, genetically and physiologically alien, sensorily austere, esthetically abstract, historically inimical. . . . Its forms are bold and suggestive. The mind is beset by light and space, the kinesthetic novelty of aridity, high temperature, and wind. The desert sky is encircling, majestic, terrible. In other habitats, the rim of sky above the horizontal is broken or obscured; here, together with the overhead portion, it is infinitely vaster than that of rolling countryside and forest lands. . . . In an unobstructed sky the clouds seem more massive, sometimes grandly reflecting the earth's curvature on their concave undersides. The angularity of desert landforms imparts a monumental architecture to the clouds as well as to the land. . . .

To the desert go prophets and hermits; through deserts go pilgrims and exiles. Here the leaders of the great religions have sought the therapeutic and spiritual values of retreat, not to escape but to find reality.

PAUL SHEPARD,
MAN IN THE LANDSCAPE:
A HISTORIC VIEW OF THE ESTHETICS OF NATURE

The bear-paw poppy, *Arctomecon californica,* is a wildflower found in an isolated corner of the Mojave Desert and nowhere else in the world. In late spring it briefly produces a delicate golden bloom, but for most of the year the plant huddles unadorned and unnoticed on the parched earth. *A. californica* is sufficiently rare that it has been classified as an endangered species. In October 1990, more than three months after McCandless left Atlanta, a National Park Service ranger named Bud Walsh was sent into the backcountry of Lake Mead National Recreation Area to tally bear-paw poppies so that the federal government might better know just how scarce the plants were.

A. californica grows only in gypsum soil of a sort that occurs in abundance along the south shore of Lake Mead, so that is where Walsh led his team of rangers to conduct the botanical survey. They turned off Temple Bar Road, drove two roadless miles down the bed of Detrital Wash, parked their rigs near the lakeshore, and started scrambling up the steep east bank of the wash, a slope of crumbly white gypsum. A few minutes later, as they neared the top of the bank, one of the rangers happened to glance back down into the wash while pausing to catch his breath. "Hey! Look down there!" he yelled. "What the hell is that?"

At the edge of the dry riverbed, in a thicket of saltbush not far from where they had parked, a large object was concealed beneath a dun-colored tarpaulin. When the rangers pulled off the tarp, they found an old yellow Datsun without license plates. A note taped to the windshield read, "This piece of shit has been abandoned. Whoever can get it out of here can have it."

The doors had been left unlocked. The floorboards were plastered with mud, apparently from a recent flash flood. When he looked inside, Walsh found a Gianini guitar, a saucepan containing $4.93 in loose change, a football, a garbage bag full of old clothes, a fishing rod and tackle, a new electric razor, a harmonica, a set of jumper cables, twenty-five pounds of rice, and in the glove compartment, the keys to the vehicle's ignition.

The rangers searched the surrounding area "for anything suspicious," according to Walsh, and then departed. Five days later another ranger returned to the abandoned vehicle, managed to jump-start it without difficulty, and drove it out to the National Park Service maintenance yard at Temple Bar. "He drove it back at sixty miles an hour," Walsh recalls. "Said the thing ran like a champ." Attempting to learn who owned the car, the rangers sent out a bulletin over the Teletype to relevant law-enforcement agencies and ran a detailed search of computer records across the Southwest to see if the Datsun's VIN was associated with any crimes. Nothing turned up.

By and by the rangers traced the car's serial number to the Hertz Corporation, the vehicle's original owner; Hertz said they had sold it as a used rental car many years earlier and had no interest in reclaiming it. "Whoa! Great!" Walsh remembers thinking. "A freebie from the road gods—a car like this will make a great undercover vehicle for drug interdiction." And indeed it did. Over the next three years the Park Service used the Datsun to make undercover drug buys that led to numerous arrests in the crime-plagued national recreation area, including the bust of a high-volume methamphetamine dealer operating out of a trailer park near Bullhead City.

"We're still getting a lot of mileage out of that old car even now," Walsh proudly reports two and a half years after finding the Datsun. "Put a few bucks of gas in the thing, and it will go all day. Real reliable. I kind of wondered why nobody ever showed up to reclaim it."

The Datsun, of course, belonged to Chris McCandless. After piloting it west out of Atlanta, he'd arrived in Lake Mead National Recreation Area on July 6, riding a giddy Emersonian high. Ignoring posted warnings that off-road driving is strictly forbidden, McCandless steered the Datsun off the pavement where it crossed a broad, sandy wash. He drove two miles down the riverbed to the south shore of the lake. The temperature was 120 degrees Fahrenheit. The empty desert stretched into the distance, shimmering in the heat. Surrounded by chollas, bur sage, and the comical scurrying of collared lizards, McCandless pitched his tent in the puny shade of a tamarisk and basked in his newfound freedom.

Detrital Wash extends for some fifty miles from Lake Mead into the mountains north of Kingman; it drains a big chunk of country. Most of the year the wash is as dry as chalk. During the summer months, however, superheated air rises from the scorched earth like bubbles from the bottom of a boiling kettle, rushing heavenward in turbulent convection currents. Frequently the updrafts create cells of muscular, anvil-headed cumulonimbus clouds that can rise thirty thousand feet or more above the Mojave. Two days after McCandless set up camp beside Lake Mead, an unusually robust wall of thunderheads reared up in the afternoon sky, and it began to rain, very hard, over much of the Detrital Valley.

McCandless was camped at the edge of the wash, a couple of feet higher than the main channel, so when the bore of brown water came rushing down from the high country, he had just enough time to gather his tent and belongings and save them from being swept away. There was nowhere to move the car, however, as the only route of egress was now a foaming, full-blown river. As it turned out, the flash flood didn't have enough power to carry away the vehicle or even to do any lasting damage. But it did get the engine wet, so wet that when McCandless tried to start the car soon thereafter, the engine wouldn't catch, and in his impatience he drained the battery.

With the battery dead there was no way to get the Datsun running. If he hoped to get the car back to a paved road, McCandless had no choice but to walk out and notify the authorities of his predicament. If he went to the rangers, however, they would have some irksome questions for him: Why had he ignored posted regulations and driven down the wash in the first place? Was he aware that the vehicle's registration had expired two years before and had not been renewed? Did he know that his driver's license had also expired, and the vehicle was uninsured as well?

Truthful responses to these queries were not likely to be well received by the rangers. McCandless could endeavor to explain that he answered to statutes of a higher order—that as a latter-day adherent of Henry David Thoreau, he took as gospel the essay "On the Duty of Civil Disobedience" and thus considered it his moral responsibility to flout the laws of the state. It was improbable, however, that deputies of the federal government would share his point of view. There would be thickets of red tape to negotiate and fines to pay. His parents would no doubt be contacted. But there was a way to avoid such aggravation: He could

Thoreau

simply abandon the Datsun and resume his odyssey on foot. And that's what he decided to do.

Instead of feeling distraught over this turn of events, moreover, McCandless was exhilarated: He saw the flash flood as an opportunity to shed unnecessary baggage. He concealed the car as best he could beneath a brown tarp, stripped it of its Virginia plates, and hid them. He buried his Winchester deer-hunting rifle and a few other possessions that he might one day want to recover. Then, in a gesture that would have done both Thoreau and Tolstoy proud, he arranged all his paper currency in a pile on the sand—a pathetic little stack of ones and fives and twenties—and put a match to it. One hundred twenty-three dollars in legal tender was promptly reduced to ash and smoke.

$ burning

We know all of this because McCandless documented the burning of his money and most of the events that followed in a journal-snapshot album he would later leave with Wayne Westerberg for safekeeping before departing for Alaska. Although the tone of the journal—written in the third person in a stilted, self-consciousness voice—often veers toward melodrama, the available evidence indicates that McCandless did not misrepresent the facts; telling the truth was a credo he took seriously.

After loading his few remaining possessions into a backpack, McCandless set out on July 10 to hike around Lake Mead. This, his journal acknowledges, turned out to be a "tremendous mistake. . . . In extreme July temperatures becomes delirious." Suffering from heat stroke, he managed to flag down some passing boaters, who gave him a lift to Callville Bay, a marina near the west end of the lake, where he stuck out his thumb and took to the road.

McCandless tramped around the West for the next two months, spellbound by the scale and power of the landscape, thrilled by minor brushes with the law, savoring the intermittent company of other vagabonds he met along the way. Allowing his life to be shaped by circumstance, he hitched to Lake Tahoe, hiked into the Sierra Nevada, and spent a week walking north on the Pacific Crest Trail before exiting the mountains and returning to the pavement.

At the end of July, he accepted a ride from a man who called himself Crazy Ernie and offered McCandless a job on a ranch in northern California; photographs of the place show an unpainted, tumbledown house surrounded by goats and chickens, bedsprings, broken televisions, shopping carts, old appliances, and mounds and mounds of garbage. After working there eleven days with six other vagabonds, it became clear to McCandless that Ernie had no intention of ever paying him, so he stole a red ten-speed bicycle from the clutter in the yard, pedaled into Chico, and ditched the bike in a mall parking lot. Then he resumed a life of constant motion, riding his thumb north and west through Red Bluff, Weaverville, and Willow Creek.

At Arcata, California, in the dripping redwood forests of the Pacific shore, McCandless turned right on U.S. Highway 101 and headed up the coast. Sixty miles south of the Oregon line, near the town of Orick, a pair of drifters in an old van pulled over to consult their map when they noticed a boy crouching in the bushes off the side of the road. "He was wearing long shorts and this really stupid hat," says Jan Burres, a forty-one-year-old rubber tramp who was traveling around the West selling knick-knacks at flea markets and swap meets with her boyfriend, Bob. "He had a book about plants with him, and he was using it to pick berries, collecting them in a gallon milk jug with the top cut off. He looked pretty pitiful, so I yelled, 'Hey, you want a ride somewhere?' I thought maybe we could give him a meal or something.

"We got to talking. He was a nice kid. Said his name was Alex. And he was big-time hungry. Hungry, hungry, *hungry*. But real happy. Said he'd been surviving on edible plants he identified from the book. Like he was real proud of it. Said he was tramping around the country, having a big old adventure. He told us about abandoning his car, about burning all his money. I said, 'Why would you want to do that?' Claimed he didn't need money. I have a son about the same age Alex was, and we've been estranged for a few years now. So I said to Bob, 'Man, we got to take this kid with us. You need to school him about some things.' Alex took a ride from us up to Orick Beach, where we were staying, and camped with us for a week. He was a really good kid. We thought the world of him. When he left, we never expected to hear from him again, but he made a point of staying in touch. For the next two years Alex sent us a postcard every month or two."

From Orick, McCandless continued north up the coast. He passed through Pistol River, Coos Bay, Seal Rock, Manzanita, Astoria; Hoquiam, Humptulips, Queets; Forks, Port Angeles, Port Townsend, Seattle. "He was alone," as James Joyce wrote of Stephen Dedalus, his artist as a young man. "He was unheeded, happy, and near to the wild heart of life. He was alone and young and wilful and wildhearted, alone amid a waste of wild air and brackish waters and the seaharvest of shells and tangle and veiled grey sunlight."

On August 10, shortly before meeting Jan Burres and Bob, McCandless had been ticketed for hitchhiking near Willow Creek, in the gold-mining country east of Eureka. In an uncharacteristic lapse, McCandless gave his parents' Annandale address when the arresting officer demanded to know his permanent place of residence. The unpaid ticket appeared in Walt and Billie's mailbox at the end of August.

Walt and Billie, terribly concerned over Chris's vanishing act, had by that time already contacted the Annandale police, who had been of no help. When the ticket arrived from California, they became frantic. One of their neighbors was the director of the U.S. Defense Intelligence Agency, and Walt approached this man, an army general, for advice. The general put him in touch with a private investigator named Peter Kalitka, who'd done contract work for both the DIA and the CIA. He was the best, the general assured Walt; if Chris was out there, Kalitka would find him.

Using the Willow Creek ticket as a starting point, Kalitka launched an extremely thorough search, chasing down leads that led as far afield as Europe and South Africa. His efforts, however, turned up nothing—until December, when he learned from an inspection of tax records that Chris had given away his college fund to OXFAM.

"That really scared us," says Walt. "By that point we had absolutely no idea what Chris could be up to. The hitchhiking ticket just didn't make any sense. He loved that Datsun so much it was mind-boggling to me that he would ever abandon it and travel on foot. Although, in retrospect, I guess it shouldn't have surprised me. Chris was very much of the school that you should own nothing except what you can carry on your back at a dead run."

As Kalitka was trying to pick up Chris's scent in California, McCandless was already far away, hitching east across the Cascade Range, across the sagebrush uplands and lava beds of the Columbia River basin, across the Idaho panhandle, into Montana. There, outside Cut Bank, he crossed paths with Wayne Westerberg and by the end of September was working for him in Carthage. When Westerberg was jailed and the work came to a halt, and with winter coming on, McCandless headed for warmer climes.

On October 28, he caught a ride with a long-haul trucker into Needles, California. "Overjoyed upon reaching the Colorado River," McCandless wrote in his journal. Then he left the highway and started walking south through the desert, following the riverbank. Twelve miles on foot brought him to Topock, Arizona, a dusty way station along Interstate 40 where the freeway intersects the California border. While he was in town, he noticed a secondhand aluminum canoe for sale and on an impulse decided to buy it and paddle it down the Colorado River to the Gulf of California, nearly four hundred miles to the south, across the border with Mexico.

This lower stretch of the river, from Hoover Dam to the gulf, has little in common with the unbridled torrent that explodes through the Grand Canyon, some 250 miles upstream from Topock. Emasculated by dams and diversion canals, the lower Colorado burbles indolently from reservoir to reservoir through some of the hottest, starkest country on the continent. McCandless was stirred by the austerity of this landscape, by its saline beauty. The desert sharpened the sweet ache of his longing, amplified it, gave shape to it in sere geology and clean slant of light.

From Topock, McCandless paddled south down Lake Havasu under a bleached dome of sky, huge and empty. He made a brief excursion up the Bill Williams River, a tributary of the Colorado, then continued downstream through the Colorado River Indian Reservation, the Cibola National Wildlife Refuge, the Imperial National Wildlife Refuge. He drifted past saguaros and alkali flats, camped beneath escarpments of naked Precambrian stone. In the distance spiky, chocolate-brown mountains floated on eerie pools of mirage. Leaving the river for a day to track a herd of wild horses, he came across a sign warning that he was trespassing on the U.S. Army's highly restricted Yuma Proving Ground. McCandless was deterred not in the least.

At the end of November, he paddled through Yuma, where he stopped long enough to replenish his provisions and send a postcard to Westerberg in care of Glory House, the Sioux Falls work-release facility where Westerberg was doing time. "Hey Wayne!" the card reads,

How's it going? I hope that your situation has improved since the time we last spoke. I've been tramping around Arizona for about a month now. This is a good state! There is all kinds of fantastic scenery and the climate is wonderful. But apart from sending greetings the main purpose of this card is to thank you once again for all your hospitality. It's rare to find a man as generous and good natured as you are. Sometimes I wish I hadn't met you though. Tramping is too easy with all this money. My days were more exciting when I was penniless and had to forage around for my next meal. I couldn't make it now without money, however, as there is very little fruiting agriculture down here at this time.

Please thank Kevin again for all the clothes he gave me, I would have froze to death without them. I hope he got that book to you. Wayne, you really should read War and Peace. I meant it when I said you had one of the highest characters of any man I'd met. That is a very powerful and highly symbolic book. It has things in it that I think you will understand. Things that escape most people. As for me, I've decided that I'm going to live this life for some time to come. The freedom and simple beauty of it is just too good to pass up. One day I'll get back to you Wayne and repay some of your kindness. A case of Jack Daniels maybe? 'Til then I'll always think of you as a friend. GOD BLESS YOU, ALEXANDER

On December 2, he reached the Morelos Dam and the Mexican border. Worried that he would be denied entry because he was carrying no identification, he sneaked into Mexico by paddling through the dam's open floodgates and shooting the spillway below. "Alex looks quickly around for signs of trouble," his journal records. "But his entry of Mexico is either unnoticed or ignored. Alexander is jubilant!"

His jubilance, however, was short-lived. Below the Morelos Dam the river turns into a maze of irrigation canals, marshland, and dead-end channels, among which McCandless repeatedly lost his way:

> Canals break off in a multitude of directions. Alex is dumbfounded. Encounters some canal officials who can speak a little English. They tell him he has not been traveling south but west and is headed for the center of the Baja Peninsula. Alex is crushed. Pleads and persists that there must be some waterway to the Gulf of California. They stare at Alex and think him crazy. But then a passionate conversation breaks out amongst them, accompanied by maps and the flourish of pencils. After 10 minutes they present to Alex a route which apparently will take him to the ocean. He is overjoyed and hope bursts back into his heart. Following the map he reverses back up the canal until he comes upon the Canal de Independencia, which he takes east. According to the map this canal should bisect the Wellteco Canal, which will turn south and flow all the way to the ocean. But his hopes are quickly smashed when the canal comes to a dead end in the middle of the desert. A reconnaissance mission reveals, however, that Alex has merely run back into the bed of the now dead and dry Colorado River. He discovers another canal about 1/2 mile on the other side of the river bed. He decides to portage to this canal.

It took McCandless most of three days to carry the canoe and his gear to the new canal. The journal entry for December 5 records,

At last! Alex finds what he believes to be the Wellteco Canal and heads south. Worries and fears return as the canal grows ever smaller. . . . Local inhabitants help him portage around a barrier. . . . Alex finds Mexicans to be warm, friendly people. Much more hospitable than Americans. . . .

12/6   Small but dangerous waterfalls litter the canal.

12/9   All hopes collapse! The canal does not reach the ocean but merely peters out into a vast swamp. Alex is utterly confounded. Decides he must be close to ocean and elects to try and work way through swamp to sea. Alex becomes progressively lost to point where he must push canoe through reeds and drag it through mud. All is in despair. Finds some dry ground to camp in swamp at sundown. Next day, on 12/10, Alex resumes quest for an opening to the sea, but only becomes more confused, traveling in circles. Completely demoralized and frustrated he lays in his canoe at day's end and weeps. But then by fantastic chance he comes upon Mexican duck hunting guides who can speak English. He tells them his story and his quest for the sea. They say there is no outlet to the sea. But then one among them agrees to tow Alex back to his basecamp [behind a small motor skiff], and drive him and the canoe [in the bed of a pickup truck] to the ocean. It is a miracle.

The duck hunters dropped him in El Golfo de Santa Clara, a fishing village on the Gulf of California. From there McCandless took to the sea, traveling south down the eastern edge of the gulf. Having reached his destination, McCandless slowed his pace, and his mood became more contemplative. He took photographs of a tarantula, plaintive sunsets, windswept dunes, the long curve of empty coastline. The journal entries become short and perfunctory. He wrote fewer than a hundred words over the month that followed.

On December 14, weary of paddling, he hauled the canoe far up the beach, climbed a sandstone bluff, and set up camp on the edge of a desolate plateau. He stayed there for ten days, until high winds forced him to seek refuge in a cave midway up the precipitous face of the bluff, where he remained for another ten days. He greeted the new year by observing the full moon as it rose over the *Gran Desierto*—the Great Desert: seventeen hundred square miles of shifting dunes, the largest expanse of pure sand desert in North America. A day later he resumed paddling down the barren shore.

His journal entry for January 11, 1991, begins "A very fateful day." After traveling some distance south, he beached the canoe on a sandbar far from shore to observe the powerful tides. An hour later violent gusts started blowing down from the desert, and the wind and tidal rips conspired to carry him out to sea. The water by this time was a chaos of whitecaps that threatened to swamp and capsize his tiny craft. The wind increased to gale force. The whitecaps grew into high, breaking waves. "In great frustration," the journal reads,

he screams and beats canoe with oar. The oar breaks. Alex has one spare oar. He calms himself. If loses second oar is dead. Finally through extreme effort and much cursing he manages to beach canoe on jetty and collapses exhausted on sand at sundown. This incident led Alexander to decide to abandon canoe and return north.

On January 16, McCandless left the stubby metal boat on a hummock of dune grass southeast of El Golfo de Santa Clara and started walking north up the deserted beach. He had not seen or talked to another soul in thirty-six days. For that entire period he subsisted on nothing but five pounds of rice and what marine life he could pull from the sea, an experience that would later convince him he could survive on similarly meager rations in the Alaska bush.

He was back at the United States border on January 18. Caught by immigration authorities trying to slip into the country without ID, he spent a night in custody before concocting a story that sprang him from the slammer, minus his .38-caliber handgun, a "beautiful Colt Python, to which he was much attached."

McCandless spent the next six weeks on the move across the Southwest, traveling as far east as Houston and as far west as the Pacific coast. To avoid being rolled by the unsavory characters who rule the streets and freeway overpasses where he slept, he learned to bury what money he had before entering a city, then recover it on the way out of town. On February 3, according to his journal, McCandless went to Los Angeles "to get a ID and a job but feels extremely uncomfortable in society now and must return to road immediately."

Six days later, camped at the bottom of the Grand Canyon with Thomas and Karin, a young German couple who had given him a ride, he wrote, "Can this be the same Alex that set out in July, 1990? Malnutrition and the road have taken their toll on his body. Over 25 pounds lost. But his spirit is <u>soaring</u>."

On February 24, seven and a half months after he abandoned the Datsun, McCandless returned to Detrital Wash. The Park Service had long since impounded the vehicle, but he unearthed his old Virginia plates, SJF-421, and a few belongings he'd buried there. Then he hitched into Las Vegas and found a job at an Italian restaurant. "Alexander buried his backpack in the desert on 2/27 and entered Las Vegas with no money and no ID," the journal tells us.

He lived on the streets with bums, tramps, and winos for several weeks. Vegas would not be the end of the story, however. On May 10, itchy feet returned and Alex left his job in Vegas, retrieved his backpack, and hit the road again, though he found that if you are stupid enough to bury a camera underground you won't be taking many pictures with it afterwards. Thus the story has no picture book for the period May 10, 1991–January 7, 1992. But this is not important. It is the experiences, the memories, the great triumphant joy of <u>living</u> to the fullest extent in which real meaning is found. <u>God it's great to be alive!</u> Thank you. Thank you.

CHAPTER FIVE

BULLHEAD CITY

The dominant primordial beast was strong in Buck, and under
the fierce conditions of trail life it grew and grew. Yet it was a
secret growth. His newborn cunning gave him poise and control.

JACK LONDON,
THE CALL OF THE WILD

All Hail the Dominant Primordial Beast!
And Captain Ahab Too!
Alexander Supertramp
May 1992

GRAFFITO FOUND INSIDE THE ABANDONED BUS
ON THE STAMPEDE TRAIL

When his camera was ruined and McCandless stopped taking
photographs, he also stopped keeping a journal, a practice he
didn't resume until he went to Alaska the next year. Not a great
deal is known, therefore, about where he traveled after departing
Las Vegas in May 1991.

From a letter McCandless sent to Jan Burres, we know he spent July and August on the Oregon coast, probably in the vicinity of Astoria, where he complained that "the fog and rain was often intolerable." In September he hitched down U.S. Highway 101 into California, then headed east into the desert again. And by early October he had landed in Bullhead City, Arizona.

Bullhead City is a community in the oxymoronic, late-twentieth-century idiom. Lacking a discernible center, the town exists as a haphazard sprawl of subdivisions and strip malls stretching for eight or nine miles along the banks of the Colorado, directly across the river from the high-rise hotels and casinos of Laughlin, Nevada. Bullhead's distinguishing civic feature is the Mohave Valley Highway, four lanes of asphalt lined with gas stations and fast-food franchises, chiropractors and video shops, auto-parts outlets and tourist traps.

On the face of it, Bullhead City doesn't seem like the kind of place that would appeal to an adherent of Thoreau and Tolstoy, an ideologue who expressed nothing but contempt for the bourgeois trappings of mainstream America. McCandless, nevertheless, took a strong liking to Bullhead. Maybe it was his affinity for the lumpen, who were well represented in the community's trailer parks and campgrounds and laundromats; perhaps he simply fell in love with the stark desert landscape that encircles the town.

In any case, when he arrived in Bullhead City, McCandless stopped moving for more than two months—probably the longest he stayed in one place from the time he left Atlanta until he went to Alaska and moved into the abandoned bus on the Stampede Trail. In a card he mailed to Westerberg in October, he says of Bullhead, "It's a good place to spend the winter and I might finally settle down and abandon my tramping life, for good. I'll see what happens when spring comes around, because that's when I tend to get really itchy feet."

At the time he wrote these words, he was holding down a full-time job, flipping Quarter Pounders at a McDonald's on the main drag, commuting to work on a bicycle. Outwardly, he was living a surprisingly conventional existence, even going so far as to open a savings account at a local bank.

Curiously, when McCandless applied for the McDonald's job, he presented himself as Chris McCandless, not as Alex, and gave his employers his real Social Security number. It was an uncharacteristic break from his cover that might easily have alerted his parents to his whereabouts—although the lapse proved to be of no consequence because the private investigator hired by Walt and Billie never caught the slip.

Two years after he sweated over the grill in Bullhead, his colleagues at the golden arches don't recall much about Chris McCandless. "One thing I do remember is that he had a thing about socks," says the assistant manager, a fleshy, garrulous man named George Dreeszen. "He always wore shoes without socks—just plain couldn't *stand* to wear socks. But McDonald's has a rule that employees have to wear appropriate footwear at all times. That means shoes *and* socks. Chris would comply with the rule, but as soon as his shift was over, bang!—the first thing he'd do is peel those socks off. I mean the very first thing. Kind of like a statement, to let us know we didn't own him, I guess. But he was a nice kid and a good worker. Real dependable."

Lori Zarza, the second assistant manager, has a somewhat different impression of McCandless. "Frankly, I was surprised he ever got hired," she says. "He could do the job—he cooked in the back—but he always worked at the same slow pace, even during the lunch rush, no matter how much you'd get on him to hurry it up. Customers would be stacked ten-deep at the counter, and he wouldn't understand why I was on his case. He just didn't make the connection. It was like he was off in his own universe.

"He was reliable, though, a body that showed up every day, so they didn't dare fire him. They only paid four twenty-five an hour, and with all the casinos right across the river starting people at six twenty-five, well, it was hard to keep bodies behind the counter.

"I don't think he ever hung out with any of the employees after work or anything. When he talked, he was always going on about trees and nature and weird stuff like that. We all thought he was missing a few screws.

"When Chris finally quit," Zarza admits, "it was probably because of me. When he first started working, he was homeless, and he'd show up for work smelling bad. It wasn't up to McDonald's standards to come in smelling the way he did. So finally they delegated me to tell him that he needed to take a bath more often. Ever since I told him, there was a clash between us. And then the other employees—they were just trying to be nice—they started asking him if he needed some soap or anything. That made him mad—you could tell. But he never showed it outright. About three weeks later, he just walked out the door and quit."

McCandless had tried to disguise the fact that he was a drifter living out of a backpack: He told his fellow employees that he lived across the river in Laughlin. Whenever they offered him a ride home after work, he made excuses and politely declined. In fact, during his first several weeks in Bullhead, McCandless camped out in the desert at the edge of town; then he started squatting in a vacant mobile home. The latter arrangement, he explained in a letter to Jan Burres, "came about this way:"

One morning I was shaving in a restroom when an old man came in, and observing me, asked me if I was "sleeping out." I told him yes, and it turned out that he had this old trailer I could stay in for free. The only problem is that he doesn't really own it. Some absentee owners are merely letting him live on their land here, in another little trailer he stays in. So I kind of have to keep things toned down and stay out of sight, because he isn't supposed to have anybody over here. It's really quite a good deal, though, for the inside of the trailer is nice, it's a house trailer, furnished, with some of the electric sockets working and a lot of living space. The only drawback is this old guy, whose name is Charlie, is something of a lunatic and it's rather difficult to get along with him sometimes.

Charlie still lives at the same address, in a small teardrop-shaped camping trailer sheathed in rust-pocked tin, without plumbing or electricity, tucked behind the much larger blue-and-white mobile home where McCandless slept. Denuded mountains are visible to the west, towering sternly above the rooftops of adjacent double-wides. A baby-blue Ford Torino rests on blocks in the unkempt yard, weeds sprouting from its engine compartment. The ammonia reek of human urine rises from a nearby oleander hedge.

"Chris? Chris?" Charlie barks, scanning porous memory banks. "Oh yeah, him. Yeah, yeah, I remember him, sure." Charlie, dressed in a sweatshirt and khaki work pants, is a frail, nervous man with rheumy eyes and a growth of white stubble across his chin. By his recollection McCandless stayed in the trailer about a month.

"Nice guy, yeah, a pretty nice guy," Charlie reports. "Didn't like to be around too many people, though. Temperamental. He meant good, but I think he had a lot of complexes—know what I'm saying? Liked to read books by that Alaska guy, Jack London. Never said much. He'd get moody, wouldn't like to be bothered. Seemed like a kid who was looking for something, looking for *something*, just didn't know what it was. I was like that once, but then I realized what I was looking for: Money! Ha! Ha hyah, hooh boy!

"But like I was saying, Alaska—yeah, he talked about going to Alaska. Maybe to find whatever it was he was looking for. Nice guy, seemed like one, anyway. Had a lot of complexes sometimes, though. Had 'em bad. When he left, was around Christmas I think, he gave me fifty bucks and a pack of cigarettes for lettin' him stay here. Thought that was mighty decent of him."

In late November, McCandless sent a postcard to Jan Burres in care of a post-office box in Niland, a small town in California's Imperial Valley. "That card we got in Niland was the first letter from him in a long time that had a return address on it," Burres remembers. "So I immediately wrote back and said we'd come see him the next weekend in Bullhead, which wasn't that far from where we were."

McCandless was thrilled to hear from Jan. "I am so glad to find you both alive and sound," he exclaimed in a letter dated December 9, 1991.

Thanks so much for the Christmas card. It's nice to be thought of this time of year. . . . I'm so excited to hear that you will be com-

ing to see me, you're welcome <u>any time</u>. It's really great to think that after almost a year and a half we shall be meeting again.

He closed the letter by drawing a map and giving detailed directions for finding the trailer on Bullhead City's Baseline Road.

Four days after receiving this letter, however, as Jan and her boyfriend, Bob, were preparing to drive up for the visit, Burres returned to their campsite one evening to find "a big backpack leaning against our van. I recognized it as Alex's. Our little dog, Sunni, sniffed him out before I did. She'd liked Alex, but I was surprised she remembered him. When the dog found him, she went nuts." McCandless explained to Burres that he'd grown tired of Bullhead, tired of punching a clock, tired of the "plastic people" he worked with, and decided to get the hell out of town.

Jan and Bob were staying three miles outside of Niland, at a place the locals call the Slabs, an old navy air base that had been abandoned and razed, leaving a grid of empty concrete foundations scattered far and wide across the desert. Come November, as the weather turns cold across the rest of the country, some five thousand snowbirds and drifters and sundry vagabonds congregate in this otherworldly setting to live on the cheap under the sun. The Slabs functions as the seasonal capital of a teeming itinerant society—a tolerant, rubber-tired culture comprising the retired, the exiled, the destitute, the perpetually unemployed. Its constituents are men and women and children of all ages, folks on the dodge from collection agencies, relationships gone sour, the law or the IRS, Ohio winters, the middle-class grind.

When McCandless arrived at the Slabs, a huge flea market—swap meet was in full swing out in the desert. Burres, as one of the vendors, had set up some folding tables displaying cheap, mostly secondhand goods for sale, and McCandless volunteered to oversee her large inventory of used paperback books.

"He helped me a lot," Burres acknowledges. "He watched the table when I needed to leave, categorized all the books, made a lot of sales. He seemed to get a real kick out of it. Alex was big on the classics: Dickens, H. G. Wells, Mark Twain, Jack London.

London was his favorite. He'd try to convince every snowbird who walked by that they should read Call of the Wild."

McCandless had been infatuated with London since childhood. London's fervent condemnation of capitalist society, his glorification of the primordial world, his championing of the great unwashed—all of it mirrored McCandless's passions. Mesmerized by London's turgid portrayal of life in Alaska and the Yukon, McCandless read and reread *The Call of the Wild, White Fang,* "To Build a Fire," "An Odyssey of the North," "The Wit of Porportuk." He was so enthralled by these tales, however, that he seemed to forget they were works of fiction, constructions of the imagination that had more to do with London's romantic sensibilities than with the actualities of life in the subarctic wilderness. McCandless conveniently overlooked the fact that London himself had spent just a single winter in the North and that he'd died by his own hand on his California estate at the age of forty, a fatuous drunk, obese and pathetic, maintaining a sedentary existence that bore scant resemblance to the ideals he espoused in print.

Among the residents of the Niland Slabs was a seventeen-year-old named Tracy, and she fell in love with McCandless during his week-long visit. "She was this sweet little thing," says Burres, "the daughter of a couple of tramps who parked their rig four vehicles down from us. And poor Tracy developed a hopeless crush on Alex. The whole time he was in Niland, she hung around making goo-goo eyes at him, bugging me to convince him to go on walks with her. Alex was nice to her, but she was too young for him. He couldn't take her seriously. Probably left her brokenhearted for a whole week at least."

Even though McCandless rebuffed Tracy's advances, Burres makes it clear that he was no recluse: "He had a *good* time when he was around people, a *real* good time. At the swap meet he'd talk and talk and talk to everybody who came by. He must have met six or seven dozen people in Niland, and he was friendly with every one of them. He needed his solitude at times, but he wasn't a hermit. He did a lot of socializing. Sometimes I think it was like he was storing up company for the times when he knew nobody would be around."

McCandless was especially attentive to Burres, flirting and clowning with her at every opportunity. "He liked to tease me and torment me," she recalls. "I'd go out back to hang clothes on the line behind the trailer, and he'd attach clothespins all over me. He was playful, like a little kid. I had puppies, and he was always putting them under laundry baskets to watch them bounce around and yelp. He'd do it till I'd get mad and have to yell at him to stop. But in truth he was real good with the dogs. They'd follow him around, cry after him, want to sleep with him. Alex just had a way with animals."

One afternoon while McCandless was tending the book table at the Niland swap meet, somebody left a portable electric organ with Burres to sell on consignment. "Alex took it over and entertained everybody all day playing it," she says. "He had an amazing voice. He drew quite a crowd. Until then I never knew he was musical."

McCandless spoke frequently to the denizens of the Slabs about his plans for Alaska. He did calisthenics each morning to get in shape for the rigors of the bush and discussed backcountry survival strategies at length with Bob, a self-styled survivalist.

"Me," says Burres, "I thought Alex had lost his mind when he told us about his 'great Alaskan odyssey,' as he called it. But he was really excited about it. Couldn't stop talking about the trip."

Despite prodding from Burres, however, McCandless revealed virtually nothing about his family. "I'd ask him," Burres says, " 'Have you let your people know what you're up to? Does your mom know you're going to Alaska? Does your dad know?' But he'd never answer. He'd just roll his eyes at me, get peeved, tell me to quit trying to mother him. And Bob would say, 'Leave him alone! He's a grown man!' I'd keep at it until he'd change the subject, though—because of what happened between me and my own son. He's out there somewhere, and I'd want someone to look after him like I tried to look after Alex."

The Sunday before McCandless left Niland, he was watching

an NFL playoff game on the television in Burres's trailer when she noticed he was rooting especially hard for the Washington Redskins. "So I asked him if he was from the D.C. area," she says. "And he answered, 'Yeah, actually I am.' That's the only thing he ever let on about his background."

The following Wednesday, McCandless announced it was time for him to be moving on. He said he needed to go to the post office in Salton City, fifty miles west of Niland, to which he'd asked the manager of the Bullhead McDonald's to send his final paycheck, general delivery. He accepted Burres's offer to drive him there, but when she tried to give him a little money for helping out at the swap meet, she recalls, "he acted real offended. I told him, 'Man, you gotta have money to get along in this world,' but he wouldn't take it. Finally I got him to take some Swiss Army knives and a few belt knives; I convinced him they'd come in handy in Alaska and that he could maybe trade them for something down the road."

After an extended argument Burres also got McCandless to accept some long underwear and other warm clothing she thought he'd need in Alaska. "He eventually took it to shut me up," she laughs, "but the day after he left, I found most of it in the van. He'd pulled it out of his pack when we weren't looking and hid it up under the seat. Alex was a great kid, but he could really make me mad sometimes."

Although Burres was concerned about McCandless, she assumed he'd come through in one piece. "I thought he'd be fine in the end," she reflects. "He was smart. He'd figured out how to paddle a canoe down to Mexico, how to hop freight trains, how to score a bed at inner-city missions. He figured all of that out on his own, and I felt sure he'd figure out Alaska, too."

CHAPTER SIX

ANZA-BORREGO

No man ever followed his genius till it misled him. Though the result were bodily weakness, yet perhaps no one can say that the consequences were to be regretted, for these were a life in conformity to higher principles. If the day and the night are such that you greet them with joy, and life emits a fragrance like flowers and sweet-scented herbs, is more elastic, more starry, more immortal,—that is your success. All nature is your congratulation, and you have cause momentarily to bless yourself. The greatest gains and values are farthest from being appreciated. We easily come to doubt if they exist. We soon forget them. They are the highest reality. . . . The true harvest of my daily life is somewhat as intangible and indescribable as the tints of morning or evening. It is a little star-dust caught, a segment of the rainbow which I have clutched.

HENRY DAVID THOREAU,
WALDEN, OR LIFE IN THE WOODS
PASSAGE HIGHLIGHTED IN ONE OF THE BOOKS FOUND
WITH CHRIS MCCANDLESS'S REMAINS

On January 4, 1993, this writer received an unusual letter, penned in a shaky, anachronistic script that suggested an elderly author. "To Whom It May Concern," the letter began.

I would like to get a copy of the magazine that carried the story of the young man (Alex McCandless) dying in Alaska. I would like to write the one that investigated the incident. I drove him from Salton City Calif. . . . in March 1992 . . . to Grand Junction Co. . . . I left Alex there to hitch-hike to S.D. He said he would keep in touch. The last I heard from him was a letter the first week in April, 1992. On our trip we took pictures, me with the camcorder + Alex with his camera.

If you have a copy of that magazine please send me the cost of that magazine. . . .

I understand he was hurt. If so I would like to know how he was injured, for he always carried enough rice in his backpack + he had arctic clothes + plenty of money.

SINCERELY,
RONALD A. FRANZ

Please do not make these facts available to anybody till I know more about his death for he was not just the common wayfarer. Please believe me.

The magazine that Franz requested was the January 1993 issue of *Outside,* which featured a cover story about the death of Chris McCandless. His letter had been addressed to the offices of *Outside* in Chicago; because I had written the McCandless piece, it was forwarded to me.

McCandless made an indelible impression on a number of people during the course of his *hegira,* most of whom spent only a few days in his company, a week or two at most. Nobody, however, was affected more powerfully by his or her brief contact with the boy than Ronald Franz, who was eighty years old when their paths intersected in January 1992.

After McCandless bid farewell to Jan Burres at the Salton City Post Office, he hiked into the desert and set up camp in a brake of creosote at the edge of Anza-Borrego Desert State Park. Hard to the east is the Salton Sea, a placid ocean in miniature, its surface more than two hundred feet below sea level, created in 1905 by a monumental engineering snafu: Not long after a canal was dug from the Colorado River to irrigate rich farmland in the Imperial Valley, the river breached its banks during a series of major floods, carved a new channel, and began to gush unabated into the Imperial Valley Canal. For more than two years the canal inadvertently diverted virtually all of the river's prodigious flow into the Salton sink. Water surged across the once-dry floor of the sink, inundating farms and settlements, eventually drowning four hundred square miles of desert and giving birth to a landlocked ocean.

Only fifty miles from the limousines and exclusive tennis clubs and lush green fairways of Palm Springs, the west shore of the Salton Sea had once been the site of intense real estate speculation. Lavish resorts were planned, grand subdivisions platted. But little of the promised development ever came to pass. These days most of the lots remain vacant and are gradually being reclaimed by the desert. Tumbleweeds scuttle down Salton City's broad, desolate boulevards. Sun-bleached FOR SALE signs line the curbs, and paint peels from uninhabited buildings. A placard in the window of the Salton Sea Realty and Development Company declares CLOSED/CERRADO. Only the rattle of the wind interrupts the spectral quiet.

Away from the lakeshore the land rises gently and then abruptly to form the desiccated, phantasmal badlands of Anza-Borrego. The *bajada* beneath the badlands is open country cut by steep-walled arroyos. Here, on a low, sun-scorched rise dotted with chollas and indigobushes and twelve-foot ocotillo stems, McCandless slept on the sand under a tarp hung from a creosote branch.

When he needed provisions, he would hitch or walk the four miles into town, where he bought rice and filled his plastic water jug at the market–liquor store–post office, a beige stucco building that serves as the cultural nexus of greater Salton City. One Thursday in mid-January, McCandless was hitching back out to the *bajada* after filling his jug when an old man, name of Ron Franz, stopped to give him a ride.

"Where's your camp?" Franz inquired.

"Out past Oh-My-God Hot Springs," McCandless replied.

"I've lived in these parts six years now, and I've never heard of any place goes by that name. Show me how to get there."

They drove for a few minutes down the Borrego-Salton Seaway, and then McCandless told him to turn left into the desert, where a rough 4-x-4 track twisted down a narrow wash. After a mile or so they arrived at a bizarre encampment, where some two hundred people had gathered to spend the winter living out of their vehicles. The community was beyond the fringe, a vision of post-apocalypse America. There were families sheltered in cheap tent trailers, aging hippies in Day-Glo vans, Charles Manson look-alikes sleeping in rusted-out Studebakers that hadn't turned over since Eisenhower was in the White House. A substantial number of those present were walking around buck naked. At the center of the camp, water from a geothermal well had been piped into a pair of shallow, steaming pools lined with rocks and shaded by palm trees: Oh-My-God Hot Springs.

McCandless, however, wasn't living right at the springs; he was camped by himself another half mile out on the *bajada*. Franz drove Alex the rest of the way, chatted with him there for a while, and then returned to town, where he lived alone, rent free, in return for managing a ramshackle apartment building.

Franz, a devout Christian, had spent most of his adult life in the army, stationed in Shanghai and Okinawa. On New Year's Eve 1957, while he was overseas, his wife and only child were killed by a drunk driver in an automobile accident. Franz's son had been due to graduate from medical school the following June. Franz started hitting the whiskey, hard.

Six months later he managed to pull himself together and quit drinking, cold turkey, but he never really got over the loss. To salve his loneliness in the years after the accident, he started unofficially "adopting" indigent Okinawan boys and girls, eventually taking fourteen of them under his wing, paying for the oldest to attend medical school in Philadelphia and another to study medicine in Japan.

When Franz met McCandless, his long-dormant paternal impulses were kindled anew. He couldn't get the young man out of his mind. The boy had said his name was Alex—he'd declined to give a surname—and that he came from West Virginia. He was polite, friendly, well-groomed.

"He seemed extremely intelligent," Franz states in an exotic brogue that sounds like a blend of Scottish, Pennsylvania Dutch, and Carolina drawl. "I thought he was too nice a kid to be living by that hot springs with those nudists and drunks and dope smokers." After attending church that Sunday, Franz decided to talk to Alex "about how he was living. Somebody needed to convince him to get an education and a job and make something of his life."

When he returned to McCandless's camp and launched into the self-improvement pitch, though, McCandless cut him off abruptly. "Look, Mr. Franz," he declared, "you don't need to worry about me. I have a college education. I'm not destitute. I'm living like this by choice." And then, despite his initial prickliness, the young man warmed to the old-timer, and the two engaged in a long conversation. Before the day was out, they had driven into Palm Springs in Franz's truck, had a meal at a nice restaurant, and taken a ride on the tramway to the top of San Jacinto Peak, at the bottom of which McCandless stopped to unearth a Mexican serape and some other possessions he'd buried for safekeeping a year earlier.

Over the next few weeks McCandless and Franz spent a lot of time together. The younger man would regularly hitch into Salton City to do his laundry and barbecue steaks at Franz's apartment. He confided that he was biding his time until spring, when he intended to go to Alaska and embark on an "ultimate adventure." He also turned the tables and started lecturing the grandfatherly figure about the shortcomings of his sedentary existence, urging the eighty-year-old to sell most of his belongings, move out of the apartment, and live on the road. Franz took these harangues in stride and in fact delighted in the boy's company.

An accomplished leatherworker, Franz taught Alex the secrets of his craft; for his first project McCandless produced a tooled leather belt, on which he created an artful pictorial record of his wanderings. *ALEX* is inscribed at the belt's left end; then the initials *C.J.M.* (for Christopher Johnson McCandless) frame a skull and crossbones. Across the strip of cowhide one sees a rendering of a two-lane blacktop, a NO U-TURN sign, a thunderstorm producing a flash flood that engulfs a car, a hitchhiker's thumb, an eagle, the Sierra Nevada, salmon cavorting in the Pacific Ocean, the Pacific Coast Highway from Oregon to Washington, the Rocky Mountains, Montana wheat fields, a South Dakota rattlesnake, Westerberg's house in Carthage, the Colorado River, a gale in the Gulf of California, a canoe beached beside a tent, Las Vegas, the initials *T.C.D.*, Morro Bay, Astoria, and at the buckle end, finally, the letter *N* (presumably representing north). Executed with remarkable skill and creativity, this belt is as astonishing as any artifact Chris McCandless left behind.

Franz grew increasingly fond of McCandless. "God, he was a smart kid," the old man rasps in a barely audible voice. He directs his gaze at a patch of sand between his feet as he makes this declaration; then he stops talking. Bending stiffly from the waist, he wipes some imaginary dirt from his pant leg. His ancient joints crack loudly in the awkward silence.

More than a minute passes before Franz speaks again; squinting at the sky, he begins to reminisce further about the time he spent in the youngster's company. Not infrequently during their visits, Franz recalls, McCandless's face would darken with anger and he'd fulminate about his parents or politicians or the endemic idiocy of mainstream American life. Worried about alienating the boy, Franz said little during such outbursts and let him rant.

One day in early February, McCandless announced that he was splitting for San Diego to earn more money for his Alaska trip.

"You don't need to go to San Diego," Franz protested. "I'll give you money if you need some."

"No. You don't get it. I'm *going* to San Diego. And I'm leaving on Monday."

"OK. I'll drive you there."

"Don't be ridiculous," McCandless scoffed.

"I need to go anyway," Franz lied, "to pick up some leather supplies."

McCandless relented. He struck his camp, stored most of his belongings in Franz's apartment—the boy didn't want to schlepp his sleeping bag or backpack around the city—and then rode with the old man across the mountains to the coast. It was raining when Franz dropped McCandless at the San Diego waterfront. "It was a very hard thing for me to do," Franz says. "I was sad to be leaving him."

On February 19, McCandless called Franz, collect, to wish him a happy eighty-first birthday; McCandless remembered the date because his own birthday had been seven days earlier: He had turned twenty-four on February 12. During this phone call he also confessed to Franz that he was having trouble finding work.

On February 28, he mailed a postcard to Jan Burres. "Hello!" it reads,

Have been living on streets of San Diego for the past week. First day I got here it rained like hell. The missions here suck and I'm getting preached to death. Not much happening in terms of jobs so I'm heading north tomorrow.

I've decided to head for Alaska no later than May 1st, but I've got to raise a little cash to outfit myself. May go back and work for a friend I have in South Dakota if he can use me. Don't know where I'm headed now but I'll write when I get there. Hope all's well with you. TAKE CARE, ALEX

On March 5, McCandless sent another card to Burres and a card to Franz as well. The missive to Burres says,

Greetings from Seattle! I'm a hobo now! That's right, I'm riding the rails now. What fun, I wish I had jumped trains earlier. The rails have some drawbacks, however. First is that one becomes absolutely filthy. Second is that one must tangle with these crazy bulls. I was sitting in a hotshot in L.A. when a bull found me with his flashlight about 10 P.M. "Get outta there before I KILL ya!" screamed the bull. I got out and saw he had drawn his revolver. He interrogated me at gunpoint, then growled, "If I ever see you around this train again I'll kill ya! Hit the road!" What a lunatic! I got the last laugh when I caught the same train 5 minutes later and rode it all the way to Oakland. I'll be in touch,

ALEX

A week later Franz's phone rang. "It was the operator," he says, "asking if I would accept a collect call from someone named Alex. When I heard his voice, it was like sunshine after a month of rain."

"Will you come pick me up?" McCandless asked.

"Yes. Where in Seattle are you?"

"Ron," McCandless laughed, "I'm not in Seattle. I'm in California, just up the road from you, in Coachella." Unable to find work in the rainy Northwest, McCandless had hopped a series of freight trains back to the desert. In Colton, California, he was discovered by another bull and thrown in jail. Upon his release he had hitchhiked to Coachella, just southeast of Palm Springs, and called Franz. As soon as he hung up the phone, Franz rushed off to pick McCandless up.

"We went to a Sizzler, where I filled him up with steak and lobster," Franz recalls, "and then we drove back to Salton City."

McCandless said that he would be staying only a day, just long enough to wash his clothes and load his backpack. He'd heard from Wayne Westerberg that a job was waiting for him at the grain elevator in Carthage, and he was eager to get there. The date was March 11, a Wednesday. Franz offered to take McCandless to Grand Junction, Colorado, which was the farthest he could drive without missing an appointment in Salton City the following Monday. To Franz's surprise and great relief, McCandless accepted the offer without argument.

Before departing, Franz gave McCandless a machete, an arctic parka, a collapsible fishing pole, and some other gear for his Alaska undertaking. Thursday at daybreak they drove out of Salton City in Franz's truck. In Bullhead City they stopped to close out McCandless's bank account and to visit Charlie's trailer, where McCandless had stashed some books and other belongings, including the journal-photo album from his canoe trip down the Colorado. McCandless then insisted on buying Franz lunch at the Golden Nugget Casino, across the river in Laughlin. Recognizing McCandless, a waitress at the Nugget gushed, "Alex! Alex! You're back!"

Franz had purchased a video camera before the trip, and he

paused now and then along the way to record the sights. Although McCandless usually ducked away whenever Franz pointed the lens in his direction, some brief footage exists of him standing impatiently in the snow above Bryce Canyon. "Ok, let's go," he protests to the camcorder after a few moments. "There's a lot more ahead, Ron." Wearing jeans and a wool sweater, McCandless looks tan, strong, healthy.

Franz reports that it was a pleasant, if hurried trip. "Sometimes we'd drive for hours without saying a word," he recalls. "Even when he was sleeping, I was happy just knowing he was there." At one point Franz dared to make a special request of McCandless. "My mother was an only child," he explains. "So was my father. And I was their only child. Now that my own boy's dead, I'm the end of the line. When I'm gone, my family will be finished, gone forever. So I asked Alex if I could adopt him, if he would be my grandson."

McCandless, uncomfortable with the request, dodged the question: "We'll talk about it when I get back from Alaska, Ron."

On March 14, Franz left McCandless on the shoulder of Interstate 70 outside Grand Junction and returned to southern California. McCandless was thrilled to be on his way north, and he was relieved as well—relieved that he had again evaded the impending threat of human intimacy, of friendship, and all the messy emotional baggage that comes with it. He had fled the claustrophobic confines of his family. He'd successfully kept Jan Burres and Wayne Westerberg at arm's length, flitting out of their lives before anything was expected of him. And now he'd slipped painlessly out of Ron Franz's life as well.

[margin note, handwritten: social distancing]

Painlessly, that is, from McCandless's perspective—although not from the old man's. One can only speculate about why Franz became so attached to McCandless so quickly, but the affection he felt was genuine, intense, and unalloyed. Franz had been living a solitary existence for many years. He had no family and few friends. A disciplined, self-reliant man, he got along remarkably well despite his age and solitude. When McCandless came into his world, however, the boy undermined the old man's meticulously constructed defenses. Franz relished being with McCandless, but their burgeoning friendship also reminded him how lonely he'd been. The boy unmasked the gaping void in Franz's life even as he helped fill it. When McCandless departed as suddenly as he'd arrived, Franz found himself deeply and unexpectedly hurt.

In early April a long letter arrived in Franz's post-office box bearing a South Dakota postmark. "Hello Ron," it says,

Alex here. I have been working up here in Carthage South Dakota for nearly two weeks now. I arrived up here three days after we parted in Grand Junction, Colorado. I hope that you made it back to Salton City without too many problems. I enjoy working here and things are going well. The weather is not very bad and many days are surprisingly mild. Some of the farmers are even already going out into their fields. It must be getting rather hot down there in Southern California by now. I wonder if you ever got a chance to get out and see how many people showed up for the March 20 Rainbow gathering there at the hotsprings. It sounds like it might have been a lot of fun, but I don't think you really understand these kind of people very well.

I will not be here in South Dakota very much longer. My friend, Wayne, wants me to stay working at the grain elevator through May and then go combining with him the entire summer, but I have my soul set entirely on my Alaskan Odyssey *and hope to be* ___ *way no later than April 15. That means I will be leaving* ___ *very long, so I need you to send any more mail I may* ___ *to the return address listed below.*

___ *really enjoy all the help you have given me and the times that we spent together. I hope that you will not be too depressed by our parting. It may be a very long time before we see each other again. But providing that I get through this Alaskan Deal in one piece you will be hearing from me again in the future. I'd like to repeat the advice I gave you before, in that I think you really should make a radical change in your lifestyle and begin to boldly do things which you may previously never have thought of doing, or been too hesitant to attempt. So many people live within un-*

living naturally

happy circumstances and yet will not take the initiative to change their situation because they are conditioned to a life of security, conformity, and conservatism, all of which may appear to give one peace of mind, but in reality nothing is more damaging to the adventurous spirit within a man than a secure future. The very basic core of a man's living spirit is his passion for adventure. The joy of life comes from our encounters with new experiences, and hence there is no greater joy than to have an endlessly changing horizon, for each day to have a new and different sun. If you want to get more out of life, Ron, you must lose your inclination for monotonous security and adopt a helter-skelter style of life that will at first appear to you to be crazy. But once you become accustomed to such a life you will see its full meaning and its incredible beauty. And so, Ron, in short, get out of Salton City and hit the Road. I guarantee you will be very glad you did. But I fear that you will ignore my advice. You think that I am stubborn, but you are even more stubborn than me. You had a wonderful chance on your drive back to see one of the greatest sights on earth, the Grand Canyon, something every American should see at least once in his life. But for some reason incomprehensible to me you wanted nothing but to bolt for home as quickly as possible, right back to the same situation which you see day after day after day. I fear you will follow this same inclination in the future and thus fail to discover all the wonderful things that God has placed around us to discover. Don't settle down and sit in one place. Move around, be nomadic, make each day a new horizon. You are still going to live a long time, Ron, and it would be a shame if you did not take the opportunity to revolutionize your life and move into an entirely new realm of experience.

You are wrong if you think Joy emanates only or principally from human relationships. God has placed it all around us. It is in everything and anything we might experience. We just have to have the courage to turn against our habitual lifestyle and engage in unconventional living.

My point is that you do not need me or anyone else around to bring this new kind of light in your life. It is simply waiting out there for you to grasp it, and all you have to do is reach for it. The only person you are fighting is yourself and your stubbornness to engage in new circumstances.

Ron, I really hope that as soon as you can you will get out of Salton City, put a little camper on the back of your pickup, and start seeing some of the great work that God has done here in the American West. You will see things and meet people and there is much to learn from them. And you must do it economy style, no motels, do your own cooking, as a general rule spend as little as possible and you will enjoy it much more immensely. I hope that the next time I see you, you will be a new man with a vast array of new adventures and experiences behind you. Don't hesitate or allow yourself to make excuses. Just get out and do it. Just get out and do it. You will be very, very glad that you did.

TAKE CARE RON,
ALEX

Please write back to:
Alex McCandless
Madison, SD 57042

Astoundingly, the eighty-one-year-old man took the brash twenty-four-year-old vagabond's advice to heart. Franz placed his furniture and most of his other possessions in a storage locker, bought a GMC Duravan, and outfitted it with bunks and camping gear. Then he moved out of his apartment and set up camp on the *bajada.*

Franz occupied McCandless's old campsite, just past the hot springs. He arranged some rocks to create a parking area for the van, transplanted prickly pears and indigobushes for "landscaping." And then he sat out in the desert, day after day after day, awaiting his young friend's return.

Ronald Franz (this is not his real name; at his request I have given him a pseudonym) looks remarkably sturdy for a man in his ninth decade who has survived two heart attacks. Nearly six feet tall, with thick arms and a barrel chest, he stands erect, his shoulders unbowed. His ears are large beyond the proportions of his other features, as are his gnarled, meaty hands. When I walk into his camp in the desert and introduce myself, he is wearing old jeans and an immaculate white T-shirt, a decorative tooled-leather belt of his own creation, white socks, scuffed black loafers. His age is betrayed only by the creases across his brow and a proud, deeply pitted nose, over which a purple filigree of veins unfolds like a finely wrought tattoo. A little more than a year after McCandless's death he regards the world through wary blue eyes.

To dispel Franz's suspicion, I hand him an assortment of photographs I'd taken on a trip to Alaska the previous summer, during which I'd retraced McCandless's terminal journey on the Stampede Trail. The first several images in the stack are landscapes—shots of the surrounding bush, the overgrown trail, distant mountains, the Sushana River. Franz studies them in silence, occasionally nodding when I explain what they depict; he seems grateful to see them.

When he comes to the pictures of the bus in which the boy died, however, he stiffens abruptly. Several of these images show McCandless's belongings inside the derelict vehicle; as soon as Franz realizes what he's seeing, his eyes mist over, he thrusts the photos back at me without examining the rest, and the old man walks away to compose himself as I mumble a lame apology.

Franz no longer lives at McCandless's campsite. A flash flood washed the makeshift road away, so he moved twenty miles out, toward the Borrego badlands, where he camps beside an isolated stand of cottonwoods. Oh-My-God Hot Springs is gone now, too, bulldozed and plugged with concrete by order of the Imperial Valley Health Commission. County officials say they eliminated the springs out of concern that bathers might become gravely ill from virulent microbes thought to flourish in the thermal pools.

"That sure could of been true," says the clerk at the Salton City store, "but most people think they bulldozed 'em 'cause the springs was starting to attract too many hippies and drifters and scum like that. Good riddance, you ask me."

For more than eight months after he said good-bye to McCandless, Franz remained at his campsite, scanning the road for the approach of a young man with a large pack, waiting patiently for Alex to return. During the last week of 1992, the day after Christmas, he picked up two hitchhikers on his way back from a trip into Salton City to check his mail. "One fella was from Mississippi, I think; the other was a Native American," Franz remembers. "On the way out to the hot springs, I started telling them about my friend Alex, and the adventure he'd set out to have in Alaska."

Suddenly, the Indian youth interrupted: "Was his name Alex McCandless?"

"Yes, that's right. So you've met him, then—"

"I hate to tell you this, mister, but your friend is dead. Froze to death up on the tundra. Just read about it in *Outdoor* magazine."

In shock, Franz interrogated the hitchhiker at length. The details rang true; his story added up. Something had gone horribly wrong. McCandless would never be coming back.

"When Alex left for Alaska," Franz remembers, "I prayed. I asked God to keep his finger on the shoulder of that one; I told him that boy was special. But he let Alex die. So on December 26, when I learned what happened, I renounced the Lord. I withdrew my church membership and became an atheist. I decided I couldn't believe in a God who would let something that terrible happen to a boy like Alex.

"After I dropped off the hitchhikers," Franz continues, "I turned my van around, drove back to the store, and bought a bottle of whiskey. And then I went out into the desert and drank it. I wasn't used to drinking, so it made me sick. Hoped it'd kill me, but it didn't. Just made me real, real sick."

CHAPTER SEVEN

CARTHAGE

There was some books. . . . One was Pilgrim's Progress, *about
a man that left his family, it didn't say why. I read considerable
in it now and then. The statements was interesting, but tough.*

MARK TWAIN,
THE ADVENTURES OF HUCKLEBERRY FINN

*It is true that many creative people fail to make mature per-
sonal relationships, and some are extremely isolated. It is also
true that, in some instances, trauma, in the shape of early separation or bereavement, has steered the potentially creative person toward developing aspects of his personality which can find
fulfillment in comparative isolation.* But this does not mean
that solitary, creative pursuits are themselves pathological. . . .

[A]*voidance behavior is a response designed to protect the
infant from behavioural disorganization. If we transfer this
concept to adult life, we can see that an avoidant infant might
very well develop into a person whose principal need was to find
some kind of meaning and order in life which was* not *entirely,
or even chiefly, dependent upon interpersonal relationships.*

ANTHONY STORR,
SOLITUDE: A RETURN TO THE SELF

The big John Deere 8020 squats silently in the canted evening
light, a long way from anywhere, surrounded by a half-mowed
field of South Dakota milo. Wayne Westerberg's muddy sneakers
protrude from the maw of the combine, as if the machine were
in the process of swallowing him whole, an overgrown metal rep-

tile digesting its prey. "Hand me that goddamn wrench, will you?" an angry, muffled voice demands from deep within the machine's innards. "Or are you guys too busy standing around with your hands in your goddamn pockets to be of any use?" The combine has broken down for the third time in as many days, and Westerberg is frantically trying to replace a hard-to-reach bushing before nightfall.

An hour later he emerges, smeared with grease and chaff but successful. "Sorry about snapping like that," Westerberg apologizes. "We've been working too many eighteen-hour days. I guess I'm getting a little snarly, it being so late in the season and all, and us being shorthanded besides. We was counting on Alex being back at work by now." Fifty days have gone by since McCandless's body was discovered in Alaska on the Stampede Trail.

Seven months earlier, on a frosty March afternoon, McCandless had ambled into the office at the Carthage grain elevator and announced that he was ready to go to work. "There we were, ringing up the morning's tickets," remembers Westerberg, "and in walks Alex with a big old backpack slung over his shoulder." He told Westerberg he planned on staying until April 15, just long enough to put together a grubstake. He needed to buy a pile of new gear, he explained, because he was going to Alaska. McCandless promised to come back to South Dakota in time to help with the autumn harvest, but he wanted to be in Fairbanks by the end of April in order to squeeze in as much time as possible up North before his return.

During those four weeks in Carthage, McCandless worked hard, doing dirty, tedious jobs that nobody else wanted to tackle: mucking out warehouses, exterminating vermin, painting, scything weeds. At one point, to reward McCandless with a task that involved slightly more skill, Westerberg attempted to teach him to operate a front-end loader. "Alex hadn't been around machinery much," Westerberg says with a shake of his head, "and it was pretty comical to watch him try to get the hang of the clutch and all those levers. He definitely wasn't what you'd call mechanically minded."

Nor was McCandless endowed with a surfeit of common sense.

Many who knew him have commented, unbidden, that he seemed to have great difficulty seeing the trees, as it were, for the forest. "Alex wasn't a total space cadet or anything," says Westerberg; "don't get me wrong. But there was gaps in his thinking. I remember once I went over to the house, walked into the kitchen, and noticed a god-awful stink. I mean it smelled nasty in there. I opened the microwave, and the bottom of it was filled with rancid grease. Alex had been using it to cook chicken, and it never occurred to him that the grease had to drain somewhere. It wasn't that he was too lazy to clean it up—Alex always kept things real neat and orderly—it was just that he hadn't noticed the grease."

Soon after McCandless returned to Carthage that spring, Westerberg introduced him to his longtime, on-again, off-again girlfriend, Gail Borah, a petite, sad-eyed woman, as slight as a heron, with delicate features and long blond hair. Thirty-five years old, divorced, a mother of two teenage children, she quickly became close to McCandless. "He was kind of shy at first," says Borah. "He acted like it was hard for him to be around people. I just figured that was because he'd spent so much time by himself.

"I had Alex over to the house for supper just about every night," Borah continues. "He was a big eater. Never left any food on his plate. Never. He was a good cook, too. Sometimes he'd have me over to Wayne's place and fix supper for everybody. Cooked a lot of rice. You'd think he would of got tired of it, but he never did. Said he could live for a month on nothing but twenty-five pounds of rice.

"Alex talked a lot when we got together," Borah recalls. "Serious stuff, like he was baring his soul, kind of. He said he could tell me things that he couldn't tell the others. You could see something was gnawing at him. It was pretty obvious he didn't get along with his family, but he never said much about any of them except Carine, his little sister. He said they were pretty close. Said she was beautiful, that when she walked down the street, guys would turn their heads and stare."

Westerberg, for his part, didn't concern himself with McCandless's family problems. "Whatever reason he had for being pissed off, I figured it must have been a good one. Now that he's dead, though, I don't know anymore. If Alex was here right now, I'd be tempted to chew him out good: 'What the hell were you thinking? Not speaking to your family for all that time, treating them like dirt!' One of the kids that works for me, fuck, he don't even have any goddamn parents, but you don't hear him bitching. Whatever the deal was with Alex's family, I guarantee you I've seen a lot worse. Knowing Alex, I think he must have just got stuck on something that happened between him and his dad and couldn't leave it be."

Westerberg's latter conjecture, as it turned out, was a fairly astute analysis of the relationship between Chris and Walt McCandless. Both father and son were stubborn and high-strung. Given Walt's need to exert control and Chris's extravagantly independent nature, polarization was inevitable. Chris submitted to Walt's authority through high school and college to a surprising degree, but the boy raged inwardly all the while. He brooded at length over what he perceived to be his father's moral shortcomings, the hypocrisy of his parents' lifestyle, the tyranny of their conditional love. Eventually, Chris rebelled—and when he finally did, it was with characteristic immoderation.

Shortly before he disappeared, Chris complained to Carine that their parents' behavior was "so irrational, so oppressive, disrespectful and insulting that I finally passed my breaking point." He went on:

> Since they won't ever take me seriously, for a few months after graduation I'm going to let them think they are right, I'm going to let them think that I'm "coming around to see their side of things" and that our relationship is stabilizing. And then, once the time is right, with one abrupt, swift action I'm going to completely knock them out of my life. I'm going to divorce them as my parents once and for all and never speak to either of those idiots again as long as I live. I'll be through with them once and for all, forever.

The chill Westerberg sensed between Alex and his parents stood in marked contrast to the warmth McCandless exhibited in

Carthage. Outgoing and extremely personable when the spirit moved him, he charmed a lot of folks. There was mail waiting for him when he arrived back in South Dakota, correspondence from people he'd met on the road, including what Westerberg remembers as "letters from a girl who had a big crush on him, someone he'd gotten to know in some Timbuktu—some campground, I think." But McCandless never mentioned any romantic entanglements to either Westerberg or Borah.

"I don't recollect Alex ever talking about any girlfriends," says Westerberg. "Although a couple of times he mentioned wanting to get married and have a family some day. You could tell he didn't take relationships lightly. He wasn't the kind of guy who would go out and pick up girls just to get laid."

It was clear to Borah, too, that McCandless hadn't spent much time cruising singles bars. "One night a bunch of us went out to a bar over in Madison," says Borah, "and it was hard to get him out on the dance floor. But once he was out there, he wouldn't sit down. We had a blast. After Alex died and all, Carine told me that as far as she knew, I was one of the only girls he ever went dancing with."

In high school McCandless had enjoyed a close rapport with two or three members of the opposite sex, and Carine recalls one instance when he got drunk and tried to bring a girl up to his bedroom in the middle of the night (they made so much noise stumbling up the stairs that Billie was awakened and sent the girl home). But there is little evidence that he was sexually active as a teenager and even less to suggest that he slept with any woman after graduating from high school. (Nor, for that matter, is there any evidence that he was ever sexually intimate with a man.) It seems that McCandless was drawn to women but remained largely or entirely celibate, as chaste as a monk.

Chastity and moral purity were qualities McCandless mulled over long and often. Indeed, one of the books found in the bus with his remains was a collection of stories that included Tolstoy's "The Kreutzer Sonata," in which the nobleman-turned-ascetic denounces "the demands of the flesh." Several such passages are starred and highlighted in the dog-eared text, the

sexual relations

margins filled with cryptic notes printed in McCandless's distinctive hand. And in the chapter on "Higher Laws" in Thoreau's *Walden*, a copy of which was also discovered in the bus, McCandless circled "Chastity is the flowering of man; and what are called Genius, Heroism, Holiness, and the like, are but various fruits which succeed it."

We Americans are titillated by sex, obsessed by it, horrified by it. When an apparently healthy person, especially a healthy young man, elects to forgo the enticements of the flesh, it shocks us, and we leer. Suspicions are aroused.

McCandless's apparent sexual innocence, however, is a corollary of a personality type that our culture purports to admire, at least in the case of its more famous adherents. His ambivalence toward sex echoes that of celebrated others who embraced wilderness with single-minded passion—Thoreau (who was a lifelong virgin) and the naturalist John Muir, most prominently—to say nothing of countless lesser-known pilgrims, seekers, misfits, and adventurers. Like not a few of those seduced by the wild, McCandless seems to have been driven by a variety of lust that supplanted sexual desire. His yearning, in a sense, was too powerful to be quenched by human contact. McCandless may have been tempted by the succor offered by women, but it paled beside the prospect of rough congress with nature, with the cosmos itself. And thus was he drawn north, to Alaska.

McCandless assured both Westerberg and Borah that when his northern sojourn was over, he would return to South Dakota, at least for the fall. After that, it would depend.

"I got the impression that this Alaska escapade was going to be his last big adventure," Westerberg offers, "and that he wanted to settle down some. He said he was going to write a book about his travels. He liked Carthage. With his education, nobody thought he was going to work at a goddamn grain elevator the rest of his life. But he definitely intended to come back here for a while, help us out at the elevator, figure out what he was going to do next."

That spring, however, McCandless's sights were fixed unflinchingly on Alaska. He talked about the trip at every opportunity. He

shared view w/ naturalists

sought out experienced hunters around town and asked them for tips about stalking game, dressing animals, curing meat. Borah drove him to the Kmart in Mitchell to shop for some last pieces of gear.

By mid-April, Westerberg was both shorthanded and very busy, so he asked McCandless to postpone his departure and work a week or two longer. McCandless wouldn't even consider it. "Once Alex made up his mind about something, there was no changing it," Westerberg laments. "I even offered to buy him a plane ticket to Fairbanks, which would have let him work an extra ten days and still get to Alaska by the end of April, but he said, 'No, I want to hitch north. Flying would be cheating. It would wreck the whole trip.'"

Two nights before McCandless was scheduled to head north, Mary Westerberg, Wayne's mother, invited him to her house for dinner. "My mom doesn't like a lot of my hired help," Westerberg says, "and she wasn't real enthusiastic about meeting Alex, either. But I kept bugging her, telling her 'You gotta meet this kid,' and so she finally had him over for supper. They hit it off immediately. The two of 'em talked nonstop for five hours."

"There was something fascinating about him," explains Mrs. Westerberg, seated at the polished walnut table where McCandless dined that night. "Alex struck me as much older than twenty-four. Everything I said, he'd demand to know more about what I meant, about why I thought this way or that. He was hungry to learn about things. Unlike most of us, he was the sort of person who insisted on living out his beliefs.

"We talked for hours about books; there aren't that many people in Carthage who like to talk about books. He went on and on about Mark Twain. Gosh, he was fun to visit with; I didn't want the night to end. I was greatly looking forward to seeing him again this fall. I can't get him out of my mind. I keep picturing his face—he sat in the same chair you're sitting in now. Considering that I only spent a few hours in Alex's company, it amazes me how much I'm bothered by his death."

On McCandless's final night in Carthage, he partied hard at the Cabaret with Westerberg's crew. The Jack Daniel's flowed freely.

To everyone's surprise, McCandless sat down at the piano, which he'd never mentioned he knew how to play, and started pounding out honky-tonk country tunes, then ragtime, then Tony Bennett numbers. And he wasn't merely a drunk inflicting his delusions of talent on a captive audience. "Alex," says Gail Borah, "could really play. I mean he was *good*. We were all blown away by it."

On the morning of April 15, everybody gathered at the elevator to see McCandless off. His pack was heavy. He had approximately one thousand dollars tucked in his boot. He left his journal and photo album with Westerberg for safekeeping and gave him the leather belt he'd made in the desert.

"Alex used to sit at the bar in the Cabaret and read that belt for hours on end," says Westerberg, "like he was translating hieroglyphics for us. Each picture he'd carved into the leather had a long story behind it."

When McCandless hugged Borah good-bye, she says, "I noticed he was crying. That frightened me. He wasn't planning on being gone all that long; I figured he wouldn't have been crying unless he intended to take some big risks and knew he might not be coming back. That's when I started having a bad feeling that we wouldn't never see Alex again."

A big tractor-semitrailer rig was idling out front; Rod Wolf, one of Westerberg's employees, needed to haul a load of sunflower seeds to Enderlin, North Dakota, and had agreed to drive McCandless to Interstate 94.

"When I let him off, he had that big damn machete hanging off his shoulder," Wolf says. "I thought, 'Jeeze, nobody's going to pick him up when they see that thing.' But I didn't say nothin' about it. I just shook his hand, wished him good luck, and told him he'd better write."

McCandless did. A week later Westerberg received a terse card with a Montana postmark:

APRIL 18. Arrived in Whitefish this morning on a freight train. I am making good time. Today I will jump the border and turn north for Alaska. Give my regards to everyone.

TAKE CARE, ALEX

Then, in early May, Westerberg received another postcard, this one from Alaska, with a photo of a polar bear on the front. It was postmarked April 27, 1992. "Greetings from Fairbanks!" it reads,

This is the last you shall hear from me Wayne. Arrived here 2 days ago. It was very difficult to catch rides in the Yukon Territory. But I finally got here.

Please return all mail I receive to the sender. It might be a very long time before I return South. If this adventure proves fatal and you don't ever hear from me again, I want you to know you're a great man. I now walk into the wild.

ALEX.

On the same date McCandless sent a card bearing a similar message to Jan Burres and Bob:

Hey Guys!

This is the last communication you shall receive from me. I now walk out to live amongst the wild. Take care, it was great knowing you.

ALEXANDER.

CHAPTER EIGHT

ALASKA

It may, after all, be the bad habit of creative talents to invest themselves in pathological extremes that yield remarkable insights but no durable way of life for those who cannot translate their psychic wounds into significant art or thought.

THEODORE ROSZAK,
"IN SEARCH OF THE MIRACULOUS"

We have in America "The Big Two-Hearted River" tradition: taking your wounds to the wilderness for a cure, a conversion, a rest, or whatever. And as in the Hemingway story, if your wounds aren't too bad, it works. But this isn't Michigan (or Faulkner's Big Woods in Mississippi, for that matter). This is Alaska.

EDWARD HOAGLAND,
"UP THE BLACK TO CHALKYITSIK"

When McCandless turned up dead in Alaska and the perplexing circumstances of his demise were reported in the news media, many people concluded that the boy must have been mentally disturbed. The article about McCandless in *Outside* generated a large volume of mail, and not a few of the letters heaped opprobrium on McCandless—and on me, as well, the author of the story, for glorifying what some thought was a foolish, pointless death.

Much of the negative mail was sent by Alaskans. "Alex is a nut in my book," wrote a resident of Healy, the hamlet at the head of the Stampede Trail. "The author describes a man who has given away a small fortune, forsaken a loving family, abandoned his car, watch and map and burned the last of his money before traipsing off into the 'wilderness' west of Healy."

"Personally I see nothing positive at all about Chris McCandless's lifestyle or wilderness doctrine," scolded another correspondent. "Entering the wilderness purposefully ill-prepared, and surviving a near-death experience does not make you a better human, it makes you damn lucky."

One reader of the *Outside* piece wondered, "Why would anyone intending to 'live off the land for a few months' forget Boy Scout rule number one: Be Prepared? Why would any son cause his parents and family such permanent and perplexing pain?"

"Krakauer is a kook if he doesn't think Chris 'Alexander Supertramp' McCandless was a kook," opined a man from North Pole, Alaska. "McCandless had already gone over the edge and just happened to hit bottom in Alaska."

The most strident criticism came in the form of a dense, multipage epistle from Ambler, a tiny Inupiat village on the Kobuk River north of the Arctic Circle. The author was a white writer and schoolteacher, formerly from Washington, D.C., named Nick Jans. Warning that it was 1:00 A.M. and he was well into a bottle of Seagram's, Jans let fly:

> Over the past 15 years, I've run into several McCandless types out in the country. Same story: idealistic, energetic young guys who overestimated themselves, underestimated the country, and ended up in trouble. McCandless was hardly unique; there's quite a few of these guys hanging around the state, so much alike that they're almost a collective cliché. The only difference is that McCandless ended up dead, with the story of his dumbassedness splashed across the media. . . . (Jack London got it right in "To

*Build a Fire." McCandless is, finally, just a pale 20th-century bur-
lesque of London's protagonist, who freezes because he ignores
advice and commits big-time hubris). . . .*

*His ignorance, which could have been cured by a USGS quad-
rant and a Boy Scout manual, is what killed him. And while I
feel for his parents, I have no sympathy for him. Such willful ignorance . . . amounts to disrespect for the land, and paradoxi-
cally demonstrates the same sort of arrogance that resulted in the
Exxon Valdez spill—just another case of underprepared, overconfident men bumbling around out there and screwing up because they lacked the requisite humility. It's all a matter of
degree.*

*McCandless's contrived asceticism and a pseudoliterary stance
compound rather than reduce the fault. . . . McCandless's post-
cards, notes, and journals . . . read like the work of an above average, somewhat histrionic high school kid—or am I missing
something?*

The prevailing Alaska wisdom held that McCandless was simply one more dreamy half-cocked greenhorn who went into the
country expecting to find answers to all his problems and instead
found only mosquitoes and a lonely death. Dozens of marginal
characters have marched off into the Alaska wilds over the years,
never to reappear. A few have lodged firmly in the state's collec-
tive memory.

There was the countercultural idealist who passed through the
village of Tanana in the early 1970s, announcing that he intended
to spend the rest of his life "communing with Nature." In mid-
winter a field biologist discovered all his belongings—two rifles,
camping gear, a diary filled with incoherent ranting about truth
and beauty and recondite ecological theory—in an empty cabin
near Tofty, its interior filled with drifted snow. No trace of the
young man was ever found.

A few years later there was the Vietnam vet who built a cabin
on the Black River east of Chalkyitsik to "get away from people."
By February he'd run out of food and starved, apparently without
making any attempt to save himself, despite the fact that there

was another cabin stocked with meat just three miles downstream. Writing about this death, Edward Hoagland observed that Alaska is "not the best site in the world for eremitic experiments or peace-love theatrics."

And then there was the wayward genius I bumped into on the shore of Prince William Sound in 1981. I was camped in the woods outside Cordova, Alaska, trying in vain to find work as a deckhand on a seine boat, biding my time until the Department of Fish and Game announced the first "opener"—the start of the commercial salmon season. One rainy afternoon while walking into town, I crossed paths with an unkempt, agitated man who appeared to be about forty. He wore a bushlike black beard and shoulder-length hair, which he kept out of his face with a headband made from a filthy nylon strap. He was walking toward me at a brisk clip, hunched beneath the considerable weight of a six-foot log balanced across one shoulder.

I said hello as he approached, he mumbled a reply, and we paused to chat in the drizzle. I didn't ask why he was carrying a sodden log into the forest, where there seemed to be plenty of logs already. After a few minutes spent exchanging earnest banalities, we went our separate ways.

From our brief conversation I deduced that I had just met the celebrated eccentric whom the locals called the Mayor of Hippie Cove—a reference to a bight of tidewater north of town that was a magnet for long-haired transients, near which the Mayor had been living for some years. Most of the residents of Hippie Cove were, like me, summer squatters who'd come to Cordova hoping to score high-paying fishing jobs or, failing that, find work in the salmon canneries. But the Mayor was different.

His real name was Gene Rosellini. He was the eldest stepson of Victor Rosellini, a wealthy Seattle restaurateur, and cousin of Albert Rosellini, the immensely popular governor of Washington State from 1957 to 1965. As a young man Gene had been a good athlete and a brilliant student. He read obsessively, practiced yoga, became expert at the martial arts. He sustained a perfect 4.0 grade-point average through high school and college. At the University of Washington and later at Seattle University, he immersed himself in anthropology, history, philosophy, and linguistics, accumulating hundreds of credit hours without collecting a degree. He saw no reason to. The pursuit of knowledge, he maintained, was a worthy objective in its own right and needed no external validation.

By and by Rosellini left academia, departed Seattle, and drifted north up the coast through British Columbia and the Alaska panhandle. In 1977, he landed in Cordova. There, in the forest at the edge of town, he decided to devote his life to an ambitious anthropological experiment.

example of breaking free from society

"I was interested in knowing if it was possible to be independent of modern technology," he told an *Anchorage Daily News* reporter, Debra McKinney, a decade after arriving in Cordova. He wondered whether humans could live as our forebears had when mammoths and saber-toothed tigers roamed the land or whether our species had moved too far from its roots to survive without gunpowder, steel, and other artifacts of civilization. With the obsessive attention to detail that characterized his brand of dogged genius, Rosellini purged his life of all but the most primitive tools, which he fashioned from native materials with his own hands.

"He became convinced that humans had devolved into progressively inferior beings," McKinney explains, "and it was his goal to return to a natural state. He was forever experimenting with different eras—Roman times, the Iron Age, the Bronze Age. By the end his lifestyle had elements of the Neolithic."

He dined on roots, berries, and seaweed, hunted game with spears and snares, dressed in rags, endured the bitter winters. He seemed to relish the hardship. His home above Hippie Cove was a windowless hovel, which he built without benefit of saw or ax: "He'd spend days," says McKinney, "grinding his way through a log with a sharp stone."

As if merely subsisting according to his self-imposed rules weren't strenuous enough, Rosellini also exercised compulsively whenever he wasn't occupied with foraging. He filled his days with calisthenics, weight lifting, and running, often with a load of rocks on his back. During one apparently typical summer he reported covering an average of eighteen miles daily.

Rosellini's "experiment" stretched on for more than a decade, but eventually he felt the question that inspired it had been answered. In a letter to a friend he wrote,

> *I began my adult life with the hypothesis that it would be possible to become a Stone Age native. For over 30 years, I programmed and conditioned myself to this end. In the last 10 of it, I would say I realistically experienced the physical, mental, and emotional reality of the Stone Age. But to borrow a Buddhist phrase, eventually came a setting face-to-face with pure reality. I learned that it is not possible for human beings as we know them to live off the land.*

Rosellini appeared to accept the failure of his hypothesis with equanimity. At the age of forty-nine, he cheerfully announced that he had "recast" his goals and next intended to "walk around the world, living out of my backpack. I want to cover 18 to 27 miles a day, seven days a week, 365 days a year."

The trip never got off the ground. In November 1991, Rosellini was discovered lying facedown on the floor of his shack with a knife through his heart. The coroner determined that the fatal wound was self-inflicted. There was no suicide note. Rosellini left no hint as to why he had decided to end his life then and in that manner. In all likelihood nobody will ever know.

Rosellini's death and the story of his outlandish existence made the front page of the *Anchorage Daily News*. The travails of John Mallon Waterman, however, attracted less attention. Born in 1952, Waterman was raised in the same Washington suburbs that gave shape to Chris McCandless. His father, Guy Waterman, is a musician and freelance writer who, among other claims to modest fame, authored speeches for presidents, ex-presidents, and other prominent Washington politicians. Waterman *père* also happens to be an expert mountaineer who taught his three sons to climb at an early age. John, the middle son, went rock climbing for the first time at thirteen.

He was a natural. John headed to the crags at every opportunity and trained obsessively when he couldn't climb. He cranked out four hundred push-ups every day and walked two and a half miles to school, fast. After walking home in the afternoon, he'd touch the front door and head back to the school to make a second round-trip.

In 1969, as a sixteen-year-old, John climbed Mt. McKinley (which he called Denali, as most Alaskans do, preferring the peak's Athapaskan name), becoming the third-youngest person to stand atop the highest landform on the continent. Over the next few years he pulled off even more impressive ascents in Alaska, Canada, and Europe. By the time he enrolled in the University of Alaska at Fairbanks, in 1973, Waterman had established a reputation as one of the most promising young alpinists in North America.

Waterman was a small person, barely five feet three inches tall, with an elfin face and the sinewy, inexhaustible physique of a gymnast. Acquaintances remember him as a socially awkward man-child with an outrageous sense of humor and a squirrelly, almost manic-depressive personality.

"When I first met John," says James Brady, a fellow climber and college friend, "he was prancing across campus in a long black cape and blue Elton John-type glasses that had a star between the lenses. He carried around a cheap guitar held together with masking tape and would serenade anybody who'd listen with long, off-key songs about his adventures. Fairbanks has always attracted a lot of weird characters, but he was wacky even by Fairbanks standards. Yeah, John was out there. A lot of people didn't know how to handle him."

It is not difficult to imagine plausible causes for Waterman's instability. His parents, Guy and Emily Waterman, divorced when he was a teen, and Guy, according to a source close to the family, "essentially abandoned his sons following the divorce. He would have nothing more to do with the boys, and it crippled

John badly. Not long after their parents split up, John and his older brother, Bill, went to visit their father—but Guy refused to see them. Shortly after that, John and Bill went to Fairbanks to live with an uncle. At one point while they were up there, John got very excited because he heard that his father was coming to Alaska to climb. But when Guy arrived in the state he never took the trouble to see his sons; he came and went without even bothering to visit. It broke John's heart."

Bill, with whom John had an extremely close relationship, lost a leg as a teenager trying to hop a freight train. In 1973, Bill posted an enigmatic letter alluding vaguely to plans for an extended trip and then disappeared without a trace; to this day nobody knows what became of him. And after John learned to climb, eight of his intimates and climbing partners were killed in accidents or committed suicide. It's not much of a stretch to posit that such a rash of misfortune dealt a serious blow to Waterman's young psyche.

In March 1978, Waterman embarked on his most astonishing expedition, a solo ascent of Mt. Hunter's southeast spur, an unclimbed route that had previously defeated three teams of elite mountaineers. Writing about the feat in *Climbing* magazine, the journalist Glenn Randall reported that Waterman described his companions on the climb as "the wind, the snow and death":

> *Cornices as airy as meringue jutted over voids a mile deep. The vertical ice walls were as crumbly as a bucket of ice-cubes half-thawed, then refrozen. They led to ridges so narrow and so steep on both sides that straddling was the easiest solution. At times the pain and loneliness overwhelmed him and he broke down and cried.*

After eighty-one days of exhausting, extremely hazardous climbing, Waterman reached the 14,573-foot summit of Hunter, which rises in the Alaska Range immediately south of Denali. Another nine weeks were required to make the only slightly less harrowing descent; in total Waterman spent 145 days alone on the mountain. When he got back to civilization, flat broke, he borrowed twenty dollars from Cliff Hudson, the bush pilot who'd flown him out of the mountains, and returned to Fairbanks, where the only work he could find was washing dishes.

Waterman was nevertheless hailed as a hero by the small fraternity of Fairbanks climbers. He gave a public slide show of the Hunter ascent that Brady calls "unforgettable. It was an incredible performance, completely uninhibited. He poured out all his thoughts and feelings, his fear of failure, his fear of death. It was like you were there with him." In the months following the epic deed, though, Waterman discovered that instead of putting his demons to rest, success had merely agitated them.

Waterman's mind began to unravel. "John was very self-critical, always analyzing himself," Brady recalls. "And he'd always been kind of compulsive. He used to carry around a stack of clipboards and notepads. He'd take copious notes, creating a complete record of everything he did during the course of each day. I remember running into him once in downtown Fairbanks. As I walked up, he got out a clipboard, logged in the time he saw me and recorded what our conversation was about—which wasn't much at all. His notes on our meeting were three or four pages down, behind all the other stuff he'd already scribbled that day. Somewhere he must have had piles and piles and piles of notes like that, which I'm sure would have made sense to no one except John."

Soon thereafter Waterman ran for the local school board on a platform promoting unrestricted sex for students and the legalization of hallucinogenic drugs. He lost the election, to nobody's surprise save his own, but immediately launched another political campaign, this time for the presidency of the United States. He ran under the banner of the Feed-the-Starving Party, the main priority of which was to ensure that nobody on the planet died of hunger.

To publicize his campaign, he laid plans to make a solo ascent of the south face of Denali, the mountain's steepest aspect, in winter, with a minimum of food. He wanted to underscore the immorality of the standard American diet. As part of his training regimen for the climb, he immersed himself in bath-tubs filled with ice.

Waterman flew to the Kahiltna Glacier in December 1979 to begin the ascent but called it off after only fourteen days. "Take me home," he reportedly told his bush pilot. "I don't want to die." Two months later, however, he prepared for a second attempt. But in Talkeetna, a village south of Denali that is the point of embarkation for most mountaineering expeditions into the Alaska Range, the cabin he was staying in caught fire and burned to rubble, incinerating both his equipment and the voluminous accumulation of notes, poetry, and personal journals that he regarded as his life's work.

Waterman was completely unhelmed by the loss. A day after the fire he committed himself to the Anchorage Psychiatric Institute but left after two weeks, convinced there was a conspiracy afoot to put him away permanently. Then, in the winter of 1981, he launched yet another solo attempt on Denali.

As if climbing the peak alone in winter weren't challenging enough, this time he decided to up the ante even further by beginning his ascent at sea level, which entailed walking 160 hard, circuitous miles from the shore of Cook Inlet just to reach the foot of the mountain. He started plodding north from tidewater in February, but his enthusiasm fizzled on the lower reaches of the Ruth Glacier, still thirty miles from the peak, so he aborted the attempt and retreated to Talkeetna. In March, however, he mustered his resolve once more and resumed his lonely trek. Before leaving town, he told the pilot Cliff Hudson, whom he regarded as a friend, "I won't be seeing you again."

It was an exceptionally cold March in the Alaska Range. Late in the month Mugs Stump crossed paths with Waterman on the upper Ruth Glacier. Stump, an alpinist of world renown who died on Denali in 1992, had just completed a difficult new route on a nearby peak, the Mooses Tooth. Shortly after his chance encounter with Waterman, Stump visited me in Seattle and remarked that "John didn't seem like he was all there. He was acting spacey and talking some crazy shit. Supposedly he was doing this big winter ascent of Denali, but he had hardly any gear with him. He was wearing a cheap one-piece snowmobile suit and wasn't even carrying a sleeping bag. All he had in the way of food was a bunch of flour, some sugar, and a big can of Crisco."

In his book *Breaking Point*, Glenn Randall writes:

> *For several weeks, Waterman lingered in the area of the Sheldon Mountain House, a small cabin perched on the side of the Ruth Glacier in the heart of the range. Kate Bull, a friend of Waterman's who was climbing in the area at the time, reported that he was run down and less cautious than usual. He used the radio he had borrowed from Cliff [Hudson] to call him and have him fly in more supplies. Then he returned the radio he had borrowed.*
>
> *"I won't be needing this any more," he said. The radio would have been his only means of calling for help.*

Waterman was last placed on the Northwest Fork of the Ruth Glacier on April 1. His tracks led toward the east buttress of Denali, straight through a labyrinth of giant crevasses, evidence that he had made no apparent effort to circumvent obvious hazards. He was not seen again; it is assumed he broke through a thin snow bridge and plummeted to his death at the bottom of one of the deep fissures. The National Park Service searched Waterman's intended route from the air for a week following his disappearance but found no sign of him. Some climbers later discovered a note atop a box of Waterman's gear inside the Sheldon Mountain House. "3-13-81," it read. "My last kiss 1:42 PM."

Perhaps inevitably, parallels have been drawn between John Waterman and Chris McCandless. Comparisons have also been drawn between McCandless and Carl McCunn, an affable absentminded Texan who moved to Fairbanks during the 1970s oil boom and found lucrative employment on the Trans-Alaska Pipeline construction project. In early March 1981, as Waterman was making his final journey into the Alaska Range, McCunn hired a bush pilot to drop him at a remote lake near the Coleen River, about seventy-five miles northeast of Fort Yukon on the southern margin of the Brooks Range.

A thirty-five-year-old amateur photographer, McCunn told friends that the main reason for the trip was to shoot pictures of wildlife. He flew into the country with five hundred rolls of film, .22- and .30-.30-caliber rifles, a shotgun, and fourteen hundred pounds of provisions. His intention was to remain in the wilderness through August. Somehow, though, he neglected to arrange for the pilot to fly him back to civilization at summer's end, and it cost McCunn his life.

This astounding oversight wasn't a great surprise to Mark Stoppel, a young Fairbanks resident who had come to know McCunn well during the nine months they worked on the pipeline together, shortly before the lanky Texan departed for the Brooks Range.

"Carl was a friendly, extremely popular, down-home sort of guy," Stoppel recalls. "And he seemed like a smart guy. But there was a side to him that was a little bit dreamy, a little bit out of touch with reality. He was flamboyant. He liked to party hard. He could be extremely responsible, but he had a tendency to wing it sometimes, to act impulsively, to get by on bravado and style. No, I guess it really doesn't surprise me that Carl went out there and forgot to arrange to be picked up. But then I'm not easily shocked. I've had several friends who drowned or got murdered or died in weird accidents. In Alaska you get used to strange stuff happening."

In late August, as the days grew shorter and the air turned sharp and autumnal in the Brooks Range, McCunn began to worry when nobody arrived to fly him out. "I think I should have used more foresight about arranging my departure," he confessed to his diary, significant portions of which were published posthumously in a five-part story by Kris Capps in the *Fairbanks Daily News–Miner.* "I'll soon find out."

Week by week he could feel the accelerating advance of winter. As his food supply grew meager, McCunn deeply regretted tossing all but a dozen of his shotgun shells into the lake. "I keep thinking of all the shotgun shells I threw away about two months ago," he wrote. "Had five boxes and when I kept seeing them sitting there I felt rather silly for having brought so many. (Felt like a war monger.) . . . real bright. Who would have known I might need them just to keep from starving."

Then, on a brisk September morning, deliverance seemed to be at hand. McCunn was stalking ducks with what remained of his ammunition when the stillness was rocked by the buzz of an airplane, which soon appeared overhead. The pilot, spotting the camp, circled twice at a low altitude for a closer look. McCunn waved wildly with a fluorescent-orange sleeping-bag cover. The aircraft was equipped with wheels rather than floats and thus couldn't land, but McCunn was certain he'd been seen and had no doubt the pilot would summon a floatplane to return for him. He was so sure of this he recorded in the journal that "I stopped waving after the first pass. I then got busy packing things up and getting ready to break camp."

But no airplane arrived that day, or the next day, or the next. Eventually, McCunn looked on the back of his hunting license and understood why. Printed on the little square of paper were drawings of emergency hand signals for communicating with aircraft from the ground. "I recall raising my right hand, shoulder high and shaking my fist on the plane's second pass," McCunn wrote. "It was a little cheer—like when your team scored a touchdown or something." Unfortunately, as he learned too late, raising a single arm is the universally recognized signal for "all OK; assistance not necessary." The signal for "SOS; send immediate help," is two upraised arms.

"That's probably why after they flew somewhat away they returned for one more pass and on that one I gave no signal at all (in fact I may have even turned my back to the plane as it passed)," McCunn mused philosophically. "They probably blew me off as a weirdo."

By the end of September, snow was piling up on the tundra, and the lake had frozen over. As the provisions he'd brought ran out, McCunn made an effort to gather rose hips and snare rabbits. At one point he managed to scavenge meat from a diseased caribou that had wandered into the lake and died. By October, however, he had metabolized most of his body fat and was having difficulty staying warm during the long, cold nights. "Certainly someone in town should have figured something must be wrong—me not being back by now," he noted. But still no plane appeared.

"It would be just like Carl to assume that somebody would magically appear to save him," says Stoppel. "He was a Teamster—he drove a truck—so he had plenty of downtime on the job, just sitting on his butt inside his rig, daydreaming, which is how he came up with the idea for the Brooks Range trip. It was a serious quest for him: He spent the better part of a year thinking about it, planning it, figuring it out, talking to me during our breaks about what gear to take. But for all the careful planning he did, he also indulged in some wild fantasies.

"For instance," Stoppel continues, "Carl didn't want to fly into the bush alone. His big dream, originally, was to go off and live in the woods with some beautiful woman. He was hot for at least a couple of different girls who worked with us, and he spent a lot of time and energy trying to talk Sue or Barbara or whoever into accompanying him—which in itself was pretty much pure fantasyland. There was no way it was going to happen. I mean, at the pipeline camp where we worked, Pump Station 7, there were probably forty guys for every woman. But Carl was a dreamin' kind of dude, and right up until he flew into the Brooks Range, he kept hoping and hoping and hoping that one of these girls would change her mind and decide to go with him."

Similarly, Stoppel explains, "Carl was the sort of guy who would have unrealistic expectations that someone would eventually figure out he was in trouble and cover for him. Even as he was on the verge of starving, he probably still imagined that Big Sue was going to fly in at the last minute with a planeload of food and have this wild romance with him. But his fantasy world was so far off the scale that nobody was able to connect with it. Carl just got hungrier and hungrier. By the time he finally understood that nobody was going to come rescue him, he'd shriveled up to the point where it was too late for him to do anything about it."

As McCunn's food supply dwindled to almost nothing, he wrote in his journal, "I'm getting more than worried. To be honest, I'm starting to be a bit scared." The thermometer dipped to minus five degrees Fahrenheit. Painful, pus-filled frostbite blisters formed on his fingers and toes.

In November he finished the last of his rations. He felt weak and dizzy; chills racked his gaunt frame. The diary recorded, "Hands and nose continue to get worse as do feet. Nose tip very swollen, blistered, and scabbed. . . . This is sure a slow and agonizing way to die." McCunn considered leaving the security of his camp and setting out on foot for Fort Yukon but concluded he wasn't strong enough, that he would succumb to exhaustion and the cold long before he got there.

"The part of the interior where Carl went is a remote, very blank part of Alaska," says Stoppel. "It gets colder than hell there in the winter. Some people in his situation could have figured out a way to walk out or maybe winter over, but to do that, you'd have to be extremely resourceful. You'd really need to have your shit together. You'd have to be a tiger, a killer, a fuckin' animal. And Carl was too laid back. He was a party boy."

"I can't go on like this, I'm afraid," McCunn wrote sometime in late November near the end of his journal, which by now filled one hundred sheets of blue-lined loose-leaf notebook paper. "Dear God in Heaven, please forgive me my weakness and my sins. Please look over my family." And then he reclined in his wall tent, placed the muzzle of the .30-.30 against his head, and jerked his thumb down on the trigger. Two months later, on February 2, 1982, Alaska State Troopers came across his camp, looked inside the tent, and discovered the emaciated corpse frozen hard as stone.

There are similarities among Rosellini, Waterman, McCunn,

and McCandless. Like Rosellini and Waterman, McCandless was a seeker and had an impractical fascination with the harsh side of nature. Like Waterman and McCunn, he displayed a staggering paucity of common sense. But unlike Waterman, McCandless wasn't mentally ill. And unlike McCunn, he didn't go into the bush assuming someone would automatically appear to save his bacon before he came to grief.

McCandless didn't conform particularly well to the bush-casualty stereotype. Although he was rash, untutored in the ways of the backcountry, and incautious to the point of foolhardiness, he wasn't incompetent—he wouldn't have lasted 113 days if he were. And he wasn't a nutcase, he wasn't a sociopath, he wasn't an outcast. McCandless was something else—although precisely *what* is hard to say. A pilgrim, perhaps.

Some insight into the tragedy of Chris McCandless can be gained by studying predecessors cut from the same exotic cloth. And in order to do that, one must look beyond Alaska, to the bald-rock canyons of southern Utah. There, in 1934, a peculiar twenty-year-old boy walked into the desert and never came out. His name was Everett Ruess.

comparison

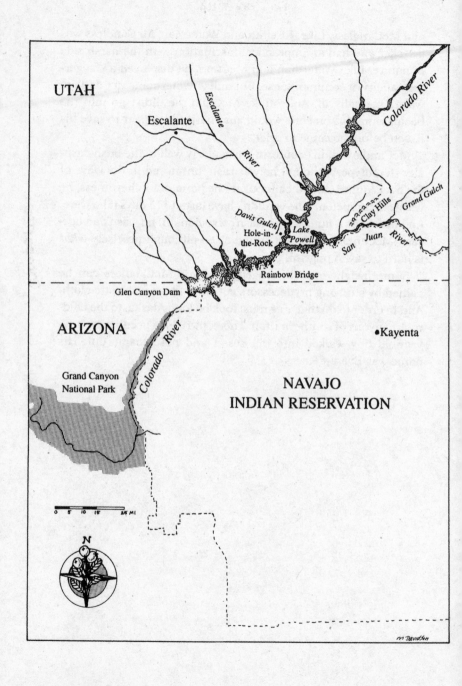

CHAPTER NINE

DAVIS GULCH

As to when I shall visit civilization, it will not be soon, I think. I have not tired of the wilderness; rather I enjoy its beauty and the vagrant life I lead, more keenly all the time. I prefer the saddle to the streetcar and star-sprinkled sky to a roof, the obscure and difficult trail, leading into the unknown, to any paved highway, and the deep peace of the wild to the discontent bred by cities. Do you blame me then for staying here, where I feel that I belong and am one with the world around me? It is true that I miss intelligent companionship, but there are so few with whom I can share the things that mean so much to me that I have learned to contain myself. It is enough that I am surrounded with beauty. . . .

Even from your scant description, I know that I could not bear the routine and humdrum of the life that you are forced to lead. I don't think I could ever settle down. I have known too much of the depths of life already, and I would prefer anything to an anticlimax.

THE LAST LETTER EVER RECEIVED FROM EVERETT RUESS,
TO HIS BROTHER, WALDO, DATED NOVEMBER 11, 1934

What Everett Ruess was after was beauty, and he conceived beauty in pretty romantic terms. We might be inclined to laugh at the extravagance of his beauty-worship if there were not something almost magnificent in his single-minded dedication to it. Esthetics as a parlor affectation is ludicrous and sometimes a little obscene; as a way of life it sometimes attains dignity. If we laugh at Everett Ruess we shall have to laugh at John Muir, because there was little difference between them except age.

WALLACE STEGNER,
MORMON COUNTRY

Davis Creek is only a trickle during most of the year and sometimes not even that. Originating at the foot of a high rock bat-
tlement known as Fiftymile Point, the stream flows just four
miles across the pink sandstone slabs of southern Utah before
surrendering its modest waters to Lake Powell, the giant reservoir that stretches one hundred ninety miles above Glen
Canyon Dam. Davis Gulch is a small watershed by any measure,
but a lovely one, and travelers through this dry, hard country
have for centuries relied on the oasis that exists at the bottom
of the slotlike defile. Eerie nine-hundred-year-old petroglyphs
and pictographs decorate its sheer walls. Crumbling stone
dwellings of the long-vanished Kayenta Anasazi, the creators of
this rock art, nestle in protective nooks. Ancient Anasazi pot-
sherds mingle in the sand with rusty tin cans discarded by turn-
of-the-century stockmen, who grazed and watered their animals
in the canyon.

For most of its short length, Davis Gulch exists as a deep, twisting gash in the slickrock, narrow enough in places to spit across,
lined by overhanging sandstone walls that bar access to the
canyon floor. There is a hidden route into the gulch at its lower
end, however. Just upstream from where Davis Creek flows into
Lake Powell, a natural ramp zigzags down from the canyon's
west rim. Not far above the creek bottom the ramp ends, and a
crude staircase appears, chiseled into the soft sandstone by Mormon cattlemen nearly a century ago.

The country surrounding Davis Gulch is a desiccated expanse
of bald rock and brick-red sand. Vegetation is lean. Shade from
the withering sun is virtually nonexistent. To descend into the
confines of the canyon, however, is to arrive in another world.
Cottonwoods lean gracefully over drifts of flowering prickly pear.
Tall grasses sway in the breeze. The ephemeral bloom of a sego
lily peeks from the toe of a ninety-foot stone arch, and canyon
wrens call back and forth in plaintive tones from a thatch of
scrub oak. High above the creek a spring seeps from the cliff face,
irrigating a growth of moss and maidenhair fern that hangs from
the rock in lush green mats.

Six decades ago in this enchanting hideaway, less than a mile downstream from where the Mormon steps meet the floor of the gulch, twenty-year-old Everett Ruess carved his nom de plume into the canyon wall below a panel of Anasazi pictographs, and he did so again in the doorway of a small masonry structure built by the Anasazi for storing grain. "NEMO 1934," he scrawled, no doubt moved by the same impulse that compelled Chris McCandless to inscribe "Alexander Supertramp/May 1992" on the wall of the Sushana bus—an impulse not so different, perhaps, from that which inspired the Anasazi to embellish the rock with their own now-indecipherable symbols. In any case, shortly after Ruess carved his mark into the sandstone, he departed Davis Gulch and mysteriously disappeared, apparently by design. An extensive search shed no light on his whereabouts. He was simply gone, swallowed whole by the desert. Sixty years later we still know next to nothing about what became of him.

Everett was born in Oakland, California, in 1914, the younger of two sons raised by Christopher and Stella Ruess. Christopher, a graduate of Harvard Divinity School, was a poet, a philosopher, and a Unitarian minister, although he earned his keep as a bureaucrat in the California penal system. Stella was a headstrong woman with bohemian tastes and driving artistic ambitions, for both herself and her kin; she self-published a literary journal, the *Ruess Quartette*, the cover of which was emblazoned with the family maxim: "Glorify the hour." A tight-knit bunch, the Ruesses were also a nomadic family, moving from Oakland to Fresno to Los Angeles to Boston to Brooklyn to New Jersey to Indiana before finally settling in southern California when Everett was fourteen.

In Los Angeles, Everett attended the Otis Art School and Hollywood High. As a sixteen-year-old he embarked on his first long solo trip, spending the summer of 1930 hitchhiking and trekking through Yosemite and Big Sur, ultimately winding up in Carmel. Two days after arriving in the latter community, he brazenly knocked on the door of Edward Weston, who was sufficiently charmed by the overwrought young man to humor him. Over the next two months the eminent photographer encouraged the boy's uneven but promising efforts at painting and block printing , and permitted Ruess to hang around his studio with his own sons, Neil and Cole.

At the end of the summer, Everett returned home only long enough to earn a high school diploma, which he received in January 1931. Less than a month later he was on the road again, tramping alone through the canyon lands of Utah, Arizona, and New Mexico, then a region nearly as sparsely populated and wrapped in mystique as Alaska is today. Except for a short, unhappy stint at UCLA (he dropped out after a single semester, to his father's lasting dismay), two extended visits with his parents, and a winter in San Francisco (where he insinuated himself into the company of Dorothea Lange, Ansel Adams, and the painter Maynard Dixon), Ruess would spend the remainder of his meteoric life on the move, living out of a backpack on very little money, sleeping in the dirt, cheerfully going hungry for days at a time.

Ruess was, in the words of Wallace Stegner, "a callow romantic, an adolescent esthete, an atavistic wanderer of the wastelands":

At eighteen, in a dream, he saw himself plodding through jungles, chinning up the ledges of cliffs, wandering through the romantic waste places of the world. No man with any of the juices of boyhood in him has forgotten those dreams. The peculiar thing about Everett Ruess was that he went out and did the things he dreamed about, not simply for a two-weeks' vacation in the civilized and trimmed wonderlands, but for months and years in the very midst of wonder. . . .

Deliberately he punished his body, strained his endurance, tested his capacity for strenuousness. He took out deliberately over trails that Indians and old timers warned him against. He tackled cliffs that more than once left him dangling halfway between talus and rim. . . . From his camps by the water pockets or the canyons or high on the timbered ridges of Navajo Mountain he wrote long, lush, enthusiastic letters to his family and friends, damning the stereotypes of civilization, chanting his barbaric adolescent yawp into the teeth of the world.

Ruess churned out many such letters, which bore the postmarks of the remote settlements through which he passed: Kayenta, Chinle, Lukachukai; Zion Canyon, Grand Canyon, Mesa Verde; Escalante, Rainbow Bridge, Canyon de Chelly. Reading this correspondence (collected in W. L. Rusho's meticulously researched biography, *Everett Ruess: A Vagabond for Beauty*), one is struck by Ruess's craving for connection with the natural world and by his almost incendiary passion for the country through which he walked. "I had some terrific experiences in the wilderness since I wrote you last—overpowering, overwhelming," he gushed to his friend Cornel Tengel. "But then I am always being overwhelmed. I require it to sustain life."

Everett Ruess's correspondence reveals uncanny parallels between Ruess and Chris McCandless. Here are excerpts from three of Ruess's letters:

> *I have been thinking more and more that I shall always be a lone wanderer of the wilderness. God, how the trail lures me. You cannot comprehend its resistless fascination for me. After all the lone trail is the best. . . . I'll never stop wandering. And when the time comes to die, I'll find the wildest, loneliest, most desolate spot there is.*

> *The beauty of this country is becoming part of me. I feel more detached from life and somehow gentler. . . . I have some good friends here, but no one who really understands why I am here or what I do. I don't know of anyone, though, who would have more than a partial understanding; I have gone too far alone.*
>
> *I have always been unsatisfied with life as most people live it. Always I want to live more intensely and richly.*

> *In my wanderings this year I have taken more chances and had more wild adventures than ever before. And what magnificent country I have seen—wild, tremendous wasteland stretches,*

[handwritten margin note: Similar mindset to McCandless]

lost mesas, blue mountains rearing upward from the vermilion sands of the desert, canyons five feet wide at the bottom and hundreds of feet deep, cloudbursts roaring down unnamed canyons, and hundreds of houses of the cliff dwellers, abandoned a thousand years ago.

A half century later McCandless sounds eerily like Ruess when he declares in a postcard to Wayne Westerberg that "I've decided that I'm going to live this life for some time to come. The freedom and simple beauty of it is just too good to pass up." And echoes of Ruess can be heard, as well, in McCandless's last letter to Ronald Franz (see pages 56–58).

Ruess was just as romantic as McCandless, if not more so, and equally heedless of personal safety. Clayborn Lockett, an archaeologist who briefly employed Ruess as a cook while excavating an Anasazi cliff dwelling in 1934, told Rusho that "he was appalled by the seemingly reckless manner in which Everett moved around dangerous cliffs."

Indeed, Ruess himself boasts in one of his letters, "Hundreds of times I have trusted my life to crumbling sandstone and nearly vertical edges in the search for water or cliff dwellings. Twice I was nearly gored to death by a wild bull. But always, so far, I've escaped unscathed and gone forth to other adventures." And in his final letter Ruess nonchalantly confesses to his brother:

I have had a few narrow escapes from rattlers and crumbling cliffs. The last misadventure occurred when Chocolatero [his burro] stirred up some wild bees. A few more stings might have been too much for me. I was three or four days getting my eyes open and recovering the use of my hands.

Also like McCandless, Ruess was undeterred by physical discomfort; at times he seemed to welcome it. "For six days I've been suffering from the semi-annual poison ivy case—my sufferings are far from over," he tells his friend Bill Jacobs. He goes on:

*For two days I couldn't tell whether I was dead or alive. I writhed
and twisted in the heat, with swarms of ants and flies crawling
over me, while the poison oozed and crusted on my face and arms
and back. I ate nothing—there was nothing to do but suffer philosophically. . . .*

I get it every time, but I refuse to be driven out of the woods.

And like McCandless, upon embarking on his terminal
odyssey, Ruess adopted a new name or, rather, a series of new
names. In a letter dated March 1, 1931, he informs his family that
he has taken to calling himself Lan Rameau and requests that
they "please respect my brush name. . . . How do you say it in
French? *Nomme de broushe,* or what?" Two months later, however, another letter explains that "I have changed my name again,
to Evert Rulan. Those who knew me formerly thought my name
was freakish and an affectation of Frenchiness." and then in August of that same year, with no explanation, he goes back to calling himself Everett Ruess and continues to do so for the next
three years—until wandering into Davis Gulch. There, for some
unknowable reason, Everett twice etched the name Nemo—Latin
for "nobody"—into the soft Navajo sandstone—and then vanished. He was twenty years old.

The last letters anyone received from Ruess were posted from
the Mormon settlement of Escalante, fifty-seven miles north of
Davis Gulch, on November 11, 1934. Addressed to his parents
and his brother, they indicate that he would be incommunicado
for "a month or two." Eight days after mailing them, Ruess en-
countered two sheepherders about a mile from the gulch and
spent two nights at their camp; these men were the last people
known to have seen the youth alive.

Some three months after Ruess departed Escalante, his parents received a bundle of unopened mail forwarded from the
postmaster at Marble Canyon, Arizona, where Everett was long
overdue. Worried, Christopher and Stella Ruess contacted the
authorities in Escalante, who organized a search party in early
March 1935. Starting from the sheep camp where Ruess was last
seen, they began combing the surrounding country and very

quickly found Everett's two burros at the bottom of Davis Gulch, grazing contentedly behind a makeshift corral fashioned from brush and tree limbs.

The burros were confined in the upper canyon, just upstream from where the Mormon steps intersect the floor of the gulch; a short distance downstream the searchers found unmistakable evidence of Ruess's camp, and then, in the doorway of an Anasazi granary below a magnificent natural arch, they came across "NEMO 1934" carved into a stone slab. Four Anasazi pots were carefully arranged on a rock nearby. Three months later searchers came across another Nemo graffito a little farther down the gulch (the rising waters of Lake Powell, which began to fill upon the completion of Glen Canyon Dam, in 1963, have long since erased both inscriptions), but except for the burros and their tack, none of Ruess's possessions—his camping paraphernalia, journals, and paintings—was ever found.

It is widely believed that Ruess fell to his death while scrambling on one or another canyon wall. Given the treacherous nature of the local topography (most of the cliffs that riddle the region are composed of Navajo sandstone, a crumbly stratum that erodes into smooth, bulging precipices) and Ruess's penchant for dangerous climbing, this is a credible scenario. Careful searches of cliffs near and far, however, have failed to unearth any human remains.

And how to account for the fact that Ruess apparently left the gulch with a heavy load of gear but without his pack animals? These bewildering circumstances have led some investigators to conclude that Ruess was murdered by a team of cattle rustlers known to have been in the area, who then stole his belongings and buried his remains or threw them into the Colorado River. This theory, too, is plausible, but no concrete evidence exists to prove it.

Shortly after Everett's disappearance his father suggested that the boy had probably been inspired to call himself Nemo by Jules Verne's *Twenty Thousand Leagues Under the Sea*—a book Everett read many times—in which the purehearted protagonist, Captain Nemo, flees civilization and severs his "every tie upon the earth." Everett's biographer, W. L. Rusho, agrees with Christopher Ruess's assessment, arguing that Everett's "withdrawal from organized society, his disdain for worldly pleasures, and his signatures as *NEMO* in Davis Gulch, all strongly suggest that he closely identified with the Jules Verne character."

Ruess's apparent fascination with Captain Nemo has fed speculation among more than a few Ruess mythographers that Everett pulled a fast one on the world after leaving Davis Gulch and is—or was—very much alive, quietly residing somewhere under an assumed identity. A year ago, while filling my truck with gas in Kingman, Arizona, I happened to strike up a conversation about Ruess with the middle-aged pump attendant, a small, twitchy man with flecks of Skoal staining the corners of his mouth. Speaking with persuasive conviction, he swore that "he knew a fella who'd definitely bumped into Ruess" in the late 1960s at a remote hogan on the Navajo Indian Reservation. According to the attendant's friend, Ruess was married to a Navajo woman, with whom he'd raised at least one child. The veracity of this and other reports of relatively recent Ruess sightings, needless to say, is extremely suspect.

Ken Sleight, who has spent as much time investigating the riddle of Everett Ruess as any other person, is convinced that the boy died in 1934 or early 1935 and believes he knows how Ruess met his end. Sleight, sixty-five years old, is a professional river guide and desert rat with a Mormon upbringing and a reputation for insolence. When Edward Abbey was writing *The Monkey Wrench Gang*, his picaresque novel about eco-terrorism in the canyon country, his pal Ken Sleight was said to have inspired the character Seldom Seen Smith. Sleight has lived in the region for forty years, visited virtually all the places Ruess visited, talked to many people who crossed paths with Ruess, taken Ruess's older brother, Waldo, into Davis Gulch to visit the site of Everett's disappearance.

"Waldo thinks Everett was murdered," Sleight says. "But I don't think so. I lived in Escalante for two years. I've talked with the folks who are accused of killing him, and I just don't think they did it. But who knows? You can't never really tell what a person does in secret. Other folks believe Everett fell off a cliff. Well, yeah, he coulda done that. It be an easy thing to do in that country. But I don't think that's what happened.

"I tell you what I think: I think he drowned."

Years ago, while hiking down Grand Gulch, a tributary of the San Juan River some forty-five miles due east of Davis Gulch, Sleight discovered the name Nemo carved into the soft mud mortar of an Anasazi granary. Sleight speculates that Ruess inscribed this Nemo not long after departing Davis Gulch.

"After corralling his burros in Davis," says Sleight, "Ruess hid all his stuff in a cave somewhere and took off, playing Captain Nemo. He had Indian friends down on the Navajo Reservation, and that's where I think he was heading." A logical route to Navajo country would have taken Ruess across the Colorado River at Hole-in-the-Rock, then along a rugged trail pioneered in 1880 by Mormon settlers across Wilson Mesa and the Clay Hills, and finally down Grand Gulch to the San Juan River, across which lay the reservation. "Everett carved his Nemo on the ruin in Grand Gulch, about a mile below where Collins Creek comes in, then continued on down to the San Juan. And when he tried to swim across the river, he drowned. That's what I think."

Sleight believes that if Ruess had made it across the river alive and reached the reservation, it would have been impossible for him to conceal his presence "even if he was still playing his Nemo game. Everett was a loner, but he liked people too damn much to stay down there and live in secret the rest of his life. A lot of us are like that—I'm like that, Ed Abbey was like that, and it sounds like this McCandless kid was like that: We like companionship, see, but we can't stand to be around people for very long. So we go get ourselves lost, come back for a while, then get the hell out again. And that's what Everett was doing.

"Everett was strange," Sleight concedes. "Kind of different. But him and McCandless, at least they tried to follow their dream. That's what was great about them. They tried. Not many do."

In attempting to understand Everett Ruess and Chris McCandless, it can be illuminating to consider their deeds in a larger context. It is helpful to look at counterparts from a distant place and a century far removed.

Off the southeastern coast of Iceland sits a low barrier island called Papós. Treeless and rocky, perpetually clobbered by gales howling off the North Atlantic, it takes its name from its first settlers, now long gone, the Irish monks known as *papar*. Walking this gnarled shore one summer afternoon, I blundered upon a matrix of faint stone rectangles embedded in the tundra: vestiges of the monks' ancient dwellings, hundreds of years older, even, than the Anasazi ruins in Davis Gulch.

The monks arrived as early as the fifth and sixth centuries A.D., having sailed and rowed from the west coast of Ireland. Setting out in small, open boats called curraghs, built from cowhide stretched over light wicker frames, they crossed one of the most treacherous stretches of ocean in the world without knowing what, if anything, they'd find on the other side.

The *papar* risked their lives—and lost them in untold droves—not in the pursuit of wealth or personal glory or to claim new lands in the name of any despot. As the great arctic explorer and Nobel laureate Fridtjof Nansen points out, "these remarkable voyages were . . . undertaken chiefly from the wish to find lonely places, where these anchorites might dwell in peace, undisturbed by the turmoil and temptations of the world." When the first handful of Norwegians showed up on the shores of Iceland in the ninth century, the *papar* decided the country had become too crowded—even though it was still all but uninhabited. The monks' response was to climb into their curraghs and row off toward Greenland. They were drawn across the storm-racked ocean, drawn west past the edge of the known world, by nothing more than a hunger of the spirit, a yearning of such queer intensity that it beggars the modern imagination.

Reading of these monks, one is moved by their courage, their reckless innocence, and the urgency of their desire. Reading of these monks, one can't help thinking of Everett Ruess and Chris McCandless.

CHAPTER TEN

FAIRBANKS

DYING IN THE WILD, A HIKER RECORDED THE TERROR

*ANCHORAGE, Sept. 12 (AP)—Last Sunday a young hiker,
stranded by an injury, was found dead at a remote camp in the
Alaskan interior. No one is yet certain who he was. But his
diary and two notes found at the camp tell a wrenching story of
his desperate and progressively futile efforts to survive.*

*The diary indicates that the man, believed to be an American
in his late 20's or early 30's, might have been injured in a fall
and that he was then stranded at the camp for more than three
months. It tells how he tried to save himself by hunting game
and eating wild plants while nonetheless getting weaker.*

*One of his two notes is a plea for help, addressed to anyone
who might come upon the camp while the hiker searched the
surrounding area for food. The second note bids the world
goodbye. . . .*

*An autopsy at the state coroner's office in Fairbanks this
week found that the man had died of starvation, probably in
late July. The authorities discovered among the man's possessions a name that they believe is his. But they have so far been
unable to confirm his identity and, until they do, have declined
to disclose the name.*

THE NEW YORK TIMES,
SEPTEMBER 13, 1992

By the time *The New York Times* picked up the story about the
hiker, the Alaska State Troopers had been trying for a week to fig-

ure out who he was. When he died, McCandless was wearing a blue sweatshirt printed with the logo of a Santa Barbara towing company; when contacted, the wrecking outfit professed to know nothing about him or how he'd acquired the shirt. Many of the entries in the brief, perplexing diary recovered with the body were terse observations of flora and fauna, which fueled speculation that McCandless was a field biologist. But that ultimately led nowhere, too.

On September 10, three days before news of the dead hiker appeared in the *Times*, the story was published on the front page of the *Anchorage Daily News*. When Jim Gallien saw the headline and the accompanying map indicating that the body had been found twenty-five miles west of Healy on the Stampede Trail, he felt the hairs bristle across the base of his scalp: Alex. Gallien still held a picture in his mind of the odd, congenial youth striding down the trail in boots two sizes too big for him—Gallien's own boots, the old brown Xtratufs he'd persuaded the kid to take. "From the newspaper article, what little information there was, it sounded like the same person," says Gallien, "so I called the state troopers and said, 'Hey, I think I gave that guy a ride.'"

"OK, sure," replied trooper Roger Ellis, the cop on the other end of the line. "What makes you think so? You're the sixth person in the last hour who's called to say they know the hiker's identity." But Gallien persisted, and the more he talked, the more Ellis's skepticism receded. Gallien described several pieces of equipment not mentioned in the newspaper account that matched gear found with the body. And then Ellis noticed that the first cryptic entry in the hiker's journal read, "Exit Fairbanks. Sitting Galliean. Rabbit Day."

The troopers had by this time developed the roll of film in the hiker's Minolta, which included several apparent self-portraits. "When they brought the pictures out to the job site where I was working," says Gallien, "there was no two ways about it. The guy in the pictures was Alex."

Because McCandless had told Gallien he was from South Dakota, the troopers immediately shifted their search there for the hiker's next of kin. An all-points bulletin turned up a missing person named McCandless from eastern South Dakota, coincidentally from a small town only twenty miles from Wayne Westerberg's home in Carthage, and for a while the troopers thought they'd found their man. But this, too, turned out to be a false lead.

Westerberg had heard nothing from the friend he knew as Alex McCandless since receiving the postcard from Fairbanks the previous spring. On September 13, he was rolling down an empty ribbon of blacktop outside Jamestown, North Dakota, leading his harvest crew home to Carthage after wrapping up the four-month cutting season in Montana, when the VHF barked to life. "Wayne!" an anxious voice crackled over the radio from one of the crew's other trucks. "This is Bob. You got your radio on?"

"Yeah, Bobby. Wayne here. What's up?"

"Quick—turn on your AM, and listen to Paul Harvey. He's talking about some kid who starved to death up in Alaska. The police don't know who he is. Sounds a whole lot like Alex."

Westerberg found the station in time to catch the tail end of the Paul Harvey broadcast, and he was forced to agree: The few sketchy details made the anonymous hiker sound distressingly like his friend.

As soon as he got to Carthage, a dispirited Westerberg phoned the Alaska State Troopers to volunteer what he knew about McCandless. By that time, however, stories about the dead hiker, including excerpts from his diary, had been given prominent play in newspapers across the country. As a consequence the troopers were swamped with calls from people claiming to know the hiker's identity, so they were even less receptive to Westerberg than they had been to Gallien. "The cop told me they'd had more than one hundred fifty calls from folks who thought Alex was their kid, their friend, their brother," says Westerberg. "Well, by then I was kind of pissed at getting the runaround, so I told him, 'Look, I'm not just another crank caller. I *know* who he is. He worked for me. I think I've even got his Social Security number around here somewhere.' "

Westerberg pawed through the files at the grain elevator until he found two W-4 forms McCandless had filled out. Across the top of the first one, dating from McCandless's initial visit to Carthage, in 1990, he had scrawled "EXEMPT EXEMPT EXEMPT EXEMPT" and given his name as Iris Fucyu. Address: "None of your damn business." Social Security number: "I forget."

But on the second form, dated March 30, 1992, two weeks before he left for Alaska, he'd signed his given name: "Chris J. McCandless." And in the blank for Social Security number he'd put down, "228-31-6704." Westerberg phoned Alaska again. This time the troopers took him seriously.

The Social Security number turned out to be genuine and placed McCandless's permanent residence in northern Virginia. Authorities in Alaska contacted law-enforcement agencies in that state, who in turn started combing phone directories for McCandlesses. Walt and Billie McCandless had by then moved to the Maryland shore and no longer had a Virginia phone number, but Walt's eldest child from his first marriage lived in Annandale and was in the book; late on the afternoon of September 17, Sam McCandless received a call from a Fairfax County homicide detective.

Sam, nine years older than Chris, had seen a short article about the hiker in *The Washington Post* a few days earlier, but, he allows, "It didn't occur to me that the hiker might be Chris. Never even crossed my mind. It's ironic because when I read the article I thought, 'Oh, my God, what a terrible tragedy. I really feel sorry for the family of this guy, whoever they are. What a sad story.'"

Sam had been raised in California and Colorado, in his mother's household, and hadn't moved to Virginia until 1987, after Chris had left the state to attend college in Atlanta, so Sam didn't know his half brother well. But when the homicide detective started asking whether the hiker sounded like anyone he knew, Sam reports, "I was pretty sure it was Chris. The fact that he'd gone to Alaska, that he'd gone off by himself—it all added up."

At the detective's request, Sam went to the Fairfax County Police Department, where an officer showed him a photograph of the hiker that had been faxed from Fairbanks. "It was an eight-by-ten enlargement," Sam recalls, "a head shot. His hair was long, and he had a beard. Chris almost always had short hair and was clean-shaven. And the face in the picture was extremely gaunt. But I knew right away. There was no doubt. It was Chris. I went home, picked up Michele, my wife, and drove out to Maryland to tell Dad and Billie. I didn't know what I was going to say. How do you tell someone that their child is dead?"

CHAPTER ELEVEN

CHESAPEAKE BEACH

*Everything had changed suddenly—the tone, the moral climate;
you didn't know what to think, whom to listen to. As if all your
life you had been led by the hand like a small child and suddenly
you were on your own, you had to learn to walk by yourself.
There was no one around, neither family nor people whose
judgment you respected. At such a time you felt the need of
committing yourself to something absolute—life or truth or
beauty—of being ruled by it in place of the man-made rules that
had been discarded. You needed to surrender to some such
ultimate purpose more fully, more unreservedly than you had
ever done in the old familiar, peaceful days, in the old life that
was now abolished and gone for good.*

BORIS PASTERNAK,
DOCTOR ZHIVAGO

PASSAGE HIGHLIGHTED IN ONE OF THE BOOKS FOUND
WITH CHRIS MCCANDLESS'S REMAINS.
"NEED FOR A PURPOSE" HAD BEEN WRITTEN
IN MCCANDLESS'S HAND IN THE MARGIN ABOVE THE PASSAGE.

Samuel Walter McCandless, Jr., fifty-six years old, is a bearded,
taciturn man with longish salt-and-pepper hair combed straight
back from a high forehead. Tall and solidly proportioned, he
wears wire-rimmed glasses that give him a professorial demeanor. Seven weeks after the body of his son turned up in

Alaska wrapped in a blue sleeping bag that Billie had sewn for Chris from a kit, Walt studies a sailboat scudding beneath the window of his waterfront townhouse. "How is it," he wonders aloud as he gazes blankly across Chesapeake Bay, "that a kid with so much compassion could cause his parents so much pain?"

The McCandless home in Chesapeake Beach, Maryland, is tastefully decorated, spotless, devoid of clutter. Floor-to-ceiling windows take in the hazy panorama of the bay. A big Chevy Suburban and a white Cadillac are parked out front, a painstakingly restored '69 Corvette sits in the garage, a thirty-foot cruising catamaran is moored at the dock. Four large squares of poster board, covered with scores of photos documenting the whole brief span of Chris's life, have occupied the dining-room table for many days now.

Moving deliberately around the display, Billie points out Chris as a toddler astride a hobby horse, Chris as a rapt eight-year-old in a yellow rain slicker on his first backpacking trip, Chris at his high school commencement. "The hardest part," says Walt, pausing over a shot of his son clowning around on a family vacation, his voice cracking almost imperceptibly, "is simply not having him around anymore. I spent a lot of time with Chris, perhaps more than with any of my other kids. I really liked his company even though he frustrated us so often."

Walt is wearing gray sweatpants, racquetball shoes, and a satin baseball jacket embroidered with the logo of the Jet Propulsion Laboratory. Despite the casual attire, he projects an air of authority. Within the ranks of his arcane field—an advanced technology called synthetic aperture radar, or SAR—he is an eminence. SAR has been a component of high-profile space missions since 1978, when the first SAR-equipped satellite, *Seasat*, was placed into orbit around the earth. NASA's project manager for that pioneering *Seasat* launch was Walt McCandless.

The first line of Walt's résumé reads "Clearance: Current U.S. Department of Defense Top Secret." A little farther down the page an account of his professional experience begins: "I perform private consulting services aligned with remote sensor and satellite system design, and associated signal processing, data reduction and information extraction tasks." Colleagues refer to him as brilliant.

Walt is accustomed to calling the shots. Taking control is something he does unconsciously, reflexively. Although he speaks softly in the unhurried cadence of the American West, his voice has an edge, and the set of his jaw betrays an undercurrent of nervous energy. Even from across the room it is apparent that some very high voltage is crackling through his wires. There is no mistaking whence Chris's intensity came.

When Walt talks, people listen. If something or someone displeases him, his eyes narrow and his speech becomes clipped. According to members of the extended family, his moods can be dark and mercurial, although they say his famous temper has lost much of its volatility in recent years. After Chris gave everybody the slip in 1990, something changed in Walt. His son's disappearance scared and chastened him. A softer, more tolerant side of his personality came to the fore.

effects of his dream

Walt grew up in Greeley, Colorado, an agricultural town on the high, windswept plains up near the Wyoming line. A bright child, and driven, he won an academic scholarship to Colorado State University in nearby Fort Collins. To make ends meet, he held down an assortment of part-time jobs through college, including one in a mortuary, but his steadiest paycheck came from playing with Charlie Novak, the leader of a popular jazz quartet. Novak's band, with Walt sitting in on piano, worked the regional lounge circuit, covering dance numbers and old standards in smoky honky-tonks up and down the Front Range. An inspired musician with considerable natural talent, Walt still plays professionally from time to time.

In 1957, the Soviets launched *Sputnik I*, casting a shadow of fear across America. In the ensuing national hysteria Congress funneled millions upon millions of dollars into the California-based aerospace industry, and the boom was on. For young Walt McCandless—just out of college, married, and with a baby on the way—*Sputnik* opened the door to opportunity. After receiving his undergraduate diploma, Walt took a job with Hughes Aircraft, which sent him to Tucson for three years, where he earned a master's degree in antenna theory at the University of Arizona. As soon as he completed his thesis—"An Analysis of Conical Helices"—he transferred to Hughes's big California operation, where the real action was, eager to make his mark in the race for space.

He bought a little bungalow in Torrance, worked hard, moved quickly up the ladder. Sam was born in 1959, and four other children—Stacy, Shawna, Shelly, and Shannon—followed in quick succession. Walt was appointed test director and section head for the *Surveyor 1* mission, the first spacecraft to make a soft landing on the moon. His star was bright and rising.

By 1965, however, his marriage was in trouble. He and his wife, Marcia, separated. Walt started dating a secretary at Hughes named Wilhelmina Johnson—everyone called her Billie—who was twenty-two years old and had dark, striking eyes. They fell in love and moved in together. Billie got pregnant. Very petite to begin with, in nine months she gained only eight pounds and never even wore maternity clothes. On February 12, 1968, Billie gave birth to a son. He was underweight, but healthy and animated. Walt bought Billie a Gianini guitar, on which she strummed lullabies to soothe the fussy newborn. Twenty-two years later, rangers from the National Park Service would find that same guitar on the backseat of a yellow Datsun abandoned near the shore of Lake Mead.

It is impossible to know what murky convergence of chromosomal matter, parent-child dynamics, and alignment of the cosmos was responsible, but Christopher Johnson McCandless came into the world with unusual gifts and a will not easily deflected from its trajectory. At the age of two, he got up in the middle of the night, found his way outside without waking his parents, and entered a house down the street to plunder a neighbor's candy drawer.

In the third grade, after receiving a high score on a standardized achievement test, Chris was placed in an accelerated program for gifted students. "He wasn't happy about it," Billie remembers, "because it meant he had to do extra schoolwork. So he spent a week trying to get himself out of the program. This little boy attempted to convince the teacher, the principal—anybody who would listen—that the test results were in error, that he really didn't belong there. We learned about it at the first PTA meeting. His teacher pulled us aside and told us that 'Chris marches to a different drummer.' She just shook her head."

"Even when we were little," says Carine, who was born three years after Chris, "he was very to himself. He wasn't antisocial—he always had friends, and everybody liked him—but he could go off and entertain himself for hours. He didn't seem to need toys or friends. He could be alone without being lonely."

When Chris was six, Walt was offered a position at NASA, prompting a move to the nation's capital. They bought a split-level house on Willet Drive in suburban Annandale. It had green shutters, a bay window, a nice yard. Four years after arriving in Virginia, Walt quit working for NASA to start a consulting firm—User Systems, Incorporated—which he and Billie ran out of their home.

Money was tight. In addition to the financial strain of exchanging a steady paycheck for the vagaries of self-employment, Walt's separation from his first wife left him with two families to support. To make a go of it, says Carine, "Mom and Dad put in incredibly long hours. When Chris and I woke up in the morning to go to school, they'd be in the office working. When we came home in the afternoon, they'd be in the office working. When we went to bed at night, they'd be in the office working. They ran a real good business together and eventually started making bunches of money, but they worked all the time."

It was a stressful existence. Both Walt and Billie are tightly wound, emotional, loath to give ground. Now and then the tension erupted in verbal sparring. In moments of anger, one or the other often threatened divorce. The rancor was more smoke than fire, says Carine, but "I think it was one of the reasons Chris and I were so close. We learned to count on each other when Mom and Dad weren't getting along."

But there were good times, too. On weekends and when school was out, the family took to the road: They drove to Virginia

Beach and the Carolina shore, to Colorado to visit Walt's kids from his first marriage, to the Great Lakes, to the Blue Ridge Mountains. "We camped out of the back of the truck, the Chevy Suburban," Walt explains. "Later we bought an Airstream trailer and traveled with that. Chris loved those trips, the longer the better. There was always a little wanderlust in the family, and it was clear early on that Chris had inherited it."

In the course of their travels, the family visited Iron Mountain, Michigan, a small mining town in the forests of the Upper Peninsula that was Billie's childhood home. She was one of six kids. Loren Johnson, Billie's father, ostensibly worked as a truck driver, "but he never held any job for long," she says.

"Billie's dad didn't quite fit into society," Walt explains. "In many ways he and Chris were a lot alike."

Loren Johnson was proud and stubborn and dreamy, a woodsman, a self-taught musician, a writer of poetry. Around Iron Mountain his rapport with the creatures of the forest was legendary. "He was always raising wildlife," says Billie. "He'd find some animal in a trap, take it home, amputate the injured limb, heal it, and then let it go again. Once my dad hit a mother deer with his truck, making an orphan of its fawn. He was crushed. But he brought the baby deer home and raised it inside the house, behind the woodstove, just like it was one of his kids."

To support his family, Loren tried a series of entrepreneurial ventures, none of them very successful. He raised chickens for a while, then mink and chinchillas. He opened a stable and sold horse rides to tourists. Much of the food he put on the table came from hunting—despite the fact that he was uncomfortable killing animals. "My dad cried every time he shot a deer," Billie says, "but we had to eat, so he did it."

He also worked as a hunting guide, which pained him even more. "Men from the city would drive up in their big Cadillacs, and my dad would take them out to his hunting camp for a week to get a trophy. He would guarantee them a buck before they left, but most of them were such lousy shots and drank so much that they couldn't hit anything, so he'd usually have to shoot the deer for them. God, he hated that."

Loren, not surprisingly, was charmed by Chris. And Chris adored his grandfather. The old man's backwoods savvy, his affinity for the wilderness, left a deep impression on the boy.

When Chris was eight, Walt took him on his first overnight backpacking trip, a three-day hike in the Shenandoah to climb Old Rag. They made the summit, and Chris carried his own pack the whole way. Hiking up the mountain became a father-son tradition; they climbed Old Rag almost every year thereafter.

When Chris was a little older, Walt took Billie and his children from both marriages to climb Longs Peak in Colorado—at 14,256 feet, the highest summit in Rocky Mountain National Park. Walt, Chris, and Walt's youngest son from his first marriage reached the 13,000-foot elevation. There, at a prominent notch called the Keyhole, Walt decided to turn around. He was tired and feeling the altitude. The route above looked slabby, exposed, dangerous. "I'd had it, OK," Walt explains, "but Chris wanted to keep going to the top. I told him no way. He was only twelve then, so all he could do was complain. If he'd been fourteen or fifteen, he would have simply gone on without me."

Walt grows quiet, staring absently into the distance. "Chris was fearless even when he was little," he says after a long pause. "He didn't think the odds applied to him. We were always trying to pull him back from the edge."

Chris was a high achiever in almost everything that caught his fancy. Academically he brought home A's with little effort. Only once did he receive a grade lower than B: an F, in high school physics. When he saw the report card, Walt made an appointment with the physics teacher to see what the problem was. "He was a retired air force colonel," Walt remembers, "an old guy, traditional, pretty rigid. He'd explained at the beginning of the semester that because he had something like two hundred students, lab reports had to be written in a particular format to make grading them a manageable proposition. Chris thought it was a stupid rule and decided to ignore it. He did his lab reports, but not in the correct format, so the teacher gave him an F. After talking with the guy, I came home and told Chris he got the grade he deserved."

Both Chris and Carine shared Walt's musical aptitude. Chris took up the guitar, piano, French horn. "It was strange to see in a kid his age," says Walt, "but he loved Tony Bennett. He'd sing numbers like 'Tender Is the Night' while I accompanied him on piano. He was good." Indeed, in a goofy video Chris made in college, he can be heard belting out "Summers by the sea/Sailboats in Capri" with impressive panache, crooning like a professional lounge singer.

A gifted French-horn player, as a teen he was a member of the American University Symphony but quit, according to Walt, after objecting to rules imposed by a high school band leader. Carine recalls that there was more to it than that: "He quit playing partly because he didn't like being told what to do but also because of me. I wanted to be like Chris, so I started to play French horn, too. And it turned out to be the one thing I was better at than he was. When I was a freshman and he was a senior, I made first chair in the senior band, and there was no way he was going to sit behind his damn sister."

Their musical rivalry seems not to have damaged the relationship between Chris and Carine, however. They'd been best friends from an early age, spending hours together building forts out of cushions and blankets in their Annandale living room. "He was always really nice to me," Carine says, "and extremely protective. He'd hold my hand when we walked down the street. When he was in junior high and I was still in grade school, he got out earlier than me, but he'd hang out at his friend Brian Paskowitz's house so we could walk home together."

Chris inherited Billie's angelic features, most notably her eyes, the black depths of which betrayed his every emotion. Although he was small—in school photographs he is always in the front row, the shortest kid in the class—Chris was strong for his size and well coordinated. He tried his hand at many sports but had little patience for learning the finer points of any of them. When he went skiing during family vacations in Colorado, he seldom bothered to turn; he'd simply crouch in a gorilla tuck, feet spread wide for stability, and point the boards straight down the hill. Likewise, says Walt, "when I tried to teach him to play golf, he refused to accept that form is everything. Chris would take the biggest swing you ever saw, every time. Sometimes he'd hit the ball three hundred yards, but more often he'd slice it into the next fairway.

"Chris had so much natural talent," Walt continues, "but if you tried to coach him, to polish his skill, to bring out that final ten percent, a wall went up. He resisted instruction of any kind. I'm a serious racquetball player, and I taught Chris to play when he was eleven. By the time he was fifteen or sixteen, he was beating me regularly. He was very, very quick and had a lot of power; but when I suggested he work on the gaps in his game, he refused to listen. Once in a tournament he came up against a forty-five-year-old man with a lot of experience. Chris won a bunch of points right out of the gate, but the guy was methodically testing him, probing for his weakness. As soon as he figured out which shot gave Chris the most trouble, that was the only shot Chris saw, and it was all over."

Nuance, strategy, and anything beyond the rudimentaries of technique were wasted on Chris. The only way he cared to tackle a challenge was head-on, right now, applying the full brunt of his extraordinary energy. And he was often frustrated as a consequence. It wasn't until he took up running, an activity that rewards will and determination more than finesse or cunning, that he found his athletic calling. At the age of ten, he entered his first running competition, a ten-kilometer road race. He finished sixty-ninth, beating more than one thousand adults, and was hooked. By the time he was in his teens, he was one of the top distance runners in the region.

When Chris was twelve, Walt and Billie bought Carine a puppy, a Shetland sheepdog named Buckley, and Chris fell into the habit of taking the pet with him on his daily training runs. "Buckley was supposedly my dog," says Carine, "but he and Chris became inseparable. Buck was fast, and he'd always beat Chris home when they went running. I remember Chris was so excited the first time he made it home before Buckley. He went tearing all over the house yelling 'I beat Buck! I beat Buck!'"

At W. T. Woodson High School—a large public institution in

Fairfax, Virginia, with a reputation for high academic standards and winning athletic teams—Chris was the captain of the cross-country squad. He relished the role and concocted novel, grueling training regimens that his teammates still remember well.

"He was really into pushing himself," explains Gordy Cucullu, a younger member of the team. "Chris invented this workout he called Road Warriors: He would lead us on long, killer runs through places like farmers' fields and construction sites, places we weren't supposed to be, and intentionally try to get us lost. We'd run as far and as fast as we could, down strange roads, through the woods, whatever. The whole idea was to lose our bearings, to push ourselves into unknown territory. Then we'd run at a slightly slower pace until we found a road we recognized and race home again at full speed. In a certain sense that's how Chris lived his entire life."

McCandless viewed running as an intensely spiritual exercise, verging on religion. "Chris would use the spiritual aspect to try to motivate us," recalls Eric Hathaway, another friend on the team. "He'd tell us to think about all the evil in the world, all the hatred, and imagine ourselves running against the forces of darkness, the evil wall that was trying to keep us from running our best. He believed doing well was all mental, a simple matter of harnessing whatever energy was available. As impressionable high school kids, we were blown away by that kind of talk."

But running wasn't exclusively an affair of the spirit; it was a competitive undertaking as well. When McCandless ran, he ran to win. "Chris was really serious about running," says Kris Maxie Gillmer, a female teammate who was perhaps McCandless's closest friend at Woodson. "I can remember standing at the finish line, watching him run, knowing how badly he wanted to do well and how disappointed he'd be if he did worse than he expected. After a bad race or even a bad time trial during practice, he could be really hard on himself. And he wouldn't want to talk about it. If I tried to console him, he'd act annoyed and brush me off. He internalized the disappointment. He'd go off alone somewhere and beat himself up.

"It wasn't just running Chris took so seriously," Gillmer adds.

"He was like that about everything. You aren't supposed to think about heavy-duty stuff in high school. But I did, and he did, too, which is why we hit it off. We'd hang out during snack break at his locker and talk about life, the state of the world, serious things. I'm black, and I could never figure out why everyone made such a big deal about race. Chris would talk to me about that kind of thing. He understood. He was always questioning stuff in the same way. I liked him a lot. He was a really good guy."

McCandless took life's inequities to heart. During his senior year at Woodson, he became obsessed with racial oppression in South Africa. He spoke seriously to his friends about smuggling weapons into that country and joining the struggle to end apartheid. "We'd get into arguments about it once in a while," recalls Hathaway. "Chris didn't like going through channels, working within the system, waiting his turn. He'd say, 'Come on, Eric, we can raise enough money to go to South Africa on our own, right now. It's just a matter of deciding to do it.' I'd counter by saying we were only a couple of kids, that we couldn't possibly make a difference. But you couldn't argue with him. He'd come back with something like 'Oh, so I guess you just don't care about right and wrong.' "

On weekends, when his high school pals were attending "keggers" and trying to sneak into Georgetown bars, McCandless would wander the seedier quarters of Washington, chatting with prostitutes and homeless people, buying them meals, earnestly suggesting ways they might improve their lives.

"Chris didn't understand how people could possibly be allowed to go hungry, especially in this country," says Billie. "He would rave about that kind of thing for hours."

On one occasion Chris picked up a homeless man from the streets of D.C., brought him home to leafy, affluent Annandale, and secretly set the guy up in the Airstream trailer his parents parked beside the garage. Walt and Billie never knew they were hosting a vagrant.

On another occasion Chris drove over to Hathaway's house and announced they were going downtown. "Cool!" Hathaway remembers thinking. "It was a Friday night, and I assumed we were headed to Georgetown to party. Instead, Chris parked down on Fourteenth Street, which at the time was a real bad part of town. Then he said, 'You know, Eric, you can read about this stuff, but you can't understand it until you live it. Tonight that's what we're going to do.' We spent the next few hours hanging out in creepy places, talking with pimps and hookers and lowlife. I was, like, *scared*.

"Toward the end of the evening, Chris asked me how much money I had. I said five dollars. He had ten. 'OK, you buy the gas,' he told me; 'I'm going to get some food.' So he spent the ten bucks on a big bag of hamburgers, and we drove around handing them out to smelly guys sleeping on grates. It was the weirdest Friday night of my life. But Chris did that kind of thing a lot."

Early in his senior year at Woodson, Chris informed his parents that he had no intention of going to college. When Walt and Billie suggested that he needed a college degree to attain a fulfilling career, Chris answered that careers were demeaning "twentieth-century inventions," more of a liability than an asset, and that he would do fine without one, thank you.

"That put us into kind of a tizzy," Walt admits. "Both Billie and I come from blue-collar families. A college degree is something we don't take lightly, OK, and we worked hard to be able to afford to send our kids to good schools. So Billie sat him down and said, 'Chris, if you really want to make a difference in the world, if you really want to help people who are less fortunate, get yourself some leverage first. Go to college, get a law degree, and then you'll be able to have a real impact.'"

"Chris brought home good grades," says Hathaway. "He didn't get into trouble, he was a high achiever, he did what he was supposed to. His parents didn't really have grounds to complain. But they got on his case about going to college; and whatever they said to him, it must have worked. Because he ended up going to Emory, even though he thought it was pointless, a waste of time and money."

It's somewhat surprising that Chris ceded to pressure from Walt and Billie about attending college when he refused to listen to them about so many other things. But there was never a shortage of apparent contradictions in the relationship between Chris and his parents. When Chris visited with Kris Gillmer, he frequently railed against Walt and Billie, portraying them as unreasonable tyrants. Yet to his male buddies—Hathaway, Cucullu, and another track star, Andy Horowitz—he scarcely complained at all. "My impression was that his parents were very nice people," says Hathaway, "no different, really, than my parents or anyone's parents. Chris just didn't like being told what to do. I think he would have been unhappy with any parents; he had trouble with the whole *idea* of parents."

McCandless's personality was puzzling in its complexity. He was intensely private but could be convivial and gregarious in the extreme. And despite his overdeveloped social conscience, he was no tight-lipped, perpetually grim do-gooder who frowned on fun. To the contrary, he enjoyed tipping a glass now and then and was an incorrigible ham.

Perhaps the greatest paradox concerned his feelings about money. Walt and Billie had both known poverty when they were young and after struggling to rise above it saw nothing wrong with enjoying the fruits of their labor. "We worked very, very hard," Billie emphasizes. "We did without when the kids were little, saved what we earned, and invested it for the future." When the future finally arrived, they didn't flaunt their modest wealth, but they bought nice clothes, some jewelry for Billie, a Cadillac. Eventually, they purchased the townhouse on the bay and the sailboat. They took the kids to Europe, skiing in Breckenridge, on a Caribbean cruise. And Chris, Billie acknowledges, "was embarrassed by all that."

Her son, the teenage Tolstoyan, believed that wealth was shameful, corrupting, inherently evil—which is ironic because Chris was a natural-born capitalist with an uncanny knack for making a buck. "Chris was always an entrepreneur," Billie says with a laugh. "Always."

As an eight-year-old, he grew vegetables behind the house in Annandale and then sold them door-to-door around the neighborhood. "Here was this cute little boy pulling a wagon full of fresh-grown beans and tomatoes and peppers," says Carine.

"Who could resist? And Chris knew it. He'd have this look on his face like 'I'm damn cute! Want to buy some beans?' By the time he came home, the wagon would be empty, and he'd have a bunch of money in his hand."

When Chris was twelve, he printed up a stack of flyers and started a neighborhood copy business, Chris's Fast Copies, offering free pickup and delivery. Using the copier in Walt and Billie's office, he paid his parents a few cents a copy, charged customers two cents less than the corner store charged, and made a tidy profit.

In 1985, following his junior year at Woodson, Chris was hired by a local building contractor to canvass neighborhoods for sales, drumming up siding jobs and kitchen remodelings. And he was astonishingly successful, a salesman without peer. In a matter of a few months, half a dozen other students were working under him, and he'd put seven thousand dollars into his bank account. He used part of the money to buy the yellow Datsun, the secondhand B210.

Chris had such an outstanding knack for selling that in the spring of 1986, as Chris's high school graduation approached, the owner of the construction company phoned Walt and offered to pay for Chris's college education if Walt would persuade his son to remain in Annandale and keep working while he went to school instead of quitting the job and going off to Emory.

"When I mentioned the offer to Chris," says Walt, "he wouldn't even consider it. He told his boss that he had other plans." As soon as high school was over, Chris declared, he was going to get behind the wheel of his new car and spend the summer driving across the country. Nobody anticipated that the journey would be the first in a series of extended transcontinental adventures. Nor could anyone in his family have foreseen that a chance discovery during this initial journey would ultimately turn him inward and away, drawing Chris and those who loved him into a morass of anger, misunderstanding, and sorrow.

CHAPTER TWELVE

ANNANDALE

Rather than love, than money, than fame, give me truth. I sat at a table where were rich food and wine in abundance, an obsequious attendance, but sincerity and truth were not; and I went away hungry from the inhospitable board. The hospitality was as cold as the ices.

HENRY DAVID THOREAU,
WALDEN, OR LIFE IN THE WOODS

PASSAGE HIGHLIGHTED IN ONE OF THE BOOKS FOUND WITH
CHRIS McCANDLESS'S REMAINS.
AT THE TOP OF THE PAGE, THE WORD "TRUTH" HAD BEEN WRITTEN
IN LARGE BLOCK LETTERS IN McCANDLESS'S HAND.

For children are innocent and love justice, while most of us are wicked and naturally prefer mercy.

G. K. CHESTERTON

In 1986, on the sultry spring weekend that Chris graduated from Woodson High School, Walt and Billie threw a party for him. Walt's birthday was June 10, just a few days away, and at the party Chris gave his father a present: a very expensive Questar telescope.

"I remember sitting there when he gave Dad the telescope," says Carine. "Chris had tossed back a few drinks that night and was pretty blitzed. He got real emotional. He was almost crying, fighting back the tears, telling Dad that even though they'd had their differences over the years, he was grateful for all the things Dad had done for him. Chris said how much he respected Dad for starting from nothing, working his way through college, busting his ass to support eight kids. It was a moving speech. Everybody there was all choked up. And then he left on his trip."

Walt and Billie didn't try to prevent Chris from going, although they persuaded him to take Walt's Texaco credit card for emergencies and exacted a promise from their son to call home every three days. "We had our hearts in our mouths the whole time he was gone," says Walt, "but there was no way to stop him."

After leaving Virginia, Chris drove south and then west across the flat Texas plains, through the heat of New Mexico and Arizona, and arrived at the Pacific coast. Initially, he honored the agreement to phone regularly, but as the summer wore on, the calls became less and less frequent. He didn't appear back home until two days before the fall term was to start at Emory. When he walked into the Annandale house, he had a scruffy beard, his hair was long and tangled, and he'd shed thirty pounds from his already lean frame.

"As soon as I heard he was home," says Carine, "I ran to his room to talk with him. He was on the bed, asleep. He was *so* thin. He looked like those paintings of Jesus on the cross. When Mom saw how much weight he'd lost, she was a total wreck. She started cooking like mad to try and put some meat back on his bones."

Near the end of his trip, it turned out, Chris had gotten lost in the Mojave Desert and had nearly succumbed to dehydration. His parents were extremely alarmed when they heard about this brush with disaster but were unsure how to persuade Chris to exercise more caution in the future. "Chris was good at almost everything he ever tried," Walt reflects, "which made him supremely overconfident. If you attempted to talk him out of something, he wouldn't argue. He'd just nod politely and then do exactly what he wanted.

"So at first I didn't say anything about the safety aspect. I played tennis with Chris, talked about other things, then eventually sat down with him to discuss the risks he'd taken. I'd learned by then that a direct approach—'By God, you better not try a stunt like that again!'—didn't work with Chris. Instead, I tried to explain that we didn't object to his travels; we just wanted him to be a little more careful and to keep us better informed of his whereabouts."

To Walt's dismay Chris bristled at this small dollop of fatherly advice. The only effect it seemed to have was to make him even less inclined to share his plans.

"Chris," says Billie, "thought we were idiots for worrying about him."

During the course of his travels, Chris had acquired a machete and a .30-06 rifle, and when Walt and Billie drove him down to Atlanta to enroll in college, he insisted on taking the big knife and the gun with him. "When we went with Chris up to his dorm room," Walt laughs, "I thought his roommate's parents were going to have a stroke on the spot. The roommate was a preppy kid from Connecticut, dressed like Joe College, and Chris walks in with a scraggly beard and worn-out clothes, looking like Jeremiah Johnson, packing a machete and a deer-hunting rifle. But you know what? Within ninety days the preppy roommate had dropped out, while Chris had made the dean's list."

To his parents' pleasant surprise, as the school year stretched on, Chris seemed thrilled to be at Emory. He shaved, trimmed his hair, and readopted the clean-cut look he'd had in high school. His grades were nearly perfect. He started writing for the school newspaper. He even talked enthusiastically about going on to get a law degree when he graduated. "Hey," Chris boasted to Walt at one point, "I think my grades will be good enough to get into Harvard Law School."

The summer after his freshman year of college, Chris returned to Annandale and worked for his parents' company, developing computer software. "The program he wrote for us that summer was flawless," says Walt. "We still use it today and have sold copies of the program to many clients. But when I asked Chris to show me how he wrote it, to explain why it worked the way it did, he refused. 'All you need to know is that it works,' he said. 'You don't need to know how or why.' Chris was just being Chris, but it infuriated me. He would have made a great CIA agent—I'm serious; I know guys who work for the CIA. He told us what he thought we needed to know and nothing more. He was that way about everything."

Many aspects of Chris's personality baffled his parents. He could be generous and caring to a fault, but he had a darker side as well, characterized by monomania, impatience, and unwavering self-absorption, qualities that seemed to intensify through his college years.

"I saw Chris at a party after his sophomore year at Emory," remembers Eric Hathaway, "and it was obvious he had changed. He seemed very introverted, almost cold. When I said 'Hey, good to see you, Chris,' his reply was cynical: 'Yeah, sure, that's what everybody says.' It was hard to get him to open up. His studies were the only thing he was interested in talking about. Social life at Emory revolved around fraternities and sororities, something Chris wanted no part of. I think when everybody started going Greek, he kind of pulled back from his old friends and got more heavily into himself."

The summer between his sophomore and junior years Chris again returned to Annandale and took a job delivering pizzas for Domino's. "He didn't care that it wasn't a cool thing to do," says Carine. "He made a pile of money. I remember he'd come home every night and do his accounting at the kitchen table. It didn't matter how tired he was; he'd figure out how many miles he drove, how much Domino's paid him for gas, how much gas actually cost, his net profits for the evening, how it compared to the same evening the week before. He kept track of everything and showed me how to do it, how to make a business work. He didn't seem interested in the money so much as the fact that he was good at making it. It was like a game, and the money was a way of keeping score."

Chris's relations with his parents, which had been unusually courteous since his graduation from high school, deteriorated significantly that summer, and Walt and Billie had no idea why. According to Billie, "He seemed mad at us more often, and he became more withdrawn—no, that's not the right word. Chris wasn't ever *withdrawn*. But he wouldn't tell us what was on his mind and spent more time by himself."

Chris's smoldering anger, it turns out, was fueled by a discovery he'd made two summers earlier, during his cross-country wanderings. When he arrived in California, he'd visited the El Segundo neighborhood where he'd spent the first six years of his life. He called on a number of old family friends who still lived there, and from their answers to his queries, Chris pieced together the facts of his father's previous marriage and subsequent divorce—facts to which he hadn't been privy.

Walt's split from his first wife, Marcia, was not a clean or amicable parting. Long after falling in love with Billie, long after she gave birth to Chris, Walt continued his relationship with Marcia in secret, dividing his time between two households, two families. Lies were told and then exposed, begetting more lies to explain away the initial deceptions. Two years after Chris was born, Walt fathered another son—Quinn McCandless—with Marcia. When Walt's double life came to light, the revelations inflicted deep wounds. All parties suffered terribly.

Eventually, Walt, Billie, Chris, and Carine moved to the East Coast. The divorce from Marcia was at long last finalized, allowing Walt and Billie to legalize their marriage. They all put the turmoil behind them as best they could and carried on with their lives. Two decades went by. Wisdom accrued. The guilt and hurt and jealous fury receded into the distant past; it appeared that the storm had been weathered. And then in 1986, Chris drove out to El Segundo, made the rounds of the old neighborhood, and learned about the episode in all its painful detail.

"Chris was the sort of person who brooded about things,"

Why he resents dad

Carine observes. "If something bothered him, he wouldn't come right out and say it. He'd keep it to himself, harboring his resentment, letting the bad feelings build and build." That seems to be what happened following the discoveries he made in El Segundo.

Children can be harsh judges when it comes to their parents, disinclined to grant clemency, and this was especially true in Chris's case. More even than most teens, he tended to see things in black and white. He measured himself and those around him by an impossibly rigorous moral code.

Curiously, Chris didn't hold everyone to the same exacting standards. One of the individuals he professed to admire greatly over the last two years of his life was a heavy drinker and incorrigible philanderer who regularly beat up his girlfriends. Chris was well aware of this man's faults yet managed to forgive them. He was also able to forgive, or overlook, the shortcomings of his literary heroes: Jack London was a notorious drunk; Tolstoy, despite his famous advocacy of celibacy, had been an enthusiastic sexual adventurer as young man and went on to father at least thirteen children, some of whom were conceived at the same time the censorious count was thundering in print against the evils of sex.

Like many people, Chris apparently judged artists and close friends by their work, not their life, yet he was temperamentally incapable of extending such lenity to his father. Whenever Walt McCandless, in his stern fashion, would dispense a fatherly admonishment to Chris, Carine, or their half siblings, Chris would fixate on his father's own less than sterling behavior many years earlier and silently denounce him as a sanctimonious hypocrite. Chris kept careful score. And over time he worked himself into a choler of self-righteous indignation that was impossible to keep bottled up.

After Chris unearthed the particulars of Walt's divorce, two years passed before his anger began to leak to the surface, but leak it eventually did. The boy could not pardon the mistakes his father had made as a young man, and he was even less willing to pardon the attempt at concealment. He later declared to Carine and others that the deception committed by Walt and Billie made his "entire childhood seem like a fiction." But he did not confront his parents with what he knew, then or ever. He chose instead to make a secret of his dark knowledge and express his rage obliquely, in silence and sullen withdrawal.

In 1988, as Chris's resentment of his parents hardened, his sense of outrage over injustice in the world at large grew. That summer, Billie remembers, "Chris started complaining about all the rich kids at Emory." More and more of the classes he took addressed such pressing social issues as racism and world hunger and inequities in the distribution of wealth. But despite his aversion to money and conspicuous consumption, Chris's political leanings could not be described as liberal.

Indeed, he delighted in ridiculing the policies of the Democratic Party and was a vocal admirer of Ronald Reagan. At Emory he went so far as to co-found a College Republican Club. Chris's seemingly anomalous political positions were perhaps best summed up by Thoreau's declaration in "Civil Disobedience": "I heartily accept the motto—That government is best which governs least.'" Beyond that his views were not easily characterized.

As assistant editorial page editor of *The Emory Wheel*, he authored scores of commentaries. In reading them half a decade later, one is reminded how young McCandless was, and how passionate. The opinions he expressed in print, argued with idiosyncratic logic, were all over the map. He lampooned Jimmy Carter and Joe Biden, called for the resignation of Attorney General Edwin Meese, lambasted Bible-thumpers of the Christian right, urged vigilance against the Soviet threat, castigated the Japanese for hunting whales, and defended Jesse Jackson as a viable presidential candidate. In a typically immoderate declaration the lead sentence of McCandless's editorial of March 1, 1988, reads, "We have now begun the third month of the year 1988, and already it is shaping up to be one of the most politically corrupt and scandalous years in modern history. . . ." Chris Morris, the editor of the paper, remembers McCandless as "intense."

To his dwindling number of confrères, McCandless appeared

to grow more intense with each passing month. As soon as classes ended in the spring of 1989, Chris took his Datsun on another prolonged, extemporaneous road trip. "We only got two cards from him the whole summer," says Walt. "The first one said, 'Headed for Guatemala.' When I read that I thought, 'Oh, my God, he's going down there to fight for the insurrectionists. They're going to line him up in front of a wall and shoot him.' Then toward the end of the summer, the second card arrived, and all it said was 'Leaving Fairbanks tomorrow, see you in a couple of weeks.' It turned out he'd changed his mind and instead of heading south had driven to Alaska."

The grinding, dusty haul up the Alaska Highway was Chris's first visit to the Far North. It was an abbreviated trip—he spent a short time around Fairbanks, then hurried south to get back to Atlanta in time for the start of fall classes—but he had been smitten by the vastness of the land, by the ghostly hue of the glaciers, by the pellucid subarctic sky. There was never any question that he would return.

During his senior year at Emory, Chris lived off campus in his bare, spartan room furnished with milk crates and a mattress on the floor. Few of his friends ever saw him outside of classes. A professor gave him a key for after-hours access to the library, where he spent much of his free time. Andy Horowitz, his close high school friend and cross-country teammate, bumped into Chris among the stacks early one morning just before graduation. Although Horowitz and McCandless were classmates at Emory, it had been two years since they'd seen each other. They talked awkwardly for a few minutes, then McCandless disappeared into a carrel.

Chris seldom contacted his parents that year, and because he had no phone, they couldn't easily contact him. Walt and Billie grew increasingly worried about their son's emotional distance. In a letter to Chris, Billie implored, "You have completely dropped away from all who love and care about you. Whatever it is—whoever you're with—do you think this is right?" Chris saw this as meddling and referred to the letter as "stupid" when he talked to Carine.

"What does she mean 'whoever I'm with'?" Chris railed at his sister. "She must be fucking nuts. You know what I bet? I bet they think I'm a homosexual. How did they ever get that idea? What a bunch of imbeciles."

In the spring of 1990, when Walt, Billie, and Carine attended Chris's graduation ceremony, they thought he seemed happy. As they watched him stride across the stage and take his diploma, he was grinning from ear to ear. He indicated that he was planning another extended trip but implied that he'd visit his family in Annandale before hitting the road. Shortly thereafter, he donated the balance of his bank account to OXFAM, loaded up his car, and vanished from their lives. From then on he scrupulously avoided contacting either his parents or Carine, the sister for whom he purportedly cared immensely.

"We were all worried when we didn't hear from him," says Carine, "and I think my parents' worry was mixed with hurt and anger. But I didn't really feel hurt by his failure to write. I knew he was happy and doing what he wanted to do; I understood that it was important for him to see how independent he could be. And he knew that if he'd written or called me, Mom and Dad would find out where he was, fly out there, and try to bring him home."

Walt does not deny this. "There's no question in my mind," he says. "If we'd had any idea where to look—OK—I would have gone there in a flash, gotten a lock on his whereabouts, and brought our boy home."

As months passed without any word of Chris—and then years—the anguish mounted. Billie never left the house without leaving a note for Chris posted on the door. "Whenever we were out driving and saw a hitchhiker," she says, "if he looked anything like Chris, we'd turn around and circle back. It was a terrible time. Night was the worst, especially when it was cold and stormy. You'd wonder, 'Where is he? Is he warm? Is he hurt? Is he lonely? Is he OK?'"

In July 1992, two years after Chris left Atlanta, Billie was asleep in Chesapeake Beach when she sat bolt upright in the middle of the night, waking Walt. "I was sure I'd heard Chris calling me," she insists, tears rolling down her cheeks. "I don't know how I'll ever get over it. I wasn't dreaming. I didn't imagine it. I heard his voice! He was begging, 'Mom! Help me!' But I couldn't help him because I didn't know where he was. And that was all he said: 'Mom! Help me!' "

CHAPTER THIRTEEN

VIRGINIA BEACH

The physical domain of the country had its counterpart in me. The trails I made led outward into the hills and swamps, but they led inward also. And from the study of things underfoot, and from reading and thinking, came a kind of exploration, myself and the land. In time the two became one in my mind. With the gathering force of an essential thing realizing itself out of early ground, I faced in myself a passionate and tenacious longing— to put away thought forever, and all the trouble it brings, all but the nearest desire, direct and searching. To take the trail and not look back. Whether on foot, on showshoes or by sled, into the summer hills and their late freezing shadows—a high blaze, a runner track in the snow would show where I had gone. Let the rest of mankind find me if it could.

JOHN HAINES,
THE STARS, THE SNOW, THE FIRE:
TWENTY-FIVE YEARS IN THE NORTHERN WILDERNESS

Two framed photographs occupy the mantel in Carine McCandless's Virginia Beach home: one of Chris as a junior in high school, the other of Chris as a seven-year-old in a pint-size suit and crooked tie, standing beside Carine, who is wearing a frilly dress and a new Easter hat. "What's amazing," says Carine as she studies these images of her brother, "is that even though the pictures were taken ten years apart, his expression is identical."

She's right: In both photos Chris stares at the lens with the same pensive, recalcitrant squint, as if he'd been interrupted in the middle of an important thought and was annoyed to be wasting his time in front of the camera. His expression is most striking in the Easter photo because it contrasts so strongly with the exuberant grin Carine wears in the same frame. "That's Chris," she says with an affectionate' smile, brushing her fingertips across the surface of the image. "He'd get that look a lot."

Lying on the floor at Carine's feet is Buckley, the Shetland sheepdog Chris had been so attached to. Now thirteen years old, he's gone white in the muzzle and hobbles around with an arthritic limp. When Max, Carine's eighteen-month-old Rottweiler, intrudes on Buckley's turf, however, the ailing little dog thinks nothing of confronting the much bigger animal with a loud bark and a flurry of well-placed nips, sending the 130-pound beast scurrying for safety.

"Chris was crazy about Buck," Carine says. "That summer he disappeared he'd wanted to take Buck with him. After he graduated from Emory, he asked Mom and Dad if he could come get Buck, but they said no, because Buckley had just been hit by a car and was still recovering. Now, of course, they second-guess the decision, even though Buck was really badly hurt; the vet said he'd never walk again after that accident. My parents can't help wondering—and I admit that I can't, either—how things might have turned out different if Chris had taken Buck with him. Chris didn't think twice about risking his own life, but he never would have put Buckley in any kind of danger. There's no way he would have taken the same kind of chances if Buck had been with him."

Standing five feet eight inches tall, Carine McCandless is the same height as her brother was, maybe an inch taller, and looks enough like him that people frequently asked if they were twins. An animated talker, she flips her waist-length hair from her face with a toss of her head as she speaks and chops the air for emphasis with small, expressive hands. She is barefoot. A gold crucifix dangles from her neck. Her neatly pressed jeans have creases down the front.

Like Chris, Carine is energetic and self-assured, a high achiever, quick to state an opinion. Also like Chris, she clashed fiercely with Walt and Billie as an adolescent. But the differences between the siblings were greater than their similarities.

Carine made peace with her parents shortly after Chris disappeared, and now, at the age of twenty-two, she calls their relationship "extremely good." She is much more gregarious than Chris was and can't imagine going off into the wilderness—or virtually anywhere else—alone. And although she shares Chris's sense of outrage over racial injustice, Carine has no objection—moral or otherwise—to wealth. She recently bought an expensive new home and regularly logs fourteen-hour days at C.A.R. Services, Incorporated, the auto-repair business she owns with her husband, Chris Fish, in the hope of making her first million at an early age.

"I was always getting on Mom and Dad's case because they worked all the time and were never around," she reflects with a self-mocking laugh, "and now look at me: I'm doing the same thing." Chris, she confesses, used to poke fun at her capitalist zeal by calling her the duchess of York, Ivana Trump McCandless, and "a rising successor to Leona Helmsley." His criticism of his sister never went beyond good-natured ribbing, however; Chris and Carine were uncommonly close. In a letter delineating his quarrels with Walt and Billie, Chris once wrote to her, "Anyway, I like to talk to you about this because you are the *only* person in the world who could possibly understand what I'm saying."

Ten months after Chris's death, Carine still grieves deeply for her brother. "I can't seem to get through a day without crying," she says with a look of puzzlement. "For some reason the worst is when I'm in the car by myself. Not once have I been able to make the twenty-minute drive from home to the shop without thinking about Chris and breaking down. I get over it, but when it happens, it's hard."

On the evening of September 17, 1992, Carine was outside giving her Rottweiler a bath when Chris Fish pulled into the driveway. She was surprised he was home so early; usually Fish worked late into the night at C.A.R. Services.

"He was acting funny," Carine recalls. "There was a terrible look on his face. He went inside, came back out, and started helping me wash Max. I knew something was wrong then, because Fish never washes the dog."

"I need to talk to you," Fish said. Carine followed him into the house, rinsed Max's collars in the kitchen sink, and went into the living room. "Fish was sitting on the couch in the dark with his head down. He looked totally hurt. Trying to joke him out of his mood, I said, 'What's *wrong* with you?' I figured his buddies must have been razzing him at work, maybe telling him they'd seen me out with another guy or something. I laughed and asked, 'Have the guys been giving you a hard time?' But he didn't laugh back. When he looked up at me, I saw that his eyes were red."

"It's your brother," Fish had said. "They found him. He's dead." Sam, Walt's oldest child, had called Fish at work and given him the news.

Carine's eyes blurred, and she felt the onset of tunnel vision. Involuntarily, she started shaking her head back and forth, back and forth. "No," she corrected him, "Chris isn't dead." Then she began to scream. Her keening was so loud and continuous that Fish worried the neighbors were going to think he was harming her and call the police.

Carine curled up on the couch in a fetal position, wailing without pause. When Fish tried to comfort her, she pushed him away and shrieked at him to leave her alone. She remained hysterical for the next five hours, but by eleven o'clock she had calmed sufficiently to throw some clothes into a bag, get into the car with Fish, and let him drive her to Walt and Billie's house in Chesapeake Beach, a four-hour trip north.

On their way out of Virginia Beach, Carine asked Fish to stop at their church. "I went in and sat at the altar for an hour or so while Fish stayed in the car," Carine remembers. "I wanted some answers from God. But I didn't get any."

Earlier in the evening Sam had confirmed that the photograph of the unknown hiker faxed down from Alaska was indeed Chris, but the coroner in Fairbanks required Chris's dental records to make a conclusive identification. It took more than a day to compare the X rays, and Billie refused to look at the faxed photo until the dental ID had been completed and there was no longer any doubt whatsoever that the starved boy found in the bus beside the Sushana River was her son.

The next day Carine and Sam flew to Fairbanks to bring home Chris's remains. At the coroner's office they were given the handful of possessions recovered with the body: Chris's rifle, a pair of binoculars, the fishing rod Ronald Franz had given him, one of the Swiss Army knives Jan Burres had given him, the book of plant lore in which his journal was written, a Minolta camera, and five rolls of film—not much else. The coroner passed some papers across her desk; Sam signed them and passed them back.

Less than twenty-four hours after landing in Fairbanks, Carine and Sam flew on to Anchorage, where Chris's body had been cremated following the autopsy at the Scientific Crime Detection Laboratory. The mortuary delivered Chris's ashes to their hotel in a plastic box. "I was surprised how big the box was," Carine says. "His name was printed wrong. The label said CHRISTOPHER R. MCCANDLESS. His middle initial is really *J*. It ticked me off that they didn't get it right. I was mad. Then I thought, 'Chris wouldn't care. He'd think it was funny.'"

They caught a plane for Maryland the next morning. Carine carried her brother's ashes in her knapsack.

During the flight home, Carine ate every scrap of food the cabin attendants set in front of her, "even though," she says, "it was that horrible stuff they serve on airplanes. I just couldn't bear the thought of throwing away food since Chris had starved to death." Over the weeks that followed, however, she found that her appetite had vanished, and she lost ten pounds, leading her friends to worry that she was becoming anorectic.

Back in Chesapeake Beach, Billie had stopped eating, too. A tiny forty-eight-year-old woman with girlish features, she lost eight pounds before her appetite finally returned. Walt reacted the other way, eating compulsively, and gained eight pounds.

A month later Billie sits at her dining room table, sifting through the pictorial record of Chris's final days. It is all she can do to force herself to examine the fuzzy snapshots. As she studies the pictures, she breaks down from time to time, weeping as only a mother who has outlived a child can weep, betraying a sense of loss so huge and irreparable that the mind balks at taking its measure. Such bereavement, witnessed at close range, makes even the most eloquent apologia for high-risk activities ring fatuous and hollow.

"I just don't understand why he had to take those kind of chances," Billie protests through her tears. "I just don't understand it at all."

CHAPTER FOURTEEN

THE STIKINE ICE CAP

*I grew up exuberant in body but with a nervy, craving mind. It
was wanting something more, something tangible. It sought for
reality intensely, always as if it were not there. . . .*
    But you see at once what I do. I climb.

JOHN MENLOVE EDWARDS,

"LETTER FROM A MAN"

*I cannot now tell exactly, it was so long ago, under what cir-
cumstances I first ascended, only that I shuddered as I went
along (I have an indistinct remembrance of having been out
overnight alone),—and then I steadily ascended along a rocky
ridge half clad with stinted trees, where wild beasts haunted, till
I lost myself quite in the upper air and clouds, seeming to pass
an imaginary line which separates a hill, mere earth heaped up,
from a mountain, into a superterranean grandeur and sublim-
ity. What distinguishes that summit above the earthly line, is
that it is unhandselled, awful, grand. It can never become familiar; you are lost the moment you set foot there. You know
the path, but wander, thrilled, over the bare and pathless rock,
as if it were solidified air and cloud. That rocky, misty summit,
secreted in the clouds, was far more thrillingly awful and sublime than the crater of a volcano spouting fire.*

HENRY DAVID THOREAU,

JOURNAL

In the final postcard he sent to Wayne Westerberg, McCandless
had written, "If this adventure proves fatal and you don't ever

hear from me again I want you to know you're a great man. I now walk into the wild." When the adventure did indeed prove fatal, this melodramatic declaration fueled considerable speculation that the boy had been bent on suicide from the beginning, that when he walked into the bush, he had no intention of ever walking out again. I'm not so sure, however.

My suspicion that McCandless's death was unplanned, that it was a terrible accident, comes from reading those few documents he left behind and from listening to the men and women who spent time with him over the final year of his life. But my sense of Chris McCandless's intentions comes, too, from a more personal perspective.

As a youth, I am told, I was willful, self-absorbed, intermittently reckless, moody. I disappointed my father in the usual ways. Like McCandless, figures of male authority aroused in me a confusing medley of corked fury and hunger to please. If something captured my undisciplined imagination, I pursued it with a zeal bordering on obsession, and from the age of seventeen until my late twenties that something was mountain climbing.

I devoted most of my waking hours to fantasizing about, and then undertaking, ascents of remote mountains in Alaska and Canada—obscure spires, steep and frightening, that nobody in the world beyond a handful of climbing geeks had ever heard of. Some good actually came of this. By fixing my sights on one summit after another, I managed to keep my bearings through some thick postadolescent fog. Climbing *mattered*. The danger bathed the world in a halogen glow that caused everything—the sweep of the rock, the orange and yellow lichens, the texture of the clouds—to stand out in brilliant relief. Life thrummed at a higher pitch. The world was made real.

In 1977, while brooding on a Colorado barstool, picking unhappily at my existential scabs, I got it into my head to climb a mountain called the Devils Thumb. An intrusion of diorite sculpted by ancient glaciers into a peak of immense and spectacular proportions, the Thumb is especially imposing from the north: Its great north wall, which had never been climbed, rises sheer and clean for six thousand feet from the glacier at its base, twice the height of Yosemite's El Capitan. I would go to Alaska, ski inland from the sea across thirty miles of glacial ice, and ascend this mighty *nordwand*. I decided, moreover, to do it alone.

I was twenty-three, a year younger than Chris McCandless when he walked into the Alaska bush. My reasoning, if one can call it that, was inflamed by the scattershot passions of youth and a literary diet overly rich in the works of Nietzsche, Kerouac, and John Menlove Edwards, the latter a deeply troubled writer and psychiatrist who, before putting an end to his life with a cyanide capsule in 1958, had been one of the preeminent British rock climbers of the day. Edwards regarded climbing as a "psycho-neurotic tendency"; he climbed not for sport but to find refuge from the inner torment that framed his existence.

As I formulated my plan to climb the Thumb, I was dimly aware that I might be getting in over my head. But that only added to the scheme's appeal. That it wouldn't be easy was the whole point.

I owned a book in which there was a photograph of the Devils Thumb, a black-and-white image taken by an eminent glaciologist named Maynard Miller. In Miller's aerial photo the mountain looked particularly sinister: a huge fin of exfoliated stone, dark and smeared with ice. The picture held an almost pornographic fascination for me. How would it feel, I wondered, to be balanced on that bladelike summit ridge, worrying over the storm clouds building in the distance, hunched against the wind and dunning cold, contemplating the drop on either side? Could a person keep a lid on his terror long enough to reach the top and get back down?

And if I did pull it off . . . I was afraid to let myself imagine the triumphant aftermath, lest I invite a jinx. But I never had any doubt that climbing the Devils Thumb would transform my life. How could it not?

I was working then as an itinerant carpenter, framing condominiums in Boulder for $3.50 an hour. One afternoon, after nine hours of humping two-by-tens and driving sixteen-penny nails, I

author's experience

told my boss I was quitting: "No, not in a couple of weeks, Steve; right now was more like what I had in mind." It took me a few hours to clear my tools and other belongings out of the crummy job-site trailer where I'd been squatting. And then I climbed into my car and departed for Alaska. I was surprised, as always, by how easy the act of leaving was, and how good it felt. The world was suddenly rich with possibility.

The Devils Thumb demarcates the Alaska–British Columbia border east of Petersburg, a fishing village accessible only by boat or plane. There was regular jet service to Petersburg, but the sum of my liquid assets amounted to a 1960 Pontiac Star Chief and two hundred dollars in cash, not even enough for one-way airfare. So I drove as far as Gig Harbor, Washington, abandoned the car, and inveigled a ride on a northbound salmon seiner.

The *Ocean Queen* was a stout, no-nonsense workboat built from thick planks of Alaska yellow cedar, rigged for long-lining and purse seining. In exchange for a ride north, I had only to take regular turns at the helm—a four-hour wheel watch every twelve hours—and help tie endless skates of halibut gear. The slow journey up the Inside Passage unfolded in a gauzy reverie of anticipation. I was under way, propelled by an imperative that was beyond my ability to control or comprehend.

Sunlight glinted off the water as we chugged up the Strait of Georgia. Slopes rose precipitously from the water's edge, bearded in a gloom of hemlock and cedar and devil's club. Gulls wheeled overhead. Off Malcolm Island the boat split a pod of seven orcas. Their dorsal fins, some as tall as a man, cut the glassy surface within spitting distance of the rail.

Our second night out, two hours before dawn, I was steering from the flying bridge when the head of a mule deer materialized in the spotlight's glare. The animal was in the middle of Fitz Hugh Sound, swimming through the cold black water more than a mile from the Canadian shore. Its retinas burned red in the blinding beam; it looked exhausted and crazed with fear. I swung the wheel to starboard, the boat slid past, and the deer bobbed twice in our wake before vanishing into the darkness.

Most of the Inside Passage follows narrow, fjordlike channels. As we passed Dundas Island, though, the vista suddenly widened. To the west now was open ocean, the full sweep of the Pacific, and the boat pitched and rolled on a twelve-foot westerly swell. Waves broke over the rail. In the distance off the starboard bow, a jumble of low, craggy peaks appeared, and my pulse quickened at the sight. Those mountains heralded the approach of my desideratum. We had arrived in Alaska.

Five days out of Gig Harbor, the *Ocean Queen* docked in Petersburg to take on fuel and water. I hopped over the gunwale, shouldered my heavy backpack, and walked down the pier in the rain. At a loss for what to do next, I took refuge under the eaves of the town library and sat on my load.

Petersburg is a small town, and prim by Alaska standards. A tall, loose-limbed woman walked by and struck up a conversation. Her name was Kai, she said, Kai Sandburn. She was cheerful, outgoing, easy to talk to. I confessed my climbing plans to her, and to my relief she neither laughed nor acted as though they were particularly strange. "When the weather's clear," she simply offered, "you can see the Thumb from town. It's pretty. It's over there, right across Frederick Sound." I followed her outstretched arm, which gestured to the east, at a low wall of clouds.

Kai invited me home for dinner. Later I unrolled my sleeping bag on her floor. Long after she fell asleep, I lay awake in the next room, listening to her peaceful exhalations. I had convinced myself for many months that I didn't really mind the absence of intimacy in my life, the lack of real human connection, but the pleasure I'd felt in this woman's company—the ring of her laughter, the innocent touch of a hand on my arm—exposed my self-deceit and left me hollow and aching.

Petersburg lies on an island; the Devils Thumb is on the mainland, rising from a frozen bald known as the Stikine Ice Cap. Vast and labyrinthine, the ice cap rides the spine of the Boundary Ranges like a carapace, from which the long blue tongues of numerous glaciers inch down toward the sea under the weight of the ages. To reach the foot of the mountain, I had to find a ride across twenty-five miles of saltwater and then ski thirty miles up one of these glaciers, the Baird, a valley of ice that hadn't seen a human footprint, I was fairly certain, in many, many years.

I shared a ride with some tree planters to the head of Thomas Bay, where I was put ashore on a gravel beach. The broad, rubble-strewn terminus of the glacier was visible a mile away. Half an hour later I scrambled up its frozen snout and began the long plod to the Thumb. The ice was bare of snow and embedded with a coarse black grit that crunched beneath the steel points of my crampons.

After three or four miles I came to the snow line and there exchanged crampons for skis. Putting the boards on my feet cut fifteen pounds from the awful load on my back and made the going faster besides. But the snow concealed many of the glacier's crevasses, increasing the danger.

In Seattle, anticipating this hazard, I'd stopped at a hardware store and purchased a pair of stout aluminum curtain rods, each ten feet long. I lashed the rods together to form a cross, then strapped the rig to the hip belt of my backpack so the poles extended horizontally over the snow. Staggering slowly up the glacier beneath my overloaded pack, bearing this ridiculous metal cross, I felt like an odd sort of *penitente*. Were I to break through the veneer of snow over a hidden crevasse, though, the curtain rods would—I hoped mightily—span the slot and keep me from dropping into the frozen depths of the Baird.

For two days I slogged steadily up the valley of ice. The weather was good, the route obvious and without major obstacles. Because I was alone, however, even the mundane seemed charged with meaning. The ice looked colder and more mysterious, the sky a cleaner shade of blue. The unnamed peaks towering over the glacier were bigger and comelier and infinitely more menacing than they would have been were I in the company of another person. And my emotions were similarly amplified: The highs were higher; the periods of despair were deeper and darker. To a self-possessed young man inebriated with the unfolding drama of his own life, all of this held enormous appeal.

Three days after leaving Petersburg, I arrived beneath the Stikine Ice Cap proper, where the long arm of the Baird joins the main body of ice. Here the glacier spills abruptly over the edge of a high plateau, dropping seaward through a gap between two mountains in a phantasmagoria of shattered ice. As I stared at the tumult from a mile away, for the first time since leaving Colorado, I was truly afraid.

The icefall was crisscrossed with crevasses and tottering seracs. From afar it brought to mind a bad train wreck, as if scores of ghostly white boxcars had derailed at the lip of the ice cap and tumbled down the slope willy-nilly. The closer I got, the more unpleasant it looked. My ten-foot curtain rods seemed a poor defense against crevasses that were forty feet across and hundreds of feet deep. Before I could plot a logical course through the icefall, the wind came up, and snow began to slant hard out of the clouds, stinging my face and reducing visibility to almost nothing.

For the better part of the day, I groped blindly through the labyrinth in the whiteout, retracing my steps from one dead end to another. Time after time I'd think I'd found a way out, only to wind up in a deep-blue cul-de-sac or stranded atop a detached pillar of ice. My efforts were lent a sense of urgency by the noises emanating from beneath my feet. A madrigal of creaks and sharp reports—the sort of protest a large fir limb makes when it's slowly bent to the breaking point—served as a reminder that it is the nature of glaciers to move, the habit of seracs to topple.

I put a foot through a snow bridge spanning a slot so deep I couldn't see the bottom of it. A little later I broke through another bridge to my waist; the poles kept me out of the hundred-foot crevasse, but after I extricated myself, I bent double with dry heaves, thinking about what it would be like to be lying in a pile at the bottom of the crevasse, waiting for death to come, with nobody aware of how or where I'd met my end.

fear of death

Night had nearly fallen by the time I emerged from the top of the serac slope onto the empty, wind-scoured expanse of the high glacial plateau. In shock and chilled to the core, I skied far enough past the icefall to put its rumblings out of earshot, pitched the tent, crawled into my sleeping bag, and shivered myself into a fitful sleep.

I had planned on spending between three weeks and a month on the Stikine Ice Cap. Not relishing the prospect of carrying a four-week load of food, heavy winter camping gear, and climbing hardware all the way up the Baird on my back, I had paid a bush pilot in Petersburg $150—the last of my cash—to have six cardboard cartons of supplies dropped from an airplane when I reached the foot of the Thumb. On his map I'd showed the pilot exactly where I intended to be and told him to give me three days to get there; he promised to fly over and make the drop as soon thereafter as the weather permitted.

On May 6, I set up a base camp on the ice cap just northeast of the Thumb and waited for the airdrop. For the next four days it snowed, nixing any chance for a flight. Too terrified of crevasses to wander far from camp, I spent most of my time recumbent in the tent—the ceiling was too low to allow my sitting upright—fighting a rising chorus of doubts.

As the days passed, I grew increasingly anxious. I had no radio nor any other means of communicating with the outside world. It had been many years since anyone had visited this part of the Stikine Ice Cap, and many more would likely pass before anyone would again. I was nearly out of stove fuel and down to a single chunk of cheese, my last package of Ramen noodles, and half a box of Cocoa Puffs. This, I figured, could sustain me for three or four more days if need be, but then what would I do? It would take only two days to ski back down the Baird to Thomas Bay, but a week or more might easily pass before a fisherman happened by who could give me a lift back to Petersburg (the tree planters with whom I'd ridden over were camped fifteen miles down the impassable headland-studded coast and could be reached only by boat or plane).

When I went to bed on the evening of May 10, it was still snowing and blowing hard. Hours later I heard a faint, momentary whine, scarcely louder than a mosquito. I tore open the tent door. Most of the clouds had lifted, but there was no airplane in sight.

The whine returned, more insistently this time. Then I saw it: a tiny red-and-white fleck high in the western sky, droning my way.

A few minutes later the plane passed directly overhead. The pilot, however, was unaccustomed to glacier flying, and he'd badly misjudged the scale of the terrain. Worried about flying too low and getting nailed by unexpected turbulence, he stayed at least a thousand feet above me—believing all the while he was just off the deck—and never saw my tent in the flat evening light. My waving and screaming were to no avail; from his altitude, I was indistinguishable from a pile of rocks. For the next hour he circled the ice cap, scanning its barren contours without success. But the pilot, to his credit, appreciated the gravity of my predicament and didn't give up. Frantic, I tied my sleeping bag to the end of one of the curtain rods and waved it for all I was worth. The plane banked sharply and headed straight at me.

The pilot buzzed my tent three times in quick succession, dropping two boxes on each pass; then the airplane disappeared over a ridge, and I was alone. As silence again settled over the glacier, I felt abandoned, vulnerable, lost. I realized that I was sobbing. Embarrassed, I halted the blubbering by screaming obscenities until I grew hoarse.

I awoke early on May 11 to clear skies and the relatively warm temperature of twenty degrees Fahrenheit. Startled by the good weather, mentally unprepared to commence the actual climb, I hurriedly packed up a rucksack nonetheless and began skiing toward the base of the Thumb. Two previous Alaska expeditions had taught me that I couldn't afford to waste a rare day of perfect weather.

A small hanging glacier extends out from the lip of the ice cap, leading up and across the north face of the Thumb like a catwalk. My plan was to follow this catwalk to a prominent rock prow in the center of the wall and thereby execute an end run around the ugly, avalanche-swept lower half of the face.

The catwalk turned out to be a series of fifty-degree ice fields blanketed with knee-deep powder snow and riddled with crevasses. The depth of the snow made the going slow and exhausting; by the time I front-pointed up the overhanging wall of the uppermost *bergschrund,* some three or four hours after leaving camp, I was thrashed. And I hadn't even gotten to the real climbing yet. That would begin immediately above, where the hanging glacier gives way to vertical rock.

The rock, exhibiting a dearth of holds and coated with six inches of crumbly rime, did not look promising, but just left of the main prow was a shallow corner glazed with frozen meltwater. This ribbon of ice led straight up for three hundred feet, and if the ice proved substantial enough to support the picks of my ice axes, the route might be feasible. I shuffled over to the bottom of the corner and gingerly swung one of my tools into the two-inch-thick ice. Solid and plastic, it was thinner than I would have liked but otherwise encouraging.

The climbing was steep and so exposed it made my head spin. Beneath my Vibram soles the wall fell away for three thousand feet to the dirty, avalanche-scarred cirque of the Witches Cauldron Glacier. Above, the prow soared with authority toward the summit ridge, a vertical half mile above. Each time I planted one of my ice axes, that distance shrank by another twenty inches.

All that held me to the mountainside, all that held me to the world, were two thin spikes of chrome molybdenum stuck half an inch into a smear of frozen water, yet the higher I climbed, the more comfortable I became. Early on a difficult climb, especially a difficult solo climb, you constantly feel the abyss pulling at your back. To resist takes a tremendous conscious effort; you don't dare let your guard down for an instant. The siren song of the void puts you on edge; it makes your movements tentative, clumsy, herky-jerky. But as the climb goes on, you grow accustomed to the exposure, you get used to rubbing shoulders with doom, you come to believe in the reliability of your hands and feet and head. You learn to trust your self-control.

By and by your attention becomes so intensely focused that you no longer notice the raw knuckles, the cramping thighs, the strain of maintaining nonstop concentration. A trancelike state settles over your efforts; the climb becomes a clear-eyed dream.

Hours slide by like minutes. The accumulated clutter of day-to-day existence—the lapses of conscience, the unpaid bills, the bungled opportunities, the dust under the couch, the inescapable prison of your genes—all of it is temporarily forgotten, crowded from your thoughts by an overpowering clarity of purpose and by the seriousness of the task at hand.

At such moments something resembling happiness actually stirs in your chest, but it isn't the sort of emotion you want to lean on very hard. In solo climbing the whole enterprise is held together with little more than chutzpah, not the most reliable adhesive. Late in the day on the north face of the Thumb, I felt the glue disintegrate with a swing of an ice ax.

I'd gained nearly seven hundred feet of altitude since stepping off the hanging glacier, all of it on crampon front points and the picks of my axes. The ribbon of frozen meltwater had ended three hundred feet up and was followed by a crumbly armor of frost feathers. Though just barely substantial enough to support body weight, the rime was plastered over the rock to a thickness of two or three feet, so I kept plugging upward. The wall, however, had been growing imperceptibly steeper, and as it did so, the frost feathers became thinner. I'd fallen into a slow, hypnotic rhythm—swing, swing; kick, kick; swing, swing; kick, kick—when my left ice ax slammed into a slab of diorite a few inches beneath the rime.

I tried left, then right, but kept striking rock. The frost feathers holding me up, it became apparent, were maybe five inches thick and had the structural integrity of stale corn bread. Below was thirty-seven hundred feet of air, and I was balanced on a house of cards. The sour taste of panic rose in my throat. My eyesight blurred, I began to hyperventilate, my calves started to shake. I shuffled a few feet farther to the right, hoping to find thicker ice, but managed only to bend an ice ax on the rock.

Awkwardly, stiff with fear, I started working my way back down. The rime gradually thickened. After descending about eighty feet, I got back on reasonably solid ground. I stopped for a long time to let my nerves settle, then leaned back from my

tools and stared up at the face above, searching for a hint of solid
ice, for some variation in the underlying rock strata, for anything
that would allow passage over the frosted slabs. I looked until my
neck ached, but nothing appeared. The climb was over. The only
place to go was down.

CHAPTER FIFTEEN

THE STIKINE ICE CAP

But we little know until tried how much of the uncontrollable there is in us, urging across glaciers and torrents, and up dangerous heights, let the judgement forbid as it may.

JOHN MUIR,
THE MOUNTAINS OF CALIFORNIA

But have you noticed the slight curl at the end of Sam II's mouth, when he looks at you? It means that he didn't want you to name him Sam II, for one thing, and for two other things it means that he has a sawed-off in his left pant leg, and a baling hook in his right pant leg, and is ready to kill you with either one of them, given the opportunity. The father is taken aback. What he usually says, in such a confrontation, is "I changed your diapers for you, little snot." This is not the right thing to say. First, it is not true (mothers change nine diapers out of ten), and second, it instantly reminds Sam II of what he is mad about. He is mad about being small when you were big, but no, that's not it, he is mad about being helpless when you were powerful, but no, not that either, he is mad about being contingent when you were necessary, not quite it, he is insane because when he loved you, you didn't notice.

DONALD BARTHELME,
THE DEAD FATHER

After coming down from the side of the Devils Thumb, heavy snow and high winds kept me inside the tent for most of the next three days. The hours passed slowly. In the attempt to hurry them along, I chain-smoked for as long as my supply of cigarettes held out, and I read. When I ran out of reading matter, I was reduced to studying the ripstop pattern woven into the tent ceiling. This I did for hours on end, flat on my back, while engaging in a heated self-debate: Should I leave for the coast as soon as the weather broke, or should I stay put long enough to make another attempt on the mountain?

In truth my escapade on the north face had rattled me, and I didn't want to go up on the Thumb again at all. But the thought of returning to Boulder in defeat wasn't very appealing, either. I could all too easily picture the smug expressions of condolence I'd receive from those who'd been certain of my failure from the get-go.

By the third afternoon of the storm, I couldn't stand it any longer: the lumps of frozen snow poking me in the back, the clammy nylon walls brushing against my face, the incredible smell drifting up from the depths of my sleeping bag. I pawed through the mess at my feet until I located a small green sack, in which there was a metal film can containing the makings of what I'd hoped would be a sort of victory cigar. I'd intended to save it for my return from the summit, but what the hey—it wasn't looking like I'd be visiting the top anytime soon. I poured most of the can's contents onto a leaf of cigarette paper, rolled it into a crooked joint, and promptly smoked it down to the roach.

The marijuana of course only made the tent seem even more cramped, more suffocating, more impossible to bear. It also made me terribly hungry. I decided a little oatmeal would put things right. Making it, however, was a long, ridiculously involved process: A potful of snow had to be gathered outside in the tempest, the stove assembled and lit, the oatmeal and sugar located, the remnants of yesterday's dinner scraped from my bowl. I'd gotten the stove going and was melting the snow when I smelled something burning. A thorough check of the stove and its environs revealed nothing. Mystified, I was ready to chalk it up to my chemically enhanced imagination when I heard something crackle at my back.

I spun around in time to see a bag of garbage—into which I'd tossed the match I'd used to light the stove—flare into a small conflagration. Beating on the fire with my hands, I had it out in a few seconds, but not before a large section of the tent's inner wall vaporized before my eyes. The built-in fly escaped the flames, so it was still more or less weatherproof; now, however, it was approximately thirty degrees colder inside.

My left palm began to sting. Examining it, I noticed the pink welt of a burn. What troubled me most, though, was that the tent wasn't even mine: I'd borrowed the expensive shelter from my father. It was new before my trip—the hangtags had still been attached—and had been lent reluctantly. For several minutes I sat dumbstruck, staring at the wreckage of the tent's once-graceful form amid the acrid scent of singed hair and melted nylon. You had to hand it to me, I thought: I had a knack for living up to the old man's worst expectations.

My father was a volatile, extremely complicated person, possessed of a brash demeanor that masked deep insecurities. If he ever in his entire life admitted to being wrong, I wasn't there to witness it. But it was my father, a weekend mountaineer, who taught me to climb. He bought me my first rope and ice ax when I was eight years old and led me into the Cascade Range to make an assault on the South Sister, a gentle ten-thousand-foot volcano not far from our Oregon home. It never occurred to him that I would one day try to shape my life around climbing.

A kind and generous man, Lewis Krakauer loved his five children deeply, in the autocratic way of fathers, but his worldview was colored by a relentlessly competitive nature. Life, as he saw it, was a contest. He read and reread the works of Stephen Potter—the English writer who coined the terms *one-upmanship* and *gamesmanship*—not as social satire but as a manual of practical stratagems. He was ambitious in the extreme, and like Walt McCandless, his aspirations extended to his progeny.

Before I'd even enrolled in kindergarten, he began preparing me for a shining career in medicine—or, failing that, law as a poor consolation. For Christmas and birthdays I received such gifts as a microscope, a chemistry set, and the *Encyclopaedia Bri-*

tannica. From elementary school through high school, my siblings and I were hectored to excel in every class, to win medals in science fairs, to be chosen princess of the prom, to win election to student government. Thereby and only thereby, we learned, could we expect to gain admission to the right college, which in turn would get us into Harvard Medical School: life's one sure path to meaningful success and lasting happiness.

My father's faith in this blueprint was unshakable. It was, after all, the path he had followed to prosperity. But I was not a clone of my father. During my teens, as I came to this realization, I veered gradually from the plotted course, and then sharply. My insurrection prompted a great deal of yelling. The windows of our home rattled with the thunder of ultimatums. By the time I left Corvallis, Oregon, to enroll in a distant college where no ivy grew, I was speaking to my father with a clenched jaw or not at all. When I graduated four years later and did not enter Harvard or any other medical school but became a carpenter and climbing bum instead, the unbridgeable gulf between us widened.

I had been granted unusual freedom and responsibility at an early age, for which I should have been grateful in the extreme, but I wasn't. Instead, I felt oppressed by the old man's expectations. It was drilled into me that anything less than winning was failure. In the impressionable way of sons, I did not consider this rhetorically; I took him at his word. And that's why later, when long-held family secrets came to light, when I noticed that this deity who asked only for perfection was himself less than perfect, that he was in fact not a deity at all—well, I wasn't able to shrug it off. I was consumed instead by a blinding rage. The revelation that he was merely human, and frightfully so, was beyond my power to forgive.

Two decades after the fact I discovered that my rage was gone, and had been for years. It had been supplanted by a rueful sympathy and something not unlike affection. I came to understand that I had baffled and infuriated my father at least as much as he had baffled and infuriated me. I saw that I had been selfish and unbending and a giant pain in the ass. He'd built a bridge of priv-

similar to Mccandless

ilege for me, a hand-paved trestle to the good life, and I repaid him by chopping it down and crapping on the wreckage.

But this epiphany occurred only after the intervention of time and misfortune, when my father's self-satisfied existence had begun to crumble beneath him. It began with the betrayal of his flesh: Thirty years after a bout with polio, the symptoms mysteriously flared anew. Crippled muscles withered further, synapses wouldn't fire, wasted legs refused to ambulate. From medical journals he deduced that he was suffering from a newly identified ailment known as post-polio syndrome. Pain, excruciating at times, filled his days like a shrill and constant noise.

In an ill-advised attempt to halt the decline, he started medicating himself. He never went anywhere without a faux leather valise stuffed with dozens of orange plastic pill bottles. Every hour or two he would fumble through the drug bag, squinting at the labels, and shake out tablets of Dexedrine and Prozac and deprenyl. He gulped pills by the fistful, grimacing, without water. Used syringes and empty ampoules appeared on the bathroom sink. To a greater and greater degree his life revolved around a self-administered pharmacopoeia of steroids, amphetamines, mood elevators, and painkillers, and the drugs addled his once-formidable mind.

As his behavior became more and more irrational, more and more delusional, the last of his friends were driven away. My long-suffering mother finally had no choice but to move out. My father crossed the line into madness and then very nearly succeeded in taking his own life—an act at which he made sure I was present.

After the suicide attempt he was placed in a psychiatric hospital near Portland. When I visited him there, his arms and legs were strapped to the rails of his bed. He was ranting incoherently and had soiled himself. His eyes were wild. Flashing in defiance one moment, in uncomprehending terror the next, they rolled far back in their sockets, giving a clear and chilling view into the state of his tortured mind. When the nurses tried to change his linens, he thrashed against his restraints and cursed them, cursed me, cursed the fates. That his foolproof life plan had in the end transported him here, to this nightmarish station, was an irony that brought me no pleasure and escaped his notice altogether.

There was another irony he failed to appreciate: His struggle to mold me in his image had been successful after all. The old walrus in fact managed to instill in me a great and burning ambition; it had simply found expression in an unintended pursuit. He never understood that the Devils Thumb was the same as medical school, only different.

I suppose it was this inherited, off-kilter ambition that kept me from admitting defeat on the Stikine Ice Cap after my initial attempt to climb the Thumb had failed, even after nearly burning the tent down. Three days after retreating from my first try, I went up on the north face again. This time I climbed only 120 feet above the *bergschrund* before lack of composure and the arrival of a snow squall forced me to turn around.

Instead of descending to my base camp on the ice cap, though, I decided to spend the night on the steep flank of the mountain, just below my high point. This proved to be a mistake. By late afternoon the squall had metastasized into another major storm. Snow fell from the clouds at the rate of an inch an hour. As I crouched inside my bivouac sack under the lip of the *bergschrund*, spindrift avalanches hissed down from the wall above and washed over me like surf, slowly burying my ledge.

It took about twenty minutes for the spindrift to inundate my bivvy sack—a thin nylon envelope shaped exactly like a Baggies sandwich bag, only bigger—to the level of the breathing slit. Four times this happened, and four times I dug myself out. After the fifth burial, I'd had enough. I threw all my gear into my pack and made a break for the base camp.

The descent was terrifying. Because of the clouds, the ground blizzard, and the flat, fading light, I couldn't tell slope from sky. I worried, with ample reason, that I might step blindly off the top of a serac and end up at the bottom of the Witches Cauldron, a vertical half mile below. When I finally arrived on the frozen plain of the ice cap, I found that my tracks had long since drifted over.

I didn't have a clue as to how to locate the tent on the featureless glacial plateau. Hoping I'd get lucky and stumble across my camp, I skied in circles for an hour—until I put a foot into a small crevasse and realized that I was acting like an idiot—that I should hunker down right where I was and wait out the storm.

I dug a shallow hole, wrapped myself in the bivvy bag, and sat on my pack in the swirling snow. Drifts piled up around me. My feet became numb. A damp chill crept down my chest from the base of my neck, where spindrift had gotten inside my parka and soaked my shirt. If only I had a cigarette, I thought, a single cigarette, I could summon the strength of character to put a good face on this fucked-up situation, on the whole fucked-up trip. I pulled the bivvy sack tighter around my shoulders. The wind ripped at my back. Beyond shame, I cradled my head in my arms and embarked on an orgy of self-pity.

I knew that people sometimes died climbing mountains. But at the age of twenty-three, personal mortality—the idea of my own death—was still largely outside my conceptual grasp. When I decamped from Boulder for Alaska, my head swimming with visions of glory and redemption on the Devils Thumb, it didn't occur to me that I might be bound by the same cause-and-effect relationships that governed the actions of others. Because I wanted to climb the mountain so badly, because I had thought about the Thumb so intensely for so long, it seemed beyond the realm of possibility that some minor obstacle like the weather or crevasses or rime-covered rock might ultimately thwart my will.

At sunset the wind died, and the ceiling lifted 150 feet off the glacier, enabling me to locate my base camp. I made it back to the tent intact, but it was no longer possible to ignore the fact that the Thumb had made hash of my plans. I was forced to acknowledge that volition alone, however powerful, was not going to get me up the north wall. I saw, finally, that nothing was.

There still existed an opportunity for salvaging the expedition, however. A week earlier I'd skied over to the southeast side of the mountain to take a look at the route by which I'd intended to descend the peak after climbing the north wall, a route that Fred Beckey, the legendary alpinist, had followed in 1946 in making the first ascent of the Thumb. During my reconnaissance, I'd noticed an obvious unclimbed line to the left of the Beckey route—a patchy network of ice angling across the southeast face—that struck me as a relatively easy way to achieve the summit. At the time, I'd considered this route unworthy of my attentions. Now, on the rebound from my calamitous entanglement with the *nordwand*, I was prepared to lower my sights.

On the afternoon of May 15, when the blizzard finally abated, I returned to the southeast face and climbed to the top of a slender ridge that abuts the upper peak like a flying buttress on a Gothic cathedral. I decided to spend the night there, on the narrow crest, sixteen hundred feet below the summit. The evening sky was cold and cloudless. I could see all the way to tidewater and beyond. At dusk I watched, transfixed, as the lights of Petersburg blinked on in the west. The closest thing I'd had to human contact since the airdrop, the distant lights triggered a flood of emotion that caught me off guard. I imagined people watching baseball on television, eating fried chicken in brightly lit kitchens, drinking beer, making love. When I lay down to sleep, I was overcome by a wrenching loneliness. I'd never felt so alone, ever.

That night I had troubled dreams, of a police bust and vampires and a gangland-style execution. I heard someone whisper, "I think he's in there. . . ." I sat bolt upright and opened my eyes. The sun was about to rise. The entire sky was scarlet. It was still clear, but a thin, wispy scum of cirrus had spread across the upper atmosphere, and a dark line of squalls was visible just above the southwestern horizon. I pulled on my boots and hurriedly strapped on my crampons. Five minutes after waking up, I was climbing away from the bivouac.

I carried no rope, no tent or bivouac gear, no hardware save my ice axes. My plan was to go light and fast, to reach the summit and make it back down before the weather turned. Pushing myself, continually out of breath, I scurried up and to the left, across small snowfields linked by ice-choked clefts and short rock steps. The climbing was almost fun—the rock was covered with large, incut holds, and the ice, though thin, never got steeper than seventy degrees—but I was anxious about the storm front racing in from the Pacific, darkening the sky.

I didn't have a watch, but in what seemed like a very short time, I was on the distinctive final ice field. By now the entire sky was smeared with clouds. It looked easier to keep angling to the left but quicker to go straight for the top. Anxious about being caught by a storm high on the peak and without shelter, I opted for the direct route. The ice steepened and thinned. I swung my left ice ax and struck rock. I aimed for another spot, and once again it glanced off unyielding diorite with a dull clank. And again, and again. It was a reprise of my first attempt on the north face. Looking between my legs, I stole a glance at the glacier more than two thousand feet below. My stomach churned.

Forty-five feet above me the wall eased back onto the sloping summit shoulder. I clung stiffly to my axes, unmoving, racked by terror and indecision. Again I looked down at the long drop to the glacier, then up, then scraped away the patina of ice above my head. I hooked the pick of my left ax on a nickel-thin lip of rock and weighted it. It held. I pulled my right ax from the ice, reached up, and twisted the pick into a crooked half-inch fissure until it jammed. Barely breathing now, I moved my feet up, scrabbling my crampon points across the verglas. Reaching as high as I could with my left arm, I swung the ax gently at the shiny, opaque surface, not knowing what I'd hit beneath it. The pick went in with a solid *whunk!* A few minutes later I was standing on a broad ledge. The summit proper, a slender rock fin sprouting a grotesque meringue of atmospheric ice, stood twenty feet directly above.

The insubstantial frost feathers ensured that those last twenty feet remained hard, scary, onerous. But then suddenly there was no place higher to go. I felt my cracked lips stretch into a painful grin. I was on top of the Devils Thumb.

Fittingly, the summit was a surreal, malevolent place, an improbably slender wedge of rock and rime no wider than a file cabinet. It did not encourage loitering. As I straddled the highest point, the south face fell away beneath my right boot for twenty-five hundred feet; beneath my left boot the north face dropped twice that distance. I took some pictures to prove I'd been there and spent a few minutes trying to straighten a bent pick. Then I stood up, carefully turned around, and headed for home.

One week later I was camped in the rain beside the sea, marveling at the sight of moss, willows, mosquitoes. The salt air carried the rich stink of tidal life. By and by a small skiff motored into Thomas Bay and pulled up on the beach not far from my tent. The man driving the boat introduced himself as Jim Freeman, a timber faller from Petersburg. It was his day off, he said; he'd made the trip to show his family the glacier and to look for bears. He asked me if I'd "been huntin', or what?"

"No," I replied sheepishly. "Actually, I just climbed the Devils Thumb. I've been over here twenty days."

Freeman fiddled with a deck cleat and said nothing. It became obvious that he didn't believe me. Nor did he seem to approve of my snarled, shoulder-length hair or the way I smelled after having gone three weeks without bathing or changing my clothes. When I asked if he could give me a lift back to town, however, he offered a grudging "I don't see why not."

The water was choppy, and the ride across Frederick Sound took two hours. Freeman gradually warmed to me as we talked. He still wasn't convinced I'd climbed the Thumb, but by the time he steered the skiff into Wrangell Narrows, he pretended to be. After docking the boat, he insisted on buying me a cheeseburger. That evening he invited me to spend the night in a junked step van parked in his backyard.

I lay down in the rear of the old truck for a while but couldn't sleep, so I got up and walked to a bar called Kito's Kave. The euphoria, the overwhelming sense of relief, that had initially accompanied my return to Petersburg faded, and an unexpected melancholy took its place. The people I chatted with in Kito's didn't seem to doubt that I'd been to the top of the Thumb; they just didn't much care. As the night wore on, the place emptied except for me and an old, toothless Tlingit man at a back table. I drank alone, putting quarters into the jukebox, playing the same five songs over and over until the barmaid yelled angrily, "Hey! Give it a fucking rest, kid!" I mumbled an apology, headed for the door, and lurched back to Freeman's step van. There, surrounded by the sweet scent of old motor oil, I lay down on the floorboards next to a gutted transmission and passed out.

Less than a month after sitting on the summit of the Thumb, I was back in Boulder, nailing up siding on the Spruce Street Townhouses, the same condos I'd been framing when I left for Alaska. I got a raise, to four bucks an hour, and at the end of the summer moved out of the job-site trailer to a cheap studio apartment west of the downtown mall.

It is easy, when you are young, to believe that what you desire is no less than what you deserve, to assume that if you want something badly enough, it is your God-given right to have it. When I decided to go to Alaska that April, like Chris McCandless, I was a raw youth who mistook passion for insight and acted according to an obscure, gap-ridden logic. I thought climbing the Devils Thumb would fix all that was wrong with my life. In the end, of course, it changed almost nothing. But I came to appreciate that mountains make poor receptacles for dreams. And I lived to tell my tale.

As a young man, I was unlike McCandless in many important regards; most notably, I possessed neither his intellect nor his lofty ideals. But I believe we were similarly affected by the skewed relationships we had with our fathers. And I suspect we had a similar intensity, a similar heedlessness, a similar agitation of the soul.

The fact that I survived my Alaska adventure and McCandless did not survive his was largely a matter of chance; had I not returned from the Stikine Ice Cap in 1977, people would have been quick to say of me—as they now say of him—that I had a death wish. Eighteen years after the event, I now recognize that I suffered from hubris, perhaps, and an appalling innocence, certainly; but I wasn't suicidal.

At that stage of my youth, death remained as abstract a concept as non-Euclidean geometry or marriage. I didn't yet appreciate its terrible finality or the havoc it could wreak on those who'd entrusted the deceased with their hearts. I was stirred by the dark mystery of mortality. I couldn't resist stealing up to the edge of doom and peering over the brink. The hint of what was concealed in those shadows terrified me, but I caught sight of something in the glimpse, some forbidden and elemental riddle that was no less compelling than the sweet, hidden petals of a woman's sex.

In my case—and, I believe, in the case of Chris McCandless—that was a very different thing from wanting to die.

CHAPTER SIXTEEN

THE ALASKA INTERIOR

I wished to acquire the simplicity, native feelings, and virtues of savage life; to divest myself of the factitious habits, prejudices and imperfections of civilization; . . . and to find, amidst the solitude and grandeur of the western wilds, more correct views of human nature and of the true interests of man. The season of snows was preferred, that I might experience the pleasure of suffering, and the novelty of danger.

ESTWICK EVANS,
*A PEDESTRIOUS TOUR, OF FOUR THOUSAND MILES,
THROUGH THE WESTERN STATES AND TERRITORIES,
DURING THE WINTER AND SPRING OF 1818*

Wilderness appealed to those bored or disgusted with man and his works. It not only offered an escape from society but also was an ideal stage for the Romantic individual to exercise the cult that he frequently made of his own soul. The solitude and total freedom of the wilderness created a perfect setting for either melancholy or exultation.

RODERICK NASH,
WILDERNESS AND THE AMERICAN MIND

On April 15, 1992, Chris McCandless departed Carthage, South Dakota, in the cab of a Mack truck hauling a load of sunflower seeds: His "great Alaskan odyssey" was under way. Three days later he crossed the Canadian border at Roosville, British Columbia, and thumbed north through Skookumchuck and Radium Junction, Lake Louise and Jasper, Prince George and Dawson Creek—where, in the town center, he took a snapshot of the signpost marking the official start of the Alaska Highway. MILE "0," the sign reads, FAIRBANKS 1,523 MILES.

Hitchhiking tends to be difficult on the Alaska Highway. It's not unusual, on the outskirts of Dawson Creek, to see a dozen or more doleful-looking men and women standing along the shoulder with extended thumbs. Some of them may wait a week or more between rides. But McCandless experienced no such delay. On April 21, just six days out of Carthage, he arrived at Liard River Hotsprings, at the threshold of the Yukon Territory.

There is a public campground at Liard River, from which a boardwalk leads half a mile across a marsh to a series of natural thermal pools. It is the most popular way-stop on the Alaska Highway, and McCandless decided to pause there for a soak in the soothing waters. When he finished bathing and attempted to catch another ride north, however, he discovered that his luck had changed. Nobody would pick him up. Two days after arriving, he was still at Liard River, impatiently going nowhere.

At six-thirty on a brisk Thursday morning, the ground still frozen hard, Gaylord Stuckey walked out on the boardwalk to the largest of the pools, expecting to have the place to himself. He was surprised, therefore, to find someone already in the steaming water, a young man who introduced himself as Alex.

Stuckey—bald and cheerful, a ham-faced sixty-three-year-old Hoosier—was en route from Indiana to Alaska to deliver a new motor home to a Fairbanks RV dealer, a part-time line of work in which he'd dabbled since retiring after forty years in the restaurant business. When he told McCandless his destination, the boy exclaimed, "Hey, that's where I'm going, too! But I've been stuck here for a couple of days now, trying to get a lift. You mind if I ride with you?"

"Oh, jiminy," Stuckey replied. "I'd love to, son, but I can't. The company I work for has a strict rule against picking up hitchhikers. It could get me canned." As he chatted with McCandless through the sulfurous mist, though, Stuckey began to reconsider: "Alex was clean-shaven and had short hair, and I could tell by the language he used that he was a real sharp fella. He wasn't what you'd call a typical hitchhiker. I'm usually leery of 'em. I figure there's probably something wrong with a guy if he can't even afford a bus ticket. So anyway, after about half an hour I said, 'I tell you what, Alex: Liard is a thousand miles from Fairbanks. I'll take you five hundred miles, as far as Whitehorse; you'll be able to get a ride the rest of the way from there.' "

A day and a half later, however, when they arrived in Whitehorse—the capital of the Yukon Territory and the largest, most cosmopolitan town on the Alaska Highway—Stuckey had come to enjoy McCandless's company so much that he changed his mind and agreed to drive the boy the entire distance. "Alex didn't come out and say too much at first," Stuckey reports. "But it's a long, slow drive. We spent a total of three days together on those washboard roads, and by the end he kind of let his guard down. I tell you what: He was a dandy kid. Real courteous, and he didn't cuss or use a lot of that there slang. You could tell he came from a nice family. Mostly he talked about his sister. He didn't get along with his folks too good, I guess. Told me his dad was a genius, a NASA rocket scientist, but he'd been a bigamist at one time—and that kind of went against Alex's grain. Said he hadn't seen his parents in a couple of years, since his college graduation."

McCandless was candid with Stuckey about his intent to spend the summer alone in the bush, living off the land. "He said it was something he'd wanted to do since he was little," says Stuckey. "Said he didn't want to see a single person, no airplanes, no sign of civilization. He wanted to prove to himself that he could make it on his own, without anybody else's help."

Stuckey and McCandless arrived in Fairbanks on the afternoon of April 25. The older man took the boy to a grocery store, where he bought a big bag of rice, "and then Alex said he wanted to go out to the university to study up on what kind of plants he could eat. Berries and things like that. I told him, 'Alex, you're too early. There's still two foot, three foot of snow on the ground. There's nothing growing yet.' But his mind was pretty well made up. He was champing at the bit to get out there and start hiking."

Stuckey drove to the University of Alaska campus, on the west end of Fairbanks, and dropped McCandless off at 5:30 P.M.

"Before I let him out," Stuckey says, "I told him, 'Alex, I've driven you a thousand miles. I've fed you and fed you for three straight days. The least you can do is send me a letter when you get back from Alaska.' And he promised he would.

"I also begged and pleaded with him to call his parents. I can't imagine anything worse than having a son out there and not knowing where he's at for years and years, not knowing whether he's living or dead. 'Here's my credit card number,' I told him. '*Please* call them!' But all he said was 'Maybe I will and maybe I won't.' After he left, I thought, 'Oh, why didn't I get his parents' phone number and call them myself?' But everything just kind of happened so quick."

After dropping McCandless at the university, Stuckey drove into town to deliver the RV to the appointed dealer, only to be told that the person responsible for checking in new vehicles had already gone home for the day and wouldn't be back until Monday morning, leaving Stuckey with two days to kill in Fairbanks before he could fly home to Indiana. On Sunday morning, with time on his hands, he returned to the campus. "I hoped to find Alex and spend another day with him, take him sightseeing or something. I looked for a couple of hours, drove all over the place, but didn't see hide or hair of him. He was already gone."

After taking his leave of Stuckey on Saturday evening, McCandless spent two days and three nights in the vicinity of Fairbanks, mostly at the university. In the campus book store, tucked away on the bottom shelf of the Alaska section, he came across a scholarly, exhaustively researched field guide to the region's edible plants, *Tanaina Plantlore/Dena'ina K'et'una: An Ethnobotany of the Dena'ina Indians of Southcentral Alaska* by Priscilla Russell Kari. From a postcard rack near the cash register, he picked out two cards of a polar bear, on which he sent his final messages to Wayne Westerberg and Jan Burres from the university post office.

Perusing the classified ads, McCandless found a used gun to

buy, a semiautomatic .22-caliber Remington with a 4-×-20 scope and a plastic stock. A model called the Nylon 66, no longer in production, it was a favorite of Alaska trappers because of its light weight and reliability. He closed the deal in a parking lot, probably paying about $125 for the weapon, and then purchased four one-hundred-round boxes of hollow-point long-rifle shells from a nearby gun shop.

At the conclusion of his preparations in Fairbanks, McCandless loaded up his pack and started hiking west from the university. Leaving the campus, he walked past the Geophysical Institute, a tall glass-and-concrete building capped with a large satellite dish. The dish, one of the most distinctive landmarks on the Fairbanks skyline, had been erected to collect data from satellites equipped with synthetic aperture radar of Walt McCandless's design. Walt had in fact visited Fairbanks during the start-up of the receiving station and had written some of the software crucial to its operation. If the Geophysical Institute prompted Chris to think of his father as he tramped by, the boy left no record of it.

Four miles west of town, in the evening's deepening chill, McCandless pitched his tent on a patch of hard-frozen ground surrounded by birch trees, not far from the crest of a bluff overlooking Gold Hill Gas & Liquor. Fifty yards from his camp was the terraced road cut of the George Parks Highway, the road that would take him to the Stampede Trail. He woke early on the morning of April 28, walked down to the highway in the predawn gloaming, and was pleasantly surprised when the first vehicle to come along pulled over to give him a lift. It was a gray Ford pickup with a bumper sticker on the back that declared, I FISH THEREFORE I AM. PETERSBURG, ALASKA. The driver of the truck, an electrician on his way to Anchorage, wasn't much older than McCandless. He said his name was Jim Gallien.

Three hours later Gallien turned his truck west off the highway and drove as far as he could down an unplowed side road. When he dropped McCandless off on the Stampede Trail, the temperature was in the low thirties—it would drop into the low teens at night—and a foot and a half of crusty spring snow covered the ground. The boy could hardly contain his excitement. He was, at long last, about to be alone in the vast Alaska wilds.

As he trudged expectantly down the trail in a fake-fur parka, his rifle slung over one shoulder, the only food McCandless carried was a ten-pound bag of long-grained rice—and the two sandwiches and bag of corn chips that Gallien had contributed. A year earlier he'd subsisted for more than a month beside the Gulf of California on five pounds of rice and a bounty of fish caught with a cheap rod and reel, an experience that made him confident he could harvest enough food to survive an extended stay in the Alaska wilderness, too.

The heaviest item in McCandless's half-full backpack was his library: nine or ten paperbound books, most of which had been given to him by Jan Burres in Niland. Among these volumes were titles by Thoreau and Tolstoy and Gogol, but McCandless was no literary snob: He simply carried what he thought he might enjoy reading, including mass-market books by Michael Crichton, Robert Pirsig, and Louis L'Amour. Having neglected to pack writing paper, he began a laconic journal on some blank pages in the back of *Tanaina Plantlore*.

The Healy terminus of the Stampede Trail is traveled by a handful of dog mushers, ski tourers, and snow-machine enthusiasts during the winter months, but only until the frozen rivers begin to break up, in late March or early April. By the time McCandless headed into the bush, there was open water flowing on most of the larger streams, and nobody had been very far down the trail for two or three weeks; only the faint remnants of a packed snow-machine track remained for him to follow.

McCandless reached the Teklanika River his second day out. Although the banks were lined with a jagged shelf of frozen overflow, no ice bridges spanned the channel of open water, so he was forced to wade. There had been a big thaw in early April, and breakup had come early in 1992, but the weather had turned cold again, so the river's volume was quite low when McCandless crossed—probably thigh-deep at most—allowing him to splash to the other side without difficulty. He never suspected that in so doing, he was crossing his Rubicon. To McCandless's inexperienced eye, there was nothing to suggest that two months hence, as the glaciers and snowfields at the Teklanika's headwater thawed in the summer heat, its discharge would multiply nine or ten times in volume, transforming the river into a deep, violent torrent that bore no resemblance to the gentle brook he'd blithely waded across in April.

From his journal we know that on April 29, McCandless fell through the ice somewhere. It probably happened as he traversed a series of melting beaver ponds just beyond the Teklanika's western bank, but there is nothing to indicate that he suffered any harm in the mishap. A day later, as the trail crested a ridge, he got his first glimpse of Mt. McKinley's high, blinding-white bulwarks, and a day after that, May 1, some twenty miles down the trail from where he was dropped by Gallien, he stumbled upon the old bus beside the Sushana River. It was outfitted with a bunk and a barrel stove, and previous visitors had left the improvised shelter stocked with matches, bug dope, and other essentials. "Magic Bus Day," he wrote in his journal. He decided to lay over for a while in the vehicle and take advantage of its crude comforts.

He was elated to be there. Inside the bus, on a sheet of weathered plywood spanning a broken window, McCandless scrawled an exultant declaration of independence:

TWO YEARS HE WALKS THE EARTH. NO PHONE, NO POOL, NO PETS, NO CIGARETTES. ULTIMATE FREEDOM. AN EXTREMIST. AN AESTHETIC VOYAGER WHOSE HOME IS THE ROAD. ESCAPED FROM ATLANTA. THOU SHALT NOT RETURN, 'CAUSE "THE WEST IS THE BEST." AND NOW AFTER TWO RAMBLING YEARS COMES THE FINAL AND GREATEST ADVENTURE. THE CLIMACTIC BATTLE TO KILL THE FALSE BEING WITHIN AND VICTORIOUSLY CONCLUDE THE SPIRITUAL REVOLUTION. TEN DAYS AND NIGHTS OF FREIGHT TRAINS AND HITCHHIKING BRING HIM TO THE GREAT WHITE NORTH. NO LONGER TO BE POISONED BY CIVILIZATION HE FLEES, AND WALKS ALONE UPON THE LAND TO BECOME LOST IN THE WILD.

ALEXANDER SUPERTRAMP
MAY 1992

Reality, however, was quick to intrude on McCandless's reverie. He had difficulty killing game, and the daily journal entries during his first week in the bush include "Weakness," "Snowed in," and "Disaster." He saw but did not shoot a grizzly on May 2, shot at but missed some ducks on May 4, and finally killed and ate a spruce grouse on May 5; but he didn't shoot anything else until May 9, when he bagged a single small squirrel, by which point he'd written "4th day famine" in the journal.

But soon thereafter his fortunes took a sharp turn for the better. By mid-May the sun was circling high in the heavens, flooding the taiga with light. The sun dipped below the northern horizon for fewer than four hours out of every twenty-four, and at midnight the sky was still bright enough to read by. Everywhere but on the north-facing slopes and in the shadowy ravines, the snowpack had melted down to bare ground, exposing the previous season's rose hips and lingonberries, which McCandless gathered and ate in great quantity.

He also became much more successful at hunting game and for the next six weeks feasted regularly on squirrel, spruce grouse, duck, goose, and porcupine. On May 22, a crown fell off one of his molars, but the event didn't seem to dampen his spirits much, because the following day he scrambled up the nameless, humplike, three-thousand-foot butte that rises directly north of the bus, giving him a view of the whole icy sweep of the Alaska Range and mile after mile of uninhabited country. His journal entry for the day is characteristically terse but unmistakably joyous: "CLIMB MOUNTAIN!"

McCandless had told Gallien that he intended to remain on the move during his stay in the bush. "I'm just going to take off and keep walking west," he'd said. "I might walk all the way to the Bering Sea." On May 5, after pausing for four days at the bus, he resumed his perambulation. From the snapshots recovered with his Minolta, it appears that McCandless lost (or intentionally left) the by now indistinct Stampede Trail and headed west and north through the hills above the Sushana River, hunting game as he went.

It was slow going. In order to feed himself, he had to devote a large part of each day to stalking animals. Moreover, as the ground thawed, his route turned into a gauntlet of boggy muskeg and impenetrable alder, and McCandless belatedly came to appreciate one of the fundamental (if counterintuitive) axioms of the North: winter, not summer, is the preferred season for traveling overland through the bush.

Faced with the obvious folly of his original ambition, to walk five hundred miles to tidewater, he reconsidered his plans. On May 19, having traveled no farther west than the Toklat River—less than fifteen miles beyond the bus—he turned around. A week later he was back at the derelict vehicle, apparently without regret. He'd decided that the Sushana drainage was plenty wild to suit his purposes and that Fairbanks bus 142 would make a fine base camp for the remainder of the summer.

Ironically, the wilderness surrounding the bus—the patch of overgrown country where McCandless was determined "to become lost in the wild"—scarcely qualifies as wilderness by Alaska standards. Less than thirty miles to the east is a major thoroughfare, the George Parks Highway. Just sixteen miles to the south, beyond an escarpment of the Outer Range, hundreds of tourists rumble daily into Denali Park over a road patrolled by the National Park Service. And unbeknownst to the Aesthetic Voyager, scattered within a six-mile radius of the bus are four cabins (although none happened to be occupied during the summer of 1992).

But despite the relative proximity of the bus to civilization, for all practical purposes McCandless was cut off from the rest of the world. He spent nearly four months in the bush all told, and during that period he didn't encounter another living soul. In the end the Sushana River site was sufficiently remote to cost him his life.

In the last week of May, after moving his few possessions into the bus, McCandless wrote a list of housekeeping chores on a parchmentlike strip of birch bark: collect and store ice from the river for refrigerating meat, cover the vehicle's missing windows with plastic, lay in a supply of firewood, clean the accumulation of old ash from the stove. And under the heading "**LONG TERM**" he drew up a list of more ambitious tasks: map the area, improvise a bathtub, collect skins and feathers to sew into clothing, construct a bridge across a nearby creek, repair mess kit, blaze a network of hunting trails.

The diary entries following his return to the bus catalog a bounty of wild meat. May 28: "Gourmet Duck!" June 1: "5 Squirrel." June 2: "Porcupine, Ptarmigan, 4 Squirrel, Grey Bird." June 3: "Another Porcupine! 4 Squirrel, 2 Grey Bird, Ash Bird." June 4: "A THIRD PORCUPINE! Squirrel, Grey Bird." On June 5, he shot a Canada goose as big as a Christmas turkey. Then, on June 9, he bagged the biggest prize of all: "MOOSE!" he recorded in the journal. Overjoyed, the proud hunter took a photograph of himself kneeling over his trophy, rifle thrust triumphantly overhead, his features distorted in a rictus of ecstasy and amazement, like some unemployed janitor who'd gone to Reno and won a million-dollar jackpot.

Although McCandless was enough of a realist to know that hunting game was an unavoidable component of living off the land, he had always been ambivalent about killing animals. That ambivalence turned to remorse soon after he shot the moose. It was relatively small, weighing perhaps six hundred or seven hundred pounds, but it nevertheless amounted to a huge quantity of meat. Believing that it was morally indefensible to waste any part of an animal that has been shot for food, McCandless spent six days toiling to preserve what he had killed before it spoiled. He butchered the carcass under a thick cloud of flies and mosquitoes, boiled the organs into a stew, and then laboriously excavated a burrow in the face of the rocky stream bank directly below the bus, in which he tried to cure, by smoking, the immense slabs of purple flesh.

Alaskan hunters know that the easiest way to preserve meat in the bush is to slice it into thin strips and then air-dry it on a makeshift rack. But McCandless, in his naïveté, relied on the advice of hunters he'd consulted in South Dakota, who advised him to smoke his meat, not an easy task under the circumstances. "Butchering extremely difficult," he wrote in the journal on June 10. "Fly and mosquito hordes. Remove intestines, liver, kidneys, one lung, steaks. Get hindquarters and leg to stream."

June 11: "Remove heart and other lung. Two front legs and head. Get rest to stream. Haul near cave. Try to protect with smoker."

June 12: "Remove half rib-cage and steaks. Can only work nights. Keep smokers going."

June 13: "Get remainder of rib-cage, shoulder and neck to cave. Start smoking."

June 14: "Maggots already! Smoking appears ineffective. Don't know, looks like disaster. I now wish I had never shot the moose. One of the greatest tragedies of my life."

At that point he gave up on preserving the bulk of the meat and abandoned the carcass to the wolves. Although he castigated himself severely for this waste of a life he'd taken, a day later McCandless appeared to regain some perspective, for his journal notes, "henceforth will learn to accept my errors, however great they be."

Shortly after the moose episode McCandless began to read Thoreau's *Walden*. In the chapter titled "Higher Laws," in which Thoreau ruminates on the morality of eating, McCandless highlighted, "when I had caught and cleaned and cooked and eaten my fish, they seemed not to have fed me essentially. It was insignificant and unnecessary, and cost more than it came to."

"THE MOOSE," McCandless wrote in the margin. And in the same passage he marked,

The repugnance to animal food is not the effect of experience, but is an instinct. It appeared more beautiful to live low and fare hard in many respects; and though I never did so, I went far enough to please my imagination. I believe that every man who has ever been earnest to preserve his higher or poetic faculties in the best condition has been particularly inclined to abstain from animal food, and from much food of any kind. . . .

It is hard to provide and cook so simple and clean a diet as will not offend the imagination; but this, I think, is to be fed when we feed the body; they should both sit down at the same table. Yet perhaps this may be done. The fruits eaten temperately need not make us ashamed of our appetites, nor interrupt the worthiest pursuits. But put an extra condiment into your dish, and it will poison you.

"YES," wrote McCandless and, two pages later, "Conscious-ness of food. Eat and cook with concentration. . . . Holy Food." On the back pages of the book that served as his journal, he de-clared:

> *I am reborn. This is my dawn. Real life has just begun.*
>
> *Deliberate Living: Conscious attention to the basics of life, and a constant attention to your immediate environment and its con-cerns, example→ A job, a task, a book; anything requiring effi-cient concentration (Circumstance has no value. It is how one relates to a situation that has value. All true meaning resides in the personal relationship to a phenomenon, what it means to you).*
>
> *The Great Holiness of **FOOD**, the Vital Heat.*
>
> *Positivism, the Insurpassable Joy of the Life Aesthetic.*
>
> *Absolute Truth and Honesty.*
>
> *Reality.*
>
> *Independence.*
>
> *Finality—Stability—Consistency.*

As McCandless gradually stopped rebuking himself for the waste of the moose, the contentment that began in mid-May re-sumed and seemed to continue through early July. Then, in the midst of this idyll, came the first of two pivotal setbacks.

Satisfied, apparently, with what he had learned during his two months of solitary life in the wild, McCandless decided to return to civilization: It was time to bring his "final and greatest adven-ture" to a close and get himself back to the world of men and women, where he could chug a beer, talk philosophy, enthrall strangers with tales of what he'd done. He seemed to have moved beyond his need to assert so adamantly his autonomy, his need to separate himself from his parents. Maybe he was prepared to for-give their imperfections; maybe he was even prepared to forgive some of his own. McCandless seemed ready, perhaps, to go home.

Or maybe not; we can do no more than speculate about what he intended to do after he walked out of the bush. There is no question, however, that he intended to walk out.

Writing on a piece of birch bark, he made a list of things to do before he departed: "Patch Jeans, Shave!, Organize pack. . . ." Shortly thereafter he propped his Minolta on an empty oil drum and took a snapshot of himself brandishing a yellow disposable razor and grinning at the camera, clean-shaven, with new patches cut from an army blanket stitched onto the knees of his filthy jeans. He looks healthy but alarmingly gaunt. Already his cheeks are sunken. The tendons in his neck stand out like taut cables.

On July 2, McCandless finished reading Tolstoy's "Family Happiness," having marked several passages that moved him:

> He was right in saying that the only certain happiness in life is to live for others. . . .

> I have lived through much, and now I think I have found what is needed for happiness. A quiet secluded life in the country, with the possibility of being useful to people to whom it is easy to do good, and who are not accustomed to have it done to them; then work which one hopes may be of some use; then rest, nature, books, music, love for one's neighbor—such is my idea of happiness. And then, on top of all that, you for a mate, and children, perhaps—what more can the heart of a man desire?

Then, on July 3, he shouldered his backpack and began the twenty-mile hike to the improved road. Two days later, halfway there, he arrived in heavy rain at the beaver ponds that blocked access to the west bank of the Teklanika River. In April they'd been frozen over and hadn't presented an obstacle. Now he must have been alarmed to find a three-acre lake covering the trail. To avoid having to wade through the murky chest-deep water, he scrambled up a steep hillside, bypassed the ponds on the north, and then dropped back down to the river at the mouth of the gorge.

When he'd first crossed the river, sixty-seven days earlier in the freezing temperatures of April, it had been an icy but gentle knee-deep creek, and he'd simply strolled across it. On July 5, however, the Teklanika was at full flood, swollen with rain and snowmelt from glaciers high in the Alaska Range, running cold and fast.

If he could reach the far shore, the remainder of the hike to the highway would be easy, but to get there he would have to negotiate a channel some one hundred feet wide. The water, opaque with glacial sediment and only a few degrees warmer than the ice it had so recently been, was the color of wet concrete. Too deep to wade, it rumbled like a freight train. The powerful current would quickly knock him off his feet and carry him away.

McCandless was a weak swimmer and had confessed to several people that he was in fact afraid of the water. Attempting to swim the numbingly cold torrent or even to paddle some sort of improvised raft across seemed too risky to consider. Just downstream from where the trail met the river, the Teklanika erupted into a chaos of boiling whitewater as it accelerated through the narrow gorge. Long before he could swim or paddle to the far shore, he'd be pulled into these rapids and drowned.

In his journal he now wrote, "Disaster. . . . Rained in. River look impossible. Lonely, scared." He concluded, correctly, that he would probably be swept to his death if he attempted to cross the Teklanika at that place, in those conditions. It would be suicidal; it was simply not an option.

If McCandless had walked a mile or so upstream, he would have discovered that the river broadened into a maze of braided channels. If he'd scouted carefully, by trial and error he might have found a place where these braids were only chest-deep. As strong as the current was running, it would have certainly knocked him off his feet, but by dog-paddling and hopping along the bottom as he drifted downstream, he could conceivably have made it across before being carried into the gorge or succumbing to hypothermia.

But it would still have been a very risky proposition, and at that point McCandless had no reason to take such a risk. He'd been fending for himself quite nicely in the country. He probably understood that if he was patient and waited, the river would eventually drop to a level where it could be safely forded. After weighing his options, therefore, he settled on the most prudent course. He turned around and began walking to the west, back toward the bus, back into the fickle heart of the bush.

CHAPTER SEVENTEEN

THE STAMPEDE TRAIL

*Nature was here something savage and awful, though beautiful.
I looked with awe at the ground I trod on, to see what the Powers
had made there, the form and fashion and material of their
work. This was that Earth of which we have heard, made out of
Chaos and Old Night. Here was no man's garden, but the
unhandselled globe. It was not lawn, nor pasture, nor mead, nor
woodland, nor lea, nor arable, nor waste land. It was the fresh
and natural surface of the planet Earth, as it was made forever
and ever,—to be the dwelling of man, we say,—so Nature made
it, and man may use it if he can. Man was not to be associated
with it. It was Matter, vast, terrific,—not his Mother Earth that
we have heard of, not for him to tread on, or to be buried in,—
no, it were being too familiar even to let his bones lie there,—
the home, this, of Necessity and Fate. There was clearly felt the
presence of a force not bound to be kind to man. It was a place
of heathenism and superstitious rites,—to be inhabited by men
nearer of kin to the rocks and to wild animals than we. . . .
What is it to be admitted to a museum, to see a myriad of
particular things, compared with being shown some star's
surface, some hard matter in its home! I stand in awe of my
body, this matter to which I am bound has become so strange
to me. I fear not spirits, ghosts, of which I am one,—that my
body might,—but I fear bodies, I tremble to meet them. What is
this Titan that has possession of me? Talk of mysteries! Think
of our life in nature,—daily to be shown matter, to come in
contact with it,—rocks, trees, wind on our cheeks! the solid
earth! the actual world! the common sense! Contact! Contact!
Who are we? where are we?*

HENRY DAVID THOREAU,
"KTAADN"

A year and a week after Chris McCandless decided not to attempt to cross the Teklanika River, I stand on the opposite bank—the eastern side, the highway side—and gaze into the churning water. I, too, hope to cross the river. I want to visit the bus. I want to see where McCandless died, to better understand why.

It is a hot, humid afternoon, and the river is livid with runoff from the fast-melting snowpack that still blankets the glaciers in the higher elevations of the Alaska Range. Today the water looks considerably lower than it looks in the photographs McCandless took twelve months ago, but to try to ford the river here, in thundering midsummer flood, is nevertheless unthinkable. The water is too deep, too cold, too fast. As I stare into the Teklanika, I can hear rocks the size of bowling balls grinding along the bottom, rolled downstream by the powerful current. I'd be swept from my feet within a few yards of leaving the bank and pushed into the canyon immediately below, which pinches the river into a boil of rapids that continues without interruption for the next five miles.

Unlike McCandless, however, I have in my backpack a 1:63,360-scale topographic map (that is, a map on which one inch represents one mile). Exquisitely detailed, it indicates that half a mile downstream, in the throat of the canyon, is a gauging station that was built by the U.S. Geological Survey. Unlike McCandless, too, I am here with three companions: Alaskans Roman Dial and Dan Solie and a friend of Roman's from California, Andrew Liske. The gauging station can't be seen from where the Stampede Trail comes down to the river, but after twenty minutes of fighting our way through a snarl of spruce and dwarf birch, Roman shouts, "I see it! There! A hundred yards farther."

We arrive to find an inch-thick steel cable spanning the gorge, stretched between a fifteen-foot tower on our side of the river and an outcrop on the far shore, four hundred feet away. The cable was erected in 1970 to chart the Teklanika's seasonal fluctuations; hydrologists traveled back and forth above the river by means of an aluminum basket that is suspended from the cable with pulleys. From the basket they would drop a weighted plumb line to measure the river's depth. The station was decommissioned nine years ago for lack of funds, at which time the basket was supposed to be chained and locked to the tower on our side—the highway side—of the river. When we climbed to the top of the tower, however, the basket wasn't there. Looking across the rushing water, I could see it over on the distant shore—the bus side—of the canyon.

Some local hunters, it turns out, had cut the chain, ridden the basket across, and secured it to the far side in order to make it harder for outsiders to cross the Teklanika and trespass on their turf. When McCandless tried to walk out of the bush one year ago the previous week, the basket was in the same place it is now, on his side of the canyon. If he'd known about it, crossing the Teklanika to safety would have been a trivial matter. Because he had no topographic map, however, he had no way of conceiving that salvation was so close at hand.

Andy Horowitz, one of McCandless's friends on the Woodson High cross-country team, had mused that Chris "was born into the wrong century. He was looking for more adventure and freedom than today's society gives people." In coming to Alaska, McCandless yearned to wander uncharted country, to find a blank spot on the map. In 1992, however, there were no more blank spots on the map—not in Alaska, not anywhere. But Chris, with his idiosyncratic logic, came up with an elegant solution to this dilemma: He simply got rid of the map. In his own mind, if nowhere else, the *terra* would thereby remain *incognita*.

Because he lacked a good map, the cable spanning the river also remained incognito. Studying the Teklanika's violent flow, McCandless thus mistakenly concluded that it was impossible to reach the eastern shore. Thinking that his escape route had been cut off, he returned to the bus—a reasonable course of action, given his topographical ignorance. But why did he then stay at the bus and starve? Why, come August, didn't he try once more to cross the Teklanika, when it would have been running significantly lower, when it would have been safe to ford?

Puzzled by these questions, and troubled, I am hoping that the rusting hulk of Fairbanks bus 142 will yield some clues. But to reach the bus, I, too, need to cross the river, and the aluminum tram is still chained to the far shore.

Standing atop the tower anchoring the eastern end of the span, I attach myself to the cable with rock-climbing hardware and begin to pull myself across, hand over hand, executing what mountaineers call a Tyrolean traverse. This turns out to be a more strenuous proposition than I had anticipated. Twenty minutes after starting out, I finally haul myself onto the outcrop on the other side, completely spent, so wasted I can barely raise my arms. After at last catching my breath, I climb into the basket— a rectangular aluminum car two feet wide by four feet long—disconnect the chain, and head back to the eastern side of the canyon to ferry my companions across.

The cable sags noticeably over the middle of the river; so when I cut loose from the outcrop, the car accelerates quickly under its own weight, rolling faster and faster along the steel strand, seeking the lowest point. It's a thrilling ride. Zipping over the rapids at twenty or thirty miles per hour, I hear an involuntary bark of fright leap from my throat before I realize that I'm in no danger and regain my composure.

After all four of us are on the western side of the gorge, thirty minutes of rough bushwhacking returns us to the Stampede Trail. The ten miles of trail we have already covered—the section between our parked vehicles and the river—were gentle, well marked, and relatively heavily traveled. But the ten miles to come have an utterly different character.

Because so few people cross the Teklanika during the spring and summer months, much of the route is indistinct and overgrown with brush. Immediately past the river the trail curves to the southwest, up the bed of a fast-flowing creek. And because beavers have built a network of elaborate dams across this creek, the route leads directly through a three-acre expanse of standing water. The beaver ponds are never more than chest deep, but the water is cold, and as we slosh forward, our feet churn the muck on the bottom into a foul-smelling miasma of decomposing slime.

The trail climbs a hill beyond the uppermost pond, then rejoins the twisting, rocky creek bed before ascending again into a jungle of scrubby vegetation. The going never gets exceedingly difficult, but the fifteen-foot-high tangle of alder pressing in from both sides is gloomy, claustrophobic, oppressive. Clouds of mosquitoes materialize out of the sticky heat. Every few minutes the insects' piercing whine is supplanted by the boom of distant thunder, rumbling over the taiga from a wall of thunderheads rearing darkly on the horizon.

Thickets of buckbrush leave a crosshatch of bloody lacerations on my shins. Piles of bear scat on the trail and, at one point, a set of fresh grizzly tracks—each print half again as long as a size-nine boot print—put me on edge. None of us has a gun. "Hey, Griz!" I yell at the undergrowth, hoping to avoid a surprise encounter. "Hey, bear! Just passing through! No reason to get riled!"

I have been to Alaska some twenty times during the past twenty years—to climb mountains, to work as a carpenter and a commercial salmon fisherman and a journalist, to goof off, to poke around. I've spent a lot of time alone in the country over the course of my many visits and usually relish it. Indeed, I had intended to make this trip to the bus by myself, and when my friend Roman invited himself and two others along, I was annoyed. Now, however, I am grateful for their company. There is something disquieting about this Gothic, overgrown landscape. It feels more malevolent than other, more remote corners of the state I know—the tundra-wrapped slopes of the Brooks Range, the cloud forests of the Alexander Archipelago, even the frozen, gale-swept heights of the Denali massif. I'm happy as hell that I'm not here alone.

At 9:00 P.M. we round a bend in the trail, and there, at the edge of a small clearing, is the bus. Pink bunches of fireweed choke the vehicle's wheel wells, growing higher than the axles. Fairbanks bus 142 is parked beside a coppice of aspen, ten yards back from the brow of a modest cliff, on a shank of high ground overlooking the confluence of the Sushana River and a smaller tributary.

It's an appealing setting, open and filled with light. It's easy to see why McCandless decided to make this his base camp.

We pause some distance away from the bus and stare at it for a while in silence. Its paint is chalky and peeling. Several windows are missing. Hundreds of delicate bones litter the clearing around the vehicle, scattered among thousands of porcupine quills: the remains of the small game that made up the bulk of McCandless's diet. And at the perimeter of this boneyard lies one much larger skeleton: that of the moose he shot, and subsequently agonized over.

When I'd questioned Gordon Samel and Ken Thompson shortly after they'd discovered McCandless's body, both men insisted—adamantly and unequivocally—that the big skeleton was the remains of a caribou, and they derided the greenhorn's ignorance in mistaking the animal he killed for a moose. "Wolves had scattered the bones some," Thompson had told me, "but it was obvious that the animal was a caribou. The kid didn't know what the hell he was doing up here."

"It was definitely a caribou," Samel had scornfully piped in. "When I read in the paper that he thought he'd shot a moose, that told me right there he wasn't no Alaskan. There's a big difference between a moose and a caribou. A real big difference. You'd have to be pretty stupid not to be able to tell them apart."

Trusting Samel and Thompson, veteran Alaskan hunters who've killed many moose and caribou between them, I duly reported McCandless's mistake in the article I wrote for *Outside*, thereby confirming the opinion of countless readers that McCandless was ridiculously ill prepared, that he had no business heading into any wilderness, let alone into the big-league wilds of the Last Frontier. Not only did McCandless die because he was stupid, one Alaska correspondent observed, but "the scope of his self-styled adventure was so small as to ring pathetic—squatting in a wrecked bus a few miles out of Healy, potting jays and squirrels, mistaking a caribou for a moose (pretty hard to do). . . . Only one word for the guy: incompetent."

Among the letters lambasting McCandless, virtually all those I received mentioned his misidentification of the caribou as proof that he didn't know the first thing about surviving in the backcountry. What the angry letter writers didn't know, however, was that the ungulate McCandless shot was exactly what he'd said it was. Contrary to what I reported in *Outside*, the animal was a moose, as a close examination of the beast's remains now indicated and several of McCandless's photographs of the kill later confirmed beyond all doubt. The boy made some mistakes on the Stampede Trail, but confusing a caribou with a moose wasn't among them.

Walking past the moose bones, I approach the vehicle and step through an emergency exit at the back. Immediately inside the door is the torn mattress, stained and moldering, on which McCandless expired. For some reason I am taken aback to find a collection of his possessions spread across its ticking: a green plastic canteen; a tiny bottle of water-purification tablets; a used-up cylinder of Chap Stick; a pair of insulated flight pants of the type sold in military-surplus stores; a paperback copy of the best-seller *O Jerusalem!*, its spine broken; wool mittens; a bottle of Muskol insect repellent; a full box of matches; and a pair of brown rubber work boots with the name Gallien written across the cuffs in faint black ink.

Despite the missing windows, the air inside the cavernous vehicle is stale and musty. "Wow," Roman remarks. "It smells like dead birds in here." A moment later I come across the source of the odor: a plastic garbage bag filled with feathers, down, and the severed wings of several birds. It appears that McCandless was saving them to insulate his clothing or perhaps to make a feather pillow.

Toward the front of the bus, McCandless's pots and dishes are stacked on a makeshift plywood table beside a kerosene lamp. A long leather scabbard is expertly tooled with the initials R. F.: the sheath for the machete Ronald Franz gave McCandless when he left Salton City.

The boy's blue toothbrush rests next to a half-empty tube of Colgate, a packet of dental floss, and the gold molar crown that, according to his journal, fell off his tooth three weeks into his sojourn. A few inches away sits a skull the size of a watermelon, thick ivory fangs jutting from its bleached maxillae. It is a bear skull, the remains of a grizzly shot by someone who visited the bus years before McCandless's tenure. A message scratched in Chris's tidy hand brackets a cranial bullet hole: ALL HAIL THE PHANTOM BEAR, THE BEAST WITHIN US ALL. ALEXANDER SUPERTRAMP. MAY 1992.

Looking up, I notice that the sheet-metal walls of the vehicle are covered with graffiti left by numerous visitors over the years. Roman points out a message he wrote when he stayed in the bus four years ago, during a traverse of the Alaska Range: NOODLE EATERS EN ROUTE TO LAKE CLARK 8/89. Like Roman, most people scrawled little more than their names and a date. The longest, most eloquent graffito is one of several inscribed by McCandless, the proclamation of joy that begins with a nod to his favorite Roger Miller song: TWO YEARS HE WALKS THE EARTH. NO PHONE, NO POOL, NO PETS, NO CIGARETTES. ULTIMATE FREEDOM. AN EXTREMIST. AN AESTHETIC VOYAGER WHOSE HOME IS THE ROAD. . . .

Immediately below this manifesto squats the stove, fabricated from a rusty oil drum. A twelve-foot section of a spruce trunk is jammed into its open doorway, and across the log are draped two pairs of torn Levi's, laid out as if to dry. One pair of jeans—waist thirty, inseam thirty-two—is patched crudely with silver duct tape; the other pair has been repaired more carefully, with scraps from a faded bedspread stitched over gaping holes in the knees and seat. This latter pair also sports a belt fashioned from a strip of blanket. McCandless, it occurs to me, must have been forced to make the belt after growing so thin that his pants wouldn't stay up without it.

Sitting down on a steel cot across from the stove to mull over this eerie tableau, I encounter evidence of McCandless's presence wherever my vision rests. Here are his toenail clippers, over there his green nylon tent spread over a missing window in the front door. His Kmart hiking boots are arranged neatly beneath the stove, as though he'd soon be returning to lace them up and hit the trail. I feel uncomfortable, as if I were intruding, a voyeur who has slipped into McCandless's bedroom while he is momentarily away. Suddenly queasy, I stumble out of the bus to walk along the river and breathe some fresh air.

An hour later we build a fire outside in the fading light. The rain squalls, now past, have rinsed the haze from the atmosphere, and distant, backlit hills stand out in crisp detail. A stripe of incandescent sky burns beneath the cloud base on the northwestern horizon. Roman unwraps some steaks from a moose he shot in the Alaska Range last September and lays them across the fire on a blackened grill, the grill McCandless used for broiling his game. Moose fat pops and sizzles into the coals. Eating the gristly meat with our fingers, we slap at mosquitoes and talk about this peculiar person whom none of us ever met, trying to get a handle on how he came to grief, trying to understand why some people seem to despise him so intensely for having died here.

By design McCandless came into the country with insufficient provisions, and he lacked certain pieces of equipment deemed essential by many Alaskans: a large-caliber rifle, map and compass, an ax. This has been regarded as evidence not just of stupidity but of the even greater sin of arrogance. Some critics have even drawn parallels between McCandless and the Arctic's most infamous tragic figure, Sir John Franklin, a nineteenth-century British naval officer whose smugness and hauteur contributed to some 140 deaths, including his own.

In 1819, the Admiralty assigned Franklin to lead an expedition into the wilderness of northwestern Canada. Two years out of England, winter overtook his small party as they plodded across an expanse of tundra so vast and empty that they christened it the Barrens, the name by which it is still known. Their food ran out. Game was scarce, forcing Franklin and his men to subsist on lichens scraped from boulders, singed deer hide, scavenged animal bones, their own boot leather, and finally one another's flesh. Before the ordeal was over, at least two men had been murdered and eaten, the suspected murderer had been summarily executed, and eight others were dead from sickness and starvation. Franklin was himself within a day or two of expiring when he and the other survivors were rescued by a band of métis.

An affable Victorian gentleman, Franklin was said to be a good-natured bumbler, dogged and clueless, with the naïve ideals of a child and a disdain for acquiring backcountry skills. He had been woefully unprepared to lead an Arctic expedition, and upon returning to England, he was known as the Man Who Ate His Shoes—yet the sobriquet was uttered more often with awe than with ridicule. He was hailed as a national hero, promoted to the rank of captain by the Admiralty, paid handsomely to write an account of his ordeal, and, in 1825, given command of a second Arctic expedition.

That trip was relatively uneventful, but in 1845, hoping finally to discover the fabled Northwest Passage, Franklin made the mistake of returning to the Arctic for a third time. He and the 128 men under his command were never heard from again. Evidence unearthed by the forty-odd expeditions sent to search for them eventually established that all had perished, the victims of scurvy, starvation, and unspeakable suffering.

When McCandless turned up dead, he was likened to Franklin not simply because both men starved but also because both were perceived to have lacked a requisite humility; both were thought to have possessed insufficient respect for the land. A century after Franklin's death, the eminent explorer Vilhjalmur Stefansson pointed out that the English explorer had never taken the trouble to learn the survival skills practiced by the Indians and the Eskimos—peoples who had managed to flourish "for generations, bringing up their children and taking care of their aged" in the same harsh country that killed Franklin. (Stefansson conveniently neglected to mention that many, many Indians and Eskimos have starved in the northern latitudes, as well.)

McCandless's arrogance was not of the same strain as Franklin's, however. Franklin regarded nature as an antagonist that would inevitably submit to force, good breeding, and Victorian discipline. Instead of living in concert with the land, instead of relying on the country for sustenance as the natives did, he attempted to insulate himself from the northern environment with ill-suited military tools and traditions. McCandless, on the other hand, went too far in the opposite direction. He tried to live en-

181

tirely off the country—and he tried to do it without bothering to master beforehand the full repertoire of crucial skills.

It probably misses the point, though, to castigate McCandless for being ill prepared. He was green, and he overestimated his resilience, but he was sufficiently skilled to last for sixteen weeks on little more than his wits and ten pounds of rice. And he was fully aware when he entered the bush that he had given himself a perilously slim margin for error. He knew precisely what was at stake.

It is hardly unusual for a young man to be drawn to a pursuit considered reckless by his elders; engaging in risky behavior is a rite of passage in our culture no less than in most others. Danger has always held a certain allure. That, in large part, is why so many teenagers drive too fast and drink too much and take too many drugs, why it has always been so easy for nations to recruit young men to go to war. It can be argued that youthful derring-do is in fact evolutionarily adaptive, a behavior encoded in our genes. McCandless, in his fashion, merely took risk-taking to its logical extreme.

He had a need to test himself in ways, as he was fond of saying, "that mattered." He possessed grand—some would say grandiose—spiritual ambitions. According to the moral absolutism that characterizes McCandless's beliefs, a challenge in which a successful outcome is assured isn't a challenge at all.

It is not merely the young, of course, who are drawn to hazardous undertakings. John Muir is remembered primarily as a no-nonsense conservationist and the founding president of the Sierra Club, but he was also a bold adventurer, a fearless scrambler of peaks, glaciers, and waterfalls whose best-known essay includes a riveting account of nearly falling to his death, in 1872, while ascending California's Mt. Ritter. In another essay Muir rapturously describes riding out a ferocious Sierra gale, by choice, in the uppermost branches of a one-hundred-foot Douglas fir:

[N]ever before did I enjoy so noble an exhilaration of motion. The slender tops fairly flapped and swished in the passionate torrent,

bending and swirling backward and forward, round and round, tracing indescribable combinations of vertical and horizontal curves, while I clung with muscles firm braced, like a bobolink on a reed.

He was thirty-six years old at the time. One suspects that Muir wouldn't have thought McCandless terribly odd or incomprehensible.

Even staid, prissy Thoreau, who famously declared that it was enough to have "traveled a good deal in Concord," felt compelled to visit the more fearsome wilds of nineteenth-century Maine and climb Mt. Katahdin. His ascent of the peak's "savage and awful, though beautiful" ramparts shocked and frightened him, but it also induced a giddy sort of awe. The disquietude he felt on Katahdin's granite heights inspired some of his most powerful writing and profoundly colored the way he thought thereafter about the earth in its coarse, undomesticated state.

Unlike Muir and Thoreau, McCandless went into the wilderness not primarily to ponder nature or the world at large but, rather, to explore the inner country of his own soul. He soon discovered, however, what Muir and Thoreau already knew: An extended stay in the wilderness inevitably directs one's attention outward as much as inward, and it is impossible to live off the land without developing both a subtle understanding of, and a strong emotional bond with, that land and all it holds.

The entries in McCandless's journal contain few abstractions about wilderness or, for that matter, few ruminations of any kind. There is scant mention of the surrounding scenery. Indeed, as Roman's friend Andrew Liske points out upon reading a photocopy of the journal, "These entries are almost entirely about what he ate. He wrote about hardly anything except food."

Andrew is not exaggerating: The journal is little more than a tally of plants foraged and game killed. It would probably be a mistake, however, to conclude thereby that McCandless failed to appreciate the beauty of the country around him, that he was unmoved by the power of the landscape. As cultural ecologist Paul Shepard has observed,

The nomadic Bedouin does not dote on scenery, paint land-
scapes, or compile a nonutilitarian natural history. . . . [H]is life
is so profoundly in transaction with nature that there is no place
for abstraction or esthetics or a "nature philosophy" which can
be separated from the rest of his life. . . . Nature and his relation-
ship to it are a deadly-serious matter, prescribed by convention,
mystery, and danger. His personal leisure is aimed away from idle
amusement or detached tampering with nature's processes. But
built into his life is awareness of that presence, of the terrain, of
the unpredictable weather, of the narrow margin by which he is
sustained.

Much the same could be said of McCandless during the
months he spent beside the Sushana River.

It would be easy to stereotype Christopher McCandless as another boy who felt too much, a loopy young man who read too
many books and lacked even a modicum of common sense. But
the stereotype isn't a good fit. McCandless wasn't some feckless
slacker, adrift and confused, racked by existential despair. To the
contrary: His life hummed with meaning and purpose. But the
meaning he wrested from existence lay beyond the comfortable
path: McCandless distrusted the value of things that came easily.
He demanded much of himself—more, in the end, than he could
deliver.

Trying to explain McCandless's unorthodox behavior, some
people have made much of the fact that like John Waterman, he
was small in stature and may have suffered from a "short man's
complex," a fundamental insecurity that drove him to prove his
manhood by means of extreme physical challenges. Others have
posited that an unresolved Oedipal conflict was at the root of his
fatal odyssey. Although there may be some truth in both hy-
potheses, this sort of posthumous off-the-rack psychoanalysis is
a dubious, highly speculative enterprise that inevitably demeans
and trivializes the absent analysand. It's not clear that much of
value is learned by reducing Chris McCandless's strange spiritual
quest to a list of pat psychological disorders.

Roman and Andrew and I stare into the embers and talk about

McCandless late into the night. Roman, thirty-two, inquisitive and outspoken, has a doctorate in biology from Stanford and an abiding distrust of conventional wisdom. He spent his adolescence in the same Washington, D.C., suburbs as McCandless and found them every bit as stifling. He first came to Alaska as a nine-year-old, to visit a trio of uncles who mined coal at Usibelli, a big strip-mine operation a few miles east of Healy, and immediately fell in love with everything about the North. Over the years that followed, he returned repeatedly to the forty-ninth state. In 1977, after graduating from high school as a sixteen-year-old at the top of his class, he moved to Fairbanks and made Alaska his permanent home.

These days Roman teaches at Alaska Pacific University, in Anchorage, and enjoys statewide renown for a long, brash string of backcountry escapades: He has—among other feats—traveled the entire 1,000-mile length of the Brooks Range by foot and paddle, skied 250 miles across the Arctic National Wildlife Refuge in subzero winter cold, traversed the 700-mile crest of the Alaska Range, and pioneered more than thirty first ascents of northern peaks and crags. And Roman doesn't see a great deal of difference between his own widely respected deeds and McCandless's adventure, except that McCandless had the misfortune to perish.

I bring up McCandless's hubris and the dumb mistakes he made—the two or three readily avoidable blunders that ended up costing him his life. "Sure, he screwed up," Roman answers, "but I admire what he was trying to do. Living completely off the land like that, month after month, is incredibly difficult. I've never done it. And I'd bet you that very few, if any, of the people who call McCandless incompetent have ever done it either, not for more than a week or two. Living in the interior bush for an extended period, subsisting on nothing except what you hunt and gather—most people have no idea how hard that actually is. And McCandless almost pulled it off.

"I guess I just can't help identifying with the guy," Roman allows as he pokes the coals with a stick. "I hate to admit it, but not so many years ago it could easily have been me in the same kind of predicament. When I first started coming to Alaska, I think I was probably a lot like McCandless: just as green, just as eager. And I'm sure there are plenty of other Alaskans who had a lot in common with McCandless when they first got here, too, including many of his critics. Which is maybe why they're so hard on him. Maybe McCandless reminds them a little too much of their former selves."

Roman's observation underscores how difficult it is for those of us preoccupied with the humdrum concerns of adulthood to recall how forcefully we were once buffeted by the passions and longings of youth. As Everett Ruess's father mused years after his twenty-year-old son vanished in the desert, "The older person does not realize the soul-flights of the adolescent. I think we all poorly understood Everett."

Roman, Andrew, and I stay up well past midnight, trying to make sense of McCandless's life and death, yet his essence remains slippery, vague, elusive. Gradually, the conversation lags and falters. When I drift away from the fire to find a place to throw down my sleeping bag, the first faint smear of dawn is already bleaching the rim of the northeastern sky. Although the mosquitoes are thick tonight and the bus would no doubt offer some refuge, I decide not to bed down inside Fairbanks 142. Nor, I note before sinking into a dreamless sleep, do the others.

CHAPTER EIGHTEEN

THE STAMPEDE TRAIL

*It is nearly impossible for modern man to imagine what it is like
to live by hunting. The life of a hunter is one of hard, seemingly
continuous overland travel.... A life of frequent concerns that
the next interception may not work, that the trap or the drive will
fail, or that the herds will not appear this season. Above all, the
life of a hunter carries with it the threat of deprivation and death
by starvation.*

JOHN M. CAMPBELL,
THE HUNGRY SUMMER

*Now what is history? It is the centuries of systematic explo-
rations of the riddle of death, with a view to overcoming death.
That's why people discover mathematical infinity and electro-
magnetic waves, that's why they write symphonies. Now, you
can't advance in this direction without a certain faith. You can't
make such discoveries without spiritual equipment. And the
basic elements of this equipment are in the Gospels. What are
they? To begin with, <u>love of one's neighbor</u>, which is the
supreme form of vital energy. Once it fills the heart of man it has
to overflow and spend itself. And then the two basic ideals of
modern man—without them he is unthinkable—the idea of <u>free
personality</u> and the idea of <u>life as sacrifice</u>.*

BORIS PASTERNAK,
DOCTOR ZHIVAGO
PASSAGE HIGHLIGHTED IN ONE OF THE BOOKS FOUND
WITH CHRISTOPHER MCCANDLESS'S REMAINS;
UNDERSCORING BY MCCANDLESS

After his attempt to depart the wilderness was stymied by the Teklanika's high flow, McCandless arrived back at the bus on July 8. It's impossible to know what was going through his mind at that point, for his journal betrays nothing. Quite possibly he was unconcerned about his escape route's having been cut off; indeed, at the time there was little reason for him to worry: It was the height of summer, the country was a fecund riot of plant and animal life, and his food supply was adequate. He probably surmised that if he bided his time until August, the Teklanika would subside enough to be crossed.

Reestablished in the corroded shell of Fairbanks 142, McCandless fell back into his routine of hunting and gathering. He read Tolstoy's "The Death of Ivan Ilych" and Michael Crichton's *Terminal Man*. He noted in his journal that it rained for a week straight. Game seems to have been plentiful: In the last three weeks of July, he killed thirty-five squirrels, four spruce grouse, five jays and woodpeckers, and two frogs, all of which he supplemented with wild potatoes, wild rhubarb, various species of berries, and large numbers of mushrooms. But despite this apparent munificence, the meat he'd been killing was very lean, and he was consuming fewer calories than he was burning. After subsisting for three months on an exceedingly marginal diet, McCandless had run up a sizable caloric deficit. He was balanced on a precarious edge. And then, in late July he made the mistake that pulled him down.

He had just finished reading *Doctor Zhivago,* a book that incited him to scribble excited notes in the margins and underline several passages:

> *Lara walked along the tracks following a path worn by pilgrims and then turned into the fields. Here she stopped and, closing her eyes, took a deep breath of the flower-scented air of the broad expanse around her. It was dearer to her than her kin, better than a lover, wiser than a book. For a moment she rediscovered the purpose of her life. She was here on earth to grasp the meaning of its wild enchantment and to call each thing by its right name, or, if this were not within her power, to give birth out of love for life to successors who would do it in her place.*

"NATURE/PURITY," he printed in bold characters at the top of the page.

> *Oh, how one wishes sometimes to escape from the meaning-less dullness of human eloquence, from all those sublime phrases, to take refuge in nature, apparently so inarticulate, or in the wordlessness of long, grinding labor, of sound sleep, of true music, or of a human understanding rendered speechless by emotion!*

McCandless starred and bracketed the paragraph and circled "refuge in nature" in black ink.

Next to "And so it turned out that only a life similar to the life of those around us, merging with it without a ripple, is genuine life, and that an unshared happiness is not happiness. . . . And this was most vexing of all," he noted, "HAPPINESS ONLY REAL WHEN SHARED."

It is tempting to regard this latter notation as further evidence that McCandless's long, lonely sabbatical had changed him in some significant way. It can be interpreted to mean that he was ready, perhaps, to shed a little of the armor he wore around his heart, that upon returning to civilization, he intended to abandon the life of a solitary vagabond, stop running so hard from intimacy, and become a member of the human community. But we will never know, because *Doctor Zhivago* was the last book Chris McCandless would ever read.

Two days after he finished the book, on July 30, there is an ominous entry in the journal: "EXTREMLY WEAK, FAULT OF POT. SEED. MUCH TROUBLE JUST TO STAND UP. STARVING. GREAT JEOPARDY." Before this note there is nothing in the journal to suggest that McCandless was in dire circumstances. He was hungry, and his meager diet had pared his body down to a feral scrawn of gristle and bone, but he seemed to be in reasonably good health. Then, after July 30, his physical condition suddenly went to hell. By August 19, he was dead.

There has been a lot of conjecture about what caused such a precipitous decline. In the days following the identification of McCandless's remains, Wayne Westerberg vaguely recalled that Chris might have purchased some seeds in South Dakota before heading north, including perhaps some potato seeds, with which he intended to plant a vegetable garden after getting established in the bush. According to one theory, McCandless never got around to planting the garden (I saw no evidence of a garden in the vicinity of the bus) and by late July had grown hungry enough to eat the seeds, which poisoned him.

Potato seeds are in fact mildly toxic after they've begun to sprout. They contain solanine, a poison that occurs in plants of the nightshade family, which causes vomiting, diarrhea, head-ache, and lethargy in the short term, and adversely affects heart rate and blood pressure when ingested over an extended period. This theory has a serious flaw, however: In order for McCandless to have been incapacitated by potato seeds, he would have had to eat many, many pounds of them; and given the light weight of his pack when Gallien dropped him off, it is extremely unlikely that he carried more than a few grams of potato seeds, if he carried any at all.

But other scenarios involve potato seeds of an entirely different variety, and these scenarios are more plausible. Pages 126 and 127 of *Tanaina Plantlore* describe a plant that is called wild potato by the Dena'ina Indians, who harvested its carrotlike root. The plant, known to botanists as *Hedysarum alpinum*, grows in gravelly soil throughout the region.

According to *Tanaina Plantlore*, "The root of the wild potato is probably the most important food of the Dena'ina, other than wild fruit. They eat it in a variety of ways—raw, boiled, baked, or fried—and enjoy it especially dipped in oil or lard, in which they also preserve it." The citation goes on to say that the best time to dig wild potatoes "is in the spring as soon as the ground thaws. . . . During the summer they evidently become dry and tough."

Priscilla Russell Kari, the author of *Tanaina Plantlore*, explained to me that "spring was a really hard time for the Dena'ina people, particularly in the past. Often the game they depended on for food didn't show up, or the fish didn't start running on time. So they depended on wild potatoes as a major staple until the fish came in late spring. It has a very sweet taste. It was—and still is—something they really like to eat."

Above ground the wild potato grows as a bushy herb, two feet tall, with stalks of delicate pink flowers reminiscent of miniature sweet-pea blossoms. Taking a cue from Kari's book, McCandless started to dig and eat wild potato roots on June 24, apparently without ill effect. On July 14, he began consuming the pealike seedpods of the plant as well, probably because the roots were becoming too tough to eat. A photograph he took during this period shows a one-gallon Ziploc plastic bag stuffed to overflowing with such seeds. And then, on July 30, the entry in his journal reads, "EXTREMELY WEAK. FAULT OF POT. SEED...."

One page after *Tanaina Plantlore* enumerates the wild potato, it describes a closely related species, wild sweet pea, *Hedysarum mackenzii*. Although a slightly smaller plant, wild sweet pea looks so much like wild potato that even expert botanists sometimes have trouble telling the species apart. There is only a single distinguishing characteristic that is absolutely reliable: On the underside of the wild potato's tiny green leaflets are conspicuous lateral veins; such veins are invisible on the leaflets of the wild sweet pea.

Kari's book warns that because wild sweet pea is so difficult to distinguish from wild potato and "is reported to be poisonous, care should be taken to identify them accurately before attempting to use the wild potato as food." Accounts of individuals being poisoned from eating *H. mackenzii* are nonexistent in modern medical literature, but the aboriginal inhabitants of the North have apparently known for millennia that wild sweet pea is toxic and remain extremely careful not to confuse *H. alpinum* with *H. mackenzii*.

To find a documented poisoning attributable to wild sweet pea, I had to go all the way back to the nineteenth-century annals of Arctic exploration. I came across what I was looking for in the journals of Sir John Richardson, a famous Scottish surgeon, naturalist, and explorer. He'd been a member of the hapless Sir John Franklin's first two expeditions and had survived both of them; it was Richardson who executed, by gunshot, the suspected murderer-cannibal on the first expedition. Richardson also happened to be the botanist who first wrote a scientific description of *H. mackenzii* and gave the plant its botanical name. In 1848, while leading an expedition through the Canadian Arctic in search of the by then missing Franklin, Richardson made a botanical comparison of *H. alpinum* and *H. mackenzii*. *H. alpinum*, he observed in his journal, *furnishes long flexible roots, which taste sweet like the liquorice, and are much eaten in the spring by the natives, but become woody and lose their juiciness and crispness as the season advances. The root of the hoary, decumbent, and less elegant, but larger-flowered* Hedysarum mackenzii *is poisonous, and nearly killed an old Indian woman at Fort Simpson, who had mistaken it for that of the preceding species. Fortunately, it proved emetic; and her stomach having rejected all that she had swallowed, she was restored to health, though her recovery was for some time doubtful.*

It was easy to imagine Chris McCandless making the same mistake as the Indian woman and becoming similarly incapacitated. From all the available evidence, there seemed to be little doubt that McCandless—rash and incautious by nature—had committed a careless blunder, confusing one plant for another, and died as a consequence. In the *Outside* article, I reported with great certainty that *H. mackenzii,* the wild sweet pea, killed the boy. Virtually every other journalist who wrote about the McCandless tragedy drew the same conclusion.

But as the months passed and I had the opportunity to ponder McCandless's death at greater length, this consensus came to seem less and less plausible. For three weeks beginning on June 24, McCandless had dug and safely eaten dozens of wild potato roots without mistaking *H. mackenzii* for *H. alpinum;* why, on July 14, when he started gathering seeds instead of roots, would he suddenly have confused the two species?

McCandless, I came to believe with increasing conviction, scrupulously steered clear of the reportedly toxic *H. mackenzii* and never ate its seeds or any other part of the plant. He was indeed poisoned, but the plant that killed him wasn't wild sweet pea. The agent of his demise was wild potato, *H. alpinum,* the species plainly identified as nontoxic in *Tanaina Plantlore*.

The book advises only that the roots of the wild potato are edible. Although it says nothing about the seeds of the species being edible, it also says nothing about the seeds being toxic. Nor have the seeds of *H. alpinum* have ever been described as toxic in any other published text. But the pea family (*Leguminosae*, to which

H. *alpinum* belongs) happens to be rife with species that pro-
duce alkaloids—chemical compounds that have powerful phar-
macological effects on humans and animals. (Morphine, caffeine,
nicotine, curare, strychnine, and mescaline are all alkaloids.)
And in many alkaloid-producing species, moreover, the toxin is
strictly localized within the plant.

"What happens with a lot of legumes," explains John Bryant, a
chemical ecologist at the University of Alaska in Fairbanks, "is
that the plants concentrate alkaloids in the seed coats in late
summer, to discourage animals from eating their seeds. Depend-
ing on the time of year, it would not be uncommon for a plant
with edible roots to have poisonous seeds. If a species does pro-
duce alkaloids, as fall approaches, the seeds are where the toxin
is most likely to be found."

During my visit to the Sushana River in 1993, I collected sam-
ples of *H. alpinum* growing within a few feet of the bus and sent
some dried seedpods from this sample to Dr. Thomas Clausen, a
colleague of Professor Bryant's in the Chemistry Department at
the University of Alaska. Although preliminary analysis by
Clausen and a graduate student, Edward Treadwell, indicated the
seeds contained traces of an alkaloid, subsequent, more thorough testing turned up no indication of any alkaloids whatsoever,
toxic or otherwise.

I was baffled. Given the alarming, unambiguous entry Mc-
Candless had scrawled in his journal on July 30, I found it hard
to believe that the enormous quantity of seeds he'd eaten just
prior to that date played no role in his death.

Long after the first edition of this book was published in 1996,
I continued to puzzle over the absence of alkaloids in the seeds
tested by Clausen and Treadwell. Over a period of several years I
doggedly sifted through the scientific literature, hoping to find a
clue that would explain this conundrum. One afternoon I came
across an article titled, "Identification of Swainsonine as a Probable Contributory Mycotoxin in Moldy Forage Mycotoxicoses."
The article described a fungus, *Rhizoctonia leguminicola*, which
commonly grows on many species of legumes during the summer
months in soggy climates. And *R. leguminicola*, it turns out, is a
variety of mold that produces a potent alkaloid called swainso-

nine—a compound well known to ranchers and veterinarians as a killer of livestock. The literature of veterinary medicine is rife with cases of animals stricken by swainsonine poisoning after eating damp forage contaminated with *R. leguminicola*.

Upon reading further about the connection between *R. leguminicola* and swainsonine, I had an epiphany: It wasn't the seeds of the wild potato that had done McCandless in; he was probably killed instead by mold that had been growing on those seeds. The dried seeds I'd sent Clausen and Treadwell had tested negative because they weren't moldy. But there was ample reason to suspect the seeds on which McCandless dined during the last two weeks of July may have been contaminated with *R. leguminicola*.

He had begun to gather and eat large quantities of wild potato seeds on July 14, during an extended period of rainy weather. Between meals he stored these green seedpods in damp, unclean Ziploc bags—an excellent culture for the proliferation of mold. If the wild potato seeds McCandless ate were contaminated with swainsonine from an eruption of *R. leguminicola*, it means the guy wasn't quite as reckless or incompetent as he has been made out to be. It means he didn't carelessly confuse one species with another. The plant that poisoned him wasn't toxic, per se; McCandless simply had the misfortune to eat moldy seeds. An innocent mistake, it was nevertheless sufficient to end his life.

The literature of veterinary medicine does not lack for cases of animals felled by swainsonine poisoning after grazing on forage contaminated with *R. leguminicola*. The most obvious symptoms of swainsonine poisoning are neurological. According to a paper published in the *Journal of the American Veterinary Medicine Association*, livestock that have ingested swainsonine show signs of "depression, a slow staggering gait, rough coat, dull eyes with a staring look, emaciation, muscular incoordination, and nervousness (especially when stressed). In addition, affected animals may become solitary and hard to handle, and may have difficulty eating and drinking."

The effects of swainsonine poisoning are chronic—the alkaloid rarely kills outright. The toxin does the deed insidiously, indirectly, by inhibiting an enzyme essential to glycoprotein metabolism. It creates a massive vapor lock, as it were, in mammalian fuel lines: The body is prevented from turning what it eats into a source of usable energy. If you ingest too much swainsonine you are bound to starve, no matter how much food you put into your stomach.

Animals will sometimes recover from swainsonine poisoning after they stop eating contaminated forage, but only if they are in fairly robust condition to begin with. In order for the toxic compound to be excreted in the urine, it first has to bind with available molecules of glucose or amino acid. A large store of proteins and sugars must be present to mop up the poison and wring it from the body.

"The problem," says Professor Bryant, "is that if you're lean and hungry to begin with, you're obviously not going to have any glucose and protein to spare, so there's no way to flush the toxin from your system. When a starving mammal ingests an alkaloid—even one as benign as caffeine—it's going to get hit much harder by it than it normally would because they lack the glucose reserves necessary to excrete the stuff. The alkaloid is simply going to accumulate in the system. If McCandless ate a big slug of these seeds while he was already in a semi-starving condition, it would have been a setup for catastrophe."

Laid low by the moldy seeds, McCandless discovered that he was suddenly far too weak to hike out and save himself. He was now too weak even to hunt effectively and thus grew weaker still, sliding closer and closer toward starvation. His life was spiraling toward the brink with awful speed.

There are no journal entries for July 31 or August 1. On August 2, the diary says only, "TERRIBLE WIND." Autumn was just around the corner. The temperature was dropping, and the days were becoming noticeably shorter: Each rotation of the earth held seven fewer minutes of daylight and seven more of cold and darkness; in the span of a single week, the night grew nearly an hour longer.

"DAY 100! MADE IT!" he noted jubilantly on August 5, proud of achieving such a significant milestone, "BUT IN WEAKEST CONDITION OF LIFE. DEATH LOOMS AS SERIOUS THREAT. TOO WEAK TO WALK OUT, HAVE LITERALLY BECOME TRAPPED IN THE WILD.—NO GAME."

If McCandless had possessed a U.S. Geological Survey topographic map, it would have alerted him to the existence of a Park Service cabin on the upper Sushana River, six miles due south of the bus, a distance he might have been able to cover even in his severely weakened state. The cabin, just inside the boundary of Denali National Park, had been stocked with a small amount of emergency food, bedding, and first-aid supplies for the use of backcountry rangers on their winter patrols. And although they aren't marked on the map, two miles even closer to the bus are a pair of private cabins—one owned by the well-known Healy dog mushers Will and Linda Forsberg; the other, by an employee of Denali National Park, Steve Carwile—where there should have been some food as well.

McCandless's apparent salvation, in other words, seemed to be only a three-hour walk upriver. This sad irony was widely noted in the aftermath of his death. But even if he had known about these cabins, they wouldn't have delivered McCandless from harm: At some point after mid-April, when the last of the cabins was vacated as the spring thaw made dog mushing and snow-machine travel problematic, somebody broke into all three cabins and vandalized them extensively. The food inside was exposed to animals and the weather, ruining it.

The damage wasn't discovered until late July, when a wildlife biologist named Paul Atkinson made the grueling ten-mile bushwhack over the Outer Range, from the road into Denali National Park to the Park Service shelter. He was shocked and baffled by the mindless destruction that greeted him. "It was obviously not the work of a bear," Atkinson reports. "I'm a bear technician, so I know what bear damage looks like. This looked like somebody had gone at the cabins with a claw hammer and bashed everything in sight. From the size of the fireweed growing up through mattresses that had been tossed outside, it was clear that the vandalism had occurred many weeks earlier."

"It was completely trashed," Will Forsberg says of his cabin. "Everything that wasn't nailed down had been wrecked. All the lamps were broken and most of the windows. The bedding and mattresses had been pulled outside and thrown in a heap, ceiling boards yanked down, fuel cans were punctured, the wood stove was removed—even a big carpet had been hauled out to rot. And

damaged cabins

all the food was gone. So the cabins wouldn't have helped Alex much even if he had found them. Or then again, maybe he did."

Forsberg considers McCandless the prime suspect. He believes McCandless blundered upon the cabins after arriving at the bus during the first week of May, flew into a rage over the intrusion of civilization on his precious wilderness experience, and systematically wrecked the buildings. This theory fails to explain, however, why McCandless didn't, then, also trash the bus.

Carwile also suspects McCandless. "It's just intuition," he explains, "but I get the feeling he was the kind of guy who might want to 'set the wilderness free.' Destroying the cabins would be a way of doing that. Or maybe it was his intense dislike of the government: He saw the sign on the Park Service cabin identifying it as such, assumed all three cabins were government property, and decided to strike a blow against Big Brother. That certainly seems within the realm of possibility."

The authorities, for their part, don't think McCandless was the vandal. "We really hit a blank on who might have done it," says Ken Kehrer, chief ranger for Denali National Park. "But Chris McCandless isn't considered a suspect by the National Park Service." In fact, there is nothing in McCandless's journal or photographs to suggest he went anywhere near the cabins. When McCandless ventured beyond the bus in early May, his pictures show that he headed north, downstream along the Sushana, the opposite direction of the cabins. And even if he had somehow chanced upon them, it's difficult to imagine him destroying the buildings without boasting of the deed in his diary.

There are no entries in McCandless's journal for August 6, 7, and 8. On August 9, he notes that he shot at a bear but missed. On August 10, he saw a caribou but didn't get a shot off, and he killed five squirrels. If a sufficient amount of swainsonine had accumulated in his body, however, this windfall of small game would have provided little nourishment. On August 11, he killed and ate one ptarmigan. On August 12, he dragged himself out of the bus to forage for berries, after posting a plea for assistance in the unlikely event that someone would stop by while he was away. Written in meticulous block letters on a page torn from Gogol's *Taras Bulba*, it reads:

S.O.S. I NEED YOUR HELP. I AM INJURED, NEAR DEATH, AND TOO WEAK TO HIKE OUT OF HERE. I AM ALL ALONE, THIS IS NO JOKE. IN THE NAME OF GOD, PLEASE REMAIN TO SAVE ME. I AM OUT COLLECTING BERRIES CLOSE BY AND SHALL RETURN THIS EVENING. THANK YOU.

He signed the note "CHRIS MCCANDLESS. AUGUST?" Recognizing the gravity of his predicament, he had abandoned the cocky moniker he'd been using for years, Alexander Supertramp, in favor of the name given to him at birth by his parents.

Many Alaskans have wondered why, in his desperation, McCandless didn't start a forest fire at this point, as a distress signal. There were two nearly full gallons of stove gas in the bus; presumably, it would have been a simple matter to start a conflagration large enough to attract the attention of passing airplanes or at least burn a giant SOS into the muskeg.

Contrary to common belief, however, the bus doesn't lie beneath any established flight path, and very few planes fly over it. Over the four days I spent on the Stampede Trail, I didn't see a single aircraft overhead, other than commercial jets flying at altitudes greater than twenty-five thousand feet. Small planes did no doubt pass within sight of the bus from time to time, but Mc-Candless would probably have had to start a fairly large forest fire to be sure of attracting their attention. And as Carine McCandless points out, "Chris would never, ever, intentionally burn down a forest, not even to save his life. Anybody who would suggest otherwise doesn't understand the first thing about my brother."

Starvation is not a pleasant way to expire. In advanced stages of famine, as the body begins to consume itself, the victim suffers muscle pain, heart disturbances, loss of hair, dizziness, shortness of breath, extreme sensitivity to cold, physical and mental exhaustion. The skin becomes discolored. In the absence of key nutrients, a severe chemical imbalance develops in the brain, inducing convulsions and hallucinations. Some people who have been brought back from the far edge of starvation, though, report that near the end the hunger vanishes, the terrible pain dissolves, and the suffering is replaced by a sublime euphoria, a sense of calm accompanied by transcendent mental clarity. It would be nice to think McCandless experienced a similar rapture.

On August 12, he wrote what would prove to be the final words in his journal: "Beautiful Blueberries." From August 13 through 18, his journal records nothing beyond a tally of the days. At some point during this week, he tore the final page from Louis L'Amour's memoir, _Education of a Wandering Man._ On one side of the page were some lines L'Amour had quoted from Robinson Jeffers's poem, "Wise Men in Their Bad Hours":

> _Death's a fierce meadowlark: but to die having made_
> _Something more equal to the centuries_
> _Than muscle and bone, is mostly to shed weakness._
> _The mountains are dead stone, the people_
> _Admire or hate their stature, their insolent quietness,_
> _The mountains are not softened or troubled_
> _And a few dead men's thoughts have the same temper._

On the other side of the page, which was blank, McCandless penned a brief adios: "I HAVE HAD A HAPPY LIFE AND THANK THE LORD. GOODBYE AND MAY GOD BLESS ALL!"

Then he crawled into the sleeping bag his mother had sewn for him and slipped into unconsciousness. He probably died on August 18, 112 days after he'd walked into the wild, 19 days before six Alaskans would happen across the bus and discover his body inside.

One of his last acts was to take a picture of himself, standing near the bus under the high Alaska sky, one hand holding his final note toward the camera lens, the other raised in a brave, beatific farewell. His face is horribly emaciated, almost skeletal. But if he pitied himself in those last difficult hours—because he was so young, because he was alone, because his body had betrayed him and his will had let him down—it's not apparent from the photograph. He is smiling in the picture, and there is no mistaking the look in his eyes: Chris McCandless was at peace, serene as a monk gone to God.

EPILOGUE

*Still, the last sad memory hovers round, and sometimes drifts
across like floating mist, cutting off sunshine and chilling the
remembrance of happier times. There have been joys too great
to be described in words, and there have been griefs upon which
I have not dared to dwell; and with these in mind I say: Climb
if you will, but remember that courage and strength are nought
without prudence, and that a momentary negligence may
destroy the happiness of a lifetime. Do nothing in haste; look well
to each step; and from the beginning think what may be the end.*

EDWARD WHYMPER,
SCRAMBLES AMONGST THE ALPS

*We sleep to time's hurdy-gurdy; we wake, if we ever wake, to the
silence of God. And then, when we wake to the deep shores of
time uncreated, then when the dazzling dark breaks over the far
slopes of time, then it's time to toss things, like our reason, and
our will; then it's time to break our necks for home.*

*There are no events but thoughts and the heart's hard turning,
the heart's slow learning where to love and whom. The rest is
merely gossip, and tales for other times.*

ANNIE DILLARD,
HOLY THE FIRM

The helicopter labors upward, *thwock-thwock-thwocking* over
the shoulder of Mt. Healy. As the altimeter needle brushes five
thousand feet, we crest a mud-colored ridge, the earth drops
away, and a breathtaking sweep of taiga fills the Plexiglas wind-
screen. In the distance I can pick out the Stampede Trail, cut-

ting a faint, crooked stripe from east to west across the landscape.

Billie McCandless is in the front passenger seat; Walt and I occupy the back. Ten hard months have passed since Sam McCandless appeared at their Chesapeake Beach doorstep to tell them Chris was dead. It is time, they have decided, to visit the place where their son met his end, to see it with their own eyes.

Walt has spent the past ten days in Fairbanks, doing contract work for NASA, developing an airborne radar system for search-and-rescue missions that will enable searchers to find the wreckage of a downed plane amid thousands of acres of densely forested country. For several days now he's been distracted, irritable, edgy. Billie, who arrived in Alaska two days ago, confided to me that the prospect of visiting the bus has been difficult for him to come to terms with. Surprisingly, she says she feels calm and centered and has been looking forward to this trip for some time.

Taking a helicopter was a last-minute change of plans. Billie wanted badly to travel overland, to follow the Stampede Trail as Chris had done. Toward that end she'd contacted Butch Killian, the Healy coal miner who'd been present when Chris's body was discovered, and he agreed to drive Walt and Billie into the bus on his all-terrain vehicle. But yesterday Killian called their hotel to say that the Teklanika River was still running high—too high, he worried, to cross safely, even with his amphibious, eight-wheeled Argo. Thus the helicopter.

Two thousand feet beneath the aircraft's skids a mottled green tweed of muskeg and spruce forest now blankets the rolling country. The Teklanika appears as a long brown ribbon thrown carelessly across the land. An unnaturally bright object comes into view near the confluence of two smaller streams: Fairbanks bus 142. It has taken us fifteen minutes to cover the distance it took Chris four days to walk.

The helicopter settles noisily onto the ground, the pilot kills the engine, and we hop down onto sandy earth. A moment later the machine lifts off in a hurricane of prop wash, leaving us surrounded by a monumental silence. As Walt and Billie stand ten yards from the bus, staring at the anomalous vehicle without speaking, a trio of jays prattles from a nearby aspen tree.

"It's smaller," Billie finally says, "than I thought it would be. I mean the bus." And then, turning to take in the surroundings: "What a pretty place. I can't believe how much this reminds me of where I grew up. Oh, Walt, it looks just like the Upper Peninsula! Chris must have loved being here."

"I have a lot of reasons for disliking Alaska, OK?" Walt answers, scowling. "But I admit it—the place has a certain beauty. I can see what appealed to Chris."

For the next thirty minutes Walt and Billie walk quietly around the decrepit vehicle, amble down to the Sushana River, visit the nearby woods.

Billie is the first to enter the bus. Walt returns from the stream to find her sitting on the mattress where Chris died, taking in the vehicle's shabby interior. For a long time she gazes silently at her son's boots under the stove, his handwriting on the walls, his toothbrush. But today there are no tears. Picking through the clutter on the table, she bends to examine a spoon with a distinctive floral pattern on the handle. "Walt, look at this," she says. "This is the silverware we had in the Annandale house."

At the front of the bus, Billie picks up a pair of Chris's patched, ragged jeans and, closing her eyes, presses them to her face. "Smell," she urges her husband with a painful smile. "They still smell like Chris." After a long beat she declares, to herself more than to anyone else, "He must have been very brave and very strong, at the end, not to do himself in."

Billie and Walt wander in and out of the bus for the next two hours. Walt installs a memorial just inside the door, a simple brass plaque inscribed with a few words. Beneath it Billie arranges a bouquet of fireweed, monkshood, yarrow, and spruce boughs. Under the bed at the rear of the bus, she leaves a suitcase stocked with a first-aid kit, canned food, other survival supplies, a note urging whoever happens to read it to "call your parents as soon as possible." The suitcase also holds a Bible that belonged to Chris when he was a child, even though, she allows, "I haven't prayed since we lost him."

Walt, in a reflective mood, has had little to say, but he appears more at ease than he has in many days. "I didn't know how I was going to react to this," he admits, gesturing toward the bus. "But now I'm glad we came." This brief visit, he says, has given him a slightly better understanding of why his boy came into this country. There is much about Chris that still baffles him and always will, but now he is a little less baffled. And for that small solace he is grateful.

"It's comforting to know Chris was here," Billie explains, "to know for certain that he spent time beside this river, that he stood on this patch of ground. So many places we've visited in the past three years—we'd wonder if possibly Chris had been there. It was terrible not knowing—not knowing anything at all.

"Many people have told me that they admire Chris for what he was trying to do. If he'd lived, I would agree with them. But he didn't, and there's no way to bring him back. You can't fix it. Most things you can fix, but not that. I don't know that you ever get over this kind of loss. The fact that Chris is gone is a sharp hurt I feel every single day. It's really hard. Some days are better than others, but it's going to be hard every day for the rest of my life."

Abruptly, the quiet is shattered by the percussive racket of the helicopter, which spirals down from the clouds and lands in a patch of fireweed. We climb inside; the chopper shoulders into the sky and then hovers for a moment before banking steeply to the southeast. For a few minutes the roof of the bus remains visible among the stunted trees, a tiny white gleam in a wild green sea, growing smaller and smaller, and then it's gone.

AFTERWORD

The debate over what killed Chris McCandless, and the related question of whether he is worthy of admiration, has been smoldering and occasionally flaring for more than two decades now. Shortly after the first edition of this book was published in January 1996, University of Alaska chemists Edward Treadwell and Thomas Clausen shot down my theory that the cause of McCandless's death was a toxic alkaloid contained in the seeds of the wild potato plant, *Hedysarum alpinum.* When Treadwell and Clausen completed chemical analyses of the wild potato seeds I'd sent them, they found no trace of any poisonous compounds. "I tore that plant apart," Dr. Clausen explained to *Men's Journal* in 2007. "There were no toxins. No alkaloids. I'd eat it myself."

Based on Treadwell's and Clausen's determination that *H. alpinum* seeds aren't toxic, I proposed a new hypothesis to explain McCandless's demise, which I included in an updated edition of this book printed in 2007: It wasn't the seeds that killed McCandless, but rather a mold growing on the seeds, which produced a toxic alkaloid.

I had no hard evidence to support this hypothesis, however, so I continued searching for information that would allow me to reconcile McCandless's unambiguous journal entry—stating he had become extremely weak and was in great jeopardy because he ate wild potato seeds—with the apparently equally unambiguous results of the chemical analyses performed by Treadwell and Clausen. These results were reinforced in 2008, moreover, when they published a peer-reviewed paper titled "Is *Hedysarum mackenziei* (Wild Sweet Pea) Actually Toxic?" in the journal *Ethnobotany Research & Applications*. Upon completing "an exhaustive comparison of the secondary chemistry between the two plants [*H. alpinum* and *H. mackenzii*] as well as a search for nitrogen containing metabolites (alkaloids) in both species," Treadwell and Clausen wrote, "no chemical basis for toxicity could be found."

In August 2013, I happened upon a paper titled "The Silent Fire: ODAP and the Death of Christopher McCandless," by Ronald Hamilton, which appeared to solve the conundrum. Hamilton's essay, posted online, presented hitherto unknown evidence that the wild potato plant was in fact highly toxic, contrary to the assurances of Treadwell, Clausen, and apparently every other expert who had ever weighed in on the subject. According to Hamilton, the toxic agent in *H. alpinum* was not an alkaloid, as I had speculated, but rather an amino acid, and it was the ultimate cause of McCandless's death.

Hamilton is neither a botanist nor a chemist; he's a writer who until recently worked as a bookbinder at the Indiana University of Pennsylvania library. As Hamilton explains it, he became acquainted with the McCandless story in 2002, when he happened upon a copy of *Into the Wild*, flipped through its pages, and suddenly thought to himself, "I know why this guy died." His hunch derived from his knowledge of Vapniarca, a little-known World War II concentration camp in what was then German-occupied Ukraine.

"I first learned about Vapniarca through a book whose title I've long forgotten," Hamilton told me. "Only the barest account of Vapniarca appeared in one of its chapters. . . . But after reading *Into the Wild* I was able to track down a manuscript about Vapniarca, which has been published online." Later, in Romania, he located the son of a man who served as an administrative official of the camp, and who sent Hamilton a trove of documents.

In 1942, as a macabre experiment, an officer at Vapniarca started feeding the Jewish inmates bread and soup made from seeds of the "grasspea," *Lathyrus sativus*, a common legume that has been known since the time of Hippocrates to be toxic. "Very quickly," Hamilton writes in "The Silent Fire,"

a Jewish doctor and inmate at the camp, Dr. Arthur
Kessler, understood what this implied, particularly when
within months, hundreds of the young male inmates of the
camp began limping and had begun to use sticks as
crutches to propel themselves about. In some cases inmates
had been rapidly reduced to crawling on their backsides to
make their ways through the compound. . . . [O]nce the inmates had ingested enough of the culprit plant, it was as if a
silent fire had been lit within their bodies. There was no
turning back from this fire—once kindled, it would burn until the person who had eaten the grasspea would ultimately
be crippled. . . . The more they'd eaten, the worse the consequences—but in any case, once the effects had begun, there
was simply no way to reverse them. . . .

Even today, at this moment, Lathyrus sativus is maim-
ing [and] crippling. . . . It is currently estimated that
[throughout the twentieth century] more than 100,000 people worldwide [suffered] from irreversible paralysis due to
the consumption of the plant. The disease is called, simply,
neurolathyrism, or more commonly, "lathyrism."

Dr. Arthur Kessler, who . . . initially recognized the sinister experiment that had been undertaken at Vapniarca, was
one of those who escaped death during those terrible times.
He retired to Israel once the war had ended and there established a clinic to care for, study, and attempt to treat the numerous victims of lathyrism from Vapniarca, many of
whom had also relocated in Israel.

The injurious substance turned out to be a neurotoxin, beta-
N-oxalyl-L-alpha-beta-diaminopropionic acid, a compound com-
monly referred to as beta-ODAP or, more often, just ODAP.
According to Hamilton, ODAP

affects different people, different sexes, and even different
age groups in different ways. It even affects people within
those age groups differently. . . . The one constant about
ODAP poisoning however, very simply put, is this: those
who will be hit the hardest are always young men between

> the ages of 15 and 25 and who are essentially starving or ingesting very limited calories, who have been engaged in heavy physical activity, and who suffer trace-element shortages from meager, unvaried diets.

ODAP was identified in 1964. It brings about paralysis by overstimulating nerve receptors, causing them to die. As Hamilton explains,

> It isn't clear why, but the most vulnerable neurons to this catastrophic breakdown are the ones that regulate leg movement. . . . And when sufficient neurons die, paralysis sets in. . . . [The condition] never gets better; it always gets worse. The signals get weaker and weaker until they simply cease altogether. The victim experiences "much trouble just to stand up." Many become rapidly too weak to walk. The only thing left for them to do at that point is to crawl. . . .

After Hamilton read *Into the Wild* and became convinced ODAP was responsible for McCandless's sad end, he approached Dr. Jonathan Southard, the assistant chair of the biochemistry department at Indiana University of Pennsylvania, and persuaded Southard to have one of his students, Wendy Gruber, test the seeds of both *H. alpinum* and *H. mackenzii* for ODAP. Upon completion of her tests in 2004, Gruber determined that ODAP appeared to be present in both species of *Hedysarum*, but her results were less than conclusive. "To be able say that ODAP is definitely present in the seeds," she reported, "we would need to use another dimension of analysis, probably by HPLC-MS"—high-pressure liquid chromatography. But Gruber possessed neither the expertise nor the resources to analyze the seeds with HPLC, so Hamilton's hypothesis remained unproven.

Hoping to learn whether Hamilton should be believed, in August 2013 I sent 150 grams of freshly collected wild potato seeds to Avomeen Analytical Services in Ann Arbor, Michigan, for HPLC analysis, which determined that the seeds contained .394 percent ODAP by weight, a concentration well within the levels known to cause lathyrism in humans. On September 12, 2013, I reported Avomeen's results in an article titled "How Chris Mc-Candless Died," which was published on *The New Yorker* website.

Five days later, Dermot Cole, a journalist in Fairbanks, posted an article titled "Krakauer's Wild Theory on McCandless Gives Short Shrift to Science" on the website *Alaska Dispatch*. Cole wrote,

> *Krakauer should take the advice of Tom Clausen, the retired organic chemist from UAF who has spent much of his career studying plants in Alaska and their properties.*
>
> *Clausen said that absent peer-reviewed scientific research he would not make any conclusions about what amounts to a highly technical and complicated scientific question.*
>
> *The difference between a popular account for a general audience and a peer-reviewed journal is that an editor or two may check the former, while the latter will be subject to critical examination aimed at uncovering sloppy work.*
>
> *Clausen said he has nothing to refute the conclusion, reached by both [Ron Hamilton] and Krakauer, that ODAP was present.*
>
> *"With that said, let me follow with the comment that I am very skeptical about the entire story," Clausen wrote in an e-mail. . . . "I would be much more convinced if I was reading the report from a credible peer-reviewed professional."*

Clausen, I realized, was right: I couldn't be absolutely certain the seeds were toxic until I did additional, more sophisticated analysis, and then published the results in a reputable peer-reviewed journal. So I embarked on another round of testing.

I began by asking Avomeen to analyze the seeds with liquid chromatography-mass spectrometry (LC-MS). This test detected a prominent seed component with a molecular mass of 176, the molecular mass of ODAP, which appeared to corroborate the earlier HPLC results. Next, Avomeen suggested that we take the analysis to an even higher resolution by using liquid chromatography-tandem mass spectrometry (LC-MS/MS). The results confirmed that the mass of the compound in question was 176, but the fragmentation-ion pattern, or "fingerprint," for this compound didn't match the fragmentation-ion fingerprint of a sample of pure ODAP that was also analyzed. ODAP, in other words, was not present in *H. alpinum* seeds. LC-MS/MS conclusively disproved Hamilton's hypothesis.

The LC-MS/MS analysis nevertheless suggested the possibility that a significant concentration of a compound structurally similar to ODAP might be present in the seeds. So I combed the scientific literature yet again, even more exhaustively this time, reading every paper I could find about toxic nonprotein amino acids with a molecular mass of 176. Eventually, to my surprise, I discovered an article by a scientist named B. A. Birdsong, published in the 1960 edition of the *Canadian Journal of Botany*, which reported that *H. alpinum* seeds contained a toxic amino acid called L-canavanine. And the mass of L-canavanine, it so happens, is 176.

My earlier searches had missed this article because I had been looking for a toxic alkaloid instead of a toxic amino acid. Clausen and Treadwell had overlooked the article as well.

Birdsong and his coauthors had determined the presence of L-canavanine in the seeds using a technique called paper chromatography-trisodium pentacyanoammonioferrate colorimetric analysis, or PCAF. Given all the controversy, and because methods for analysis of plant constituents have advanced significantly during the fifty-four years since Birdsong's investigation, I asked Avomeen to evaluate the presence of L-canavanine in the seeds using LC-MS/MS, the same technique that had disproved the presence of ODAP. When the Avomeen scientists completed their work, they determined that *H. alpinum* seeds do indeed contain a significant concentration of L-canavanine—1.2 percent by weight.

L-canavanine, it turns out, is an antimetabolite stored in the seeds of many leguminous species to ward off predators, and its toxicity in animals is well documented in the scientific literature. Numerous cases have been observed of cattle poisoned after foraging on jack beans, *Canavalia ensiformis*, the seeds of which contain about 2.5 percent L-canavanine by dry weight; symptoms included stiffness of the hindquarters, progressive weakness, emphysema, and hemorrhages of the lymph glands.

Although there have been few clinical or epidemiological studies on canavanine-induced illness in humans, there have been anecdotal reports of toxic effects in people who ingested jackbean seeds. An article published in the prestigious German journal *Die Pharmazie* observed that "the scattered reports about poisoning by this plant probably stand in no relation to actual number of incidences that are caused by it in agricultural practice, because the cause is so difficult to recognize."

Dr. Jonathan Southard, Dr. Ying Long, Dr. Andrew Kolbert, Dr. Shri Thanedar, and I coauthored a paper titled "Presence of L-canavanine in *Hedysarum alpinum* seeds and its potential role in the death of Chris McCandless," which was published in the peer-reviewed journal *Wilderness and Environmental Medicine* in October 2014. In the conclusion of our paper, we wrote,

> Our results confirmed the presence of L-canavanine (an antimetabolite with demonstrated toxicity in mammals) as a significant component of H. alpinum seeds. . . . In the case of Christopher McCandless, there is evidence that H. alpinum seeds constituted a significant portion of his meager diet during a period before his death. Based on this and what is known about the toxic effects of L-canavanine, we make the logical conclusion that under these conditions, it is highly likely that the ingestion of relatively large amounts of this antimetabolite was a contributing factor to his death.
>
> The death of Chris McCandless should serve as a caveat to other foragers: Even when some parts of a plant are known to be edible, other parts of the same species may contain dangerous concentrations of toxic compounds. Additionally, there may be seasonal, as well as ecotypic, variations in the concentrations of L-canavanine between various communities of H. alpinum. Further studies are needed to determine the range of L-canavanine concentrations among different populations of the plant. Given the known toxic properties of L-canavanine and its established presence in H. alpinum seeds, it seems prudent to use caution before ingesting these seeds, especially as a significant part of the diet.

Although Ron Hamilton was wrong about ODAP's role in the death of McCandless, he was correct that *H. alpinum* seeds are poisonous, and that an amino acid, rather than an alkaloid, is the toxic constituent. I am tremendously grateful to Hamilton for publishing "The Silent Fire: ODAP and the Death of Christopher McCandless," because if he hadn't, it is unlikely I would have stumbled upon Birdsong's article, and thus would never have learned about the presence of L-canavanine in *H. alpinum* seeds. Near the end of "The Silent Fire," Hamilton mused,

> It might be said that Christopher McCandless did indeed starve to death in the Alaskan wild, but this only because he'd been poisoned, and the poison had rendered him too weak to move about, to hunt or forage, and, toward the end, "extremely weak," "too weak to walk out," and, having "much trouble just to stand up." He wasn't truly starving in the most technical sense of that condition. . . . [But] it wasn't arrogance that had killed him, it was ignorance . . . , which must be forgiven, for the facts underlying his death were to remain unrecognized to all, scientists and lay people alike, literally for decades.

Confirmation that toxic seeds were at least partly responsible for McCandless's death is unlikely to persuade many Alaskans to regard him in a more sympathetic light, but it may prevent other backcountry foragers from accidentally poisoning themselves. Had McCandless's guidebook to edible plants warned that *H. alpinum* seeds contain a "highly toxic secondary plant constituent," as L-canavanine is described in the scientific literature, he probably would have walked out of the wild in late August with no more difficulty than when he walked into it in April, and would still be alive today. If that were the case, Chris McCandless would now be forty-six years old.

Jon Krakauer
April 2015

Acknowledgments

Writing this book would have been impossible without considerable assistance from the McCandless family. I am deeply indebted to Walt McCandless, Billie McCandless, Carine McCandless, Sam McCandless, and Shelly McCandless Garcia. They gave me full access to Chris's papers, letters, and photographs and talked with me at great length. No family member made any attempt to exert control over the book's content or direction, despite knowing that some material would be extremely painful to see in print. At the family's request, twenty percent of the royalties generated by sales of *Into the Wild* will be donated to a scholarship fund in Chris McCandless's name.

I am grateful to Doug Stumpf, who acquired the manuscript for Villard Books/Random House, and to David Rosenthal and Ruth Fecych, who edited the book with skill and care following Doug's premature departure. Thanks, also, to Annik LaFarge, Adam Rothberg, Dan Rembert, Dennis Ambrose, Laura Taylor, Diana Frost, Deborah Foley, and Abigail Winograd at Villard/Random House for their assistance.

This book began as an article in *Outside* magazine. I would like to thank Mark Bryant and Laura Hohnhold for assigning me the piece and shaping it so adroitly. Adam Horowitz, Greg Cliburn, Kiki Yablon, Larry Burke, Lisa Chase, Dan Ferrara, Sue Smith, Will Dana, Alex Heard, Donovan Webster, Kathy Martin, Brad Wetzler, and Jaqueline Lee worked on the article as well.

Special gratitude is owed to Linda Mariam Moore, Roman Dial, David Roberts, Sharon Roberts, Matt Hale, and Ed Ward for providing invaluable advice and criticism; to Margaret Davidson for creating the splendid maps; and to John Ware, my agent nonpareil.

Important contributions were also made by Dennis Burnett, Chris Fish, Eric Hathaway, Gordy Cucullu, Andy Horowitz, Kris Maxie Gillmer, Wayne Westerberg, Mary Westerberg, Gail Borah, Rod Wolf, Jan Burres, Ronald Franz, Gaylord Stuckey, Jim Gallien, Ken Thompson, Gordon Samel, Ferdie Swanson, Butch Killian, Paul Atkinson, Steve Carwile, Ken Kehrer, Bob Burroughs, Berle Mercer, Will Forsberg, Nick Jans, Mark Stoppel, Dan Solie, Andrew Liske, Peggy Dial, James Brady, Cliff Hudson, the late Mugs Stump, Kate Bull, Roger Ellis, Ken Sleight, Bud Walsh, Lori Zarza, George Dreeszen, Sharon Dreeszen, Eddie Dickson, Priscilla Russell, Arthur Kruckeberg, Paul Reichart, Doug Ewing, Sarah Gage, Mike Ralphs, Richard Keeler, Nancy J. Turner, Glen Wagner, Tom Clausen, John Bryant, Edward Treadwell, Lew Krakauer, Carol Krakauer, Karin Krakauer, Wendy Krakauer, Sarah Krakauer, Andrew Krakauer, Ruth Selig, and Peggy Langrall.

I benefited from the published work of journalists Johnny Dodd, Kris Capps, Steve Young, W. L. Rusho, Chip Brown, Glenn Randall, Jonathan Waterman, Debra McKinney, T. A. Badger, and Adam Biegel.

For providing inspiration, hospitality, friendship, and sage counsel, I am grateful to Kai Sandburn, Randy Babich, Jim Freeman, Steve Rottler, Fred Beckey, Maynard Miller, Jim Doherty, David Quammen, Tim Cahill, Rosalie Stewart, Shannon Costello, Alison Jo Stewart, Maureen Costello, Ariel Kohn, Kelsi Krakauer,

Miriam Kohn, Deborah Shaw, Nick Miller, Greg Child, Dan Cauthorn, Kitty Calhoun Grissom, Colin Grissom, Dave Jones, Fran Kaul, David Trione, Dielle Havlis, Pat Joseph, Lee Joseph, Pierret Vogt, Paul Vogt, Ralph Moore, Mary Moore, and Woodrow O. Moore.

JON KRAKAUER

INTO THE WILD

Jon Krakauer is the author of eight books and has received an Academy Award in Literature from the American Academy of Arts and Letters. According to the award citation, "Krakauer combines the tenacity and courage of the finest tradition of investigative journalism with the stylish subtlety and profound insight of the born writer."

www.jonkrakauer.com

Endorsed by Jon Krakauer as an invaluable source for further insight into Chris McCandless and his life story, Carine McCandless, Chris's sister, is available for select readings, speaking engagements and lectures. To inquire about a possible appearance, please contact Penguin Random House Speakers Bureau at speakers@penguinrandomhouse.com.

MISSOULA
Rape and the Justice System in a College Town

Missoula, Montana, is a typical college town, home to a highly regarded state university whose football team inspires a passionately loyal fan base. Between January 2008 and May 2012, hundreds of students reported sexual assaults to the local police. Few of the cases were properly handled by either the university or local authorities. In this, Missoula is also typical. In these pages, acclaimed journalist Jon Krakauer investigates a spate of campus rapes that occurred in Missoula over a four-year period. Taking the town as a case study, Krakauer documents the experiences of five victims: their fear and self-doubt in the aftermath; the skepticism directed at them by police, prosecutors, and the public; their bravery in pushing forward and what it cost them. These stories cut through abstract ideological debate about acquaintance rape to demonstrate that it does not happen because women are sending mixed signals or seeking attention. They are victims of a terrible crime, deserving of fairness from our justice system. Rigorously researched, rendered in incisive prose, *Missoula* stands as an essential call to action.

Current Affairs

INTO THIN AIR
A Personal Account of the Mt. Everest Disaster

When Jon Krakauer reached the summit of Mt. Everest in the early afternoon of May 10, 1996, he hadn't slept in fifty-seven hours and was reeling from the brain-altering effects of oxygen deprivation. As he turned to begin the perilous descent from 29,028 feet (the cruising altitude of an Airbus jetliner), twenty other climbers were still pushing doggedly to the top, unaware that the sky had begun to roil with clouds. The storm, which claimed five lives and left countless more, including Krakauer's, in guilt-ridden disarray, would also provide the impetus for his epic account of the disaster.

Nonfiction/Adventure

THREE CUPS OF DECEIT
How Greg Mortenson, Humanitarian Hero, Lost His Way

Greg Mortenson, the bestselling author of *Three Cups of Tea*, is a man who has built a global reputation as a selfless humanitarian and children's crusader. But, as Jon Krakauer demonstrates in this extensively researched and penetrating book, Mortenson is not all that he appears to be. Based on wide-ranging interviews with former employees, board members, and others who have intimate knowledge of Mortenson and his charity, the Central Asia Institute, *Three Cups of Deceit* uncovers multiple layers of deception behind Mortenson's public image. Was his crusade really inspired by a desire to repay the kindness of villagers who nursed him back to health when he became lost on his descent down K2? Was he abducted and held for eight days by the Taliban? Has his charity built all of the schools that he has claimed? This book is a passionately argued plea for the truth and a tragic tale of good intentions gone very wrong.

Current Affairs

UNDER THE BANNER OF HEAVEN
A Story of Violent Faith

At the core of *Under the Banner of Heaven* is an appalling double murder committed by two Mormon Fundamentalist brothers, Ron and Dan Lafferty, who insist they received a revelation from God commanding them to kill their blameless victims. Beginning with a meticulously researched account of this "divinely inspired" crime, Krakauer constructs a multilayered, bone-chilling narrative of messianic delusion, savage violence, and unyielding faith.

Nonfiction

ANCHOR BOOKS
Available wherever books are sold.
www.anchorbooks.com